Feast of Faith

Confessions of a Eucharistic Pilgrim

Joan Carter McHugh

Lake Forest, Illinois

Published by Witness Ministries.

For additional copies and Information write to:

       Witness Ministries
       825 So. Waukegan Rd. A8-200
       Lake Forest, IL 60045

Dedication

To Tom McHugh

Patient Husband

Dearest Friend

Companion on my Pilgrimage

More tortuous than all else is the human heart,
beyond remedy; who can understand it?
I, the Lord, alone probe the mind and test the heart,
To reward everyone according to his ways,
according to the merit of his deeds.

—Jeremiah 17,9-11

Contents

Preface

To introduce a new book to the public requires one thoroughly to have reviewed and pondered the text. Happily, I also edited the book and became profoundly engaged in the insights and personality of Joan McHugh as writer and pilgrim and inner traveler. Many of those who travel never explore themselves and return home unchanged. Both the charm and the relevance of this book is the self-revelation of the writer—like Augustine's *Confessions*. She grows up again throughout these chapters; she relives the anxiety and triumphs and above all the relationships of her past. But her experiences are evoked during her encounters with the saints and Eucharistic miracles on her pilgrimage.

Thus the visible, outer journey is translated into an invisible, inner journey—which is after all the significant pilgrimage in life. In the end it is the soul that matters, and reaching the kingdom of God is the bottom line.

The candor of the author is matched by the touching narrations from her past life up to the present (which may startle the reader), yet was the thrust of the book from the beginning. The work is sentimental without being saccharine, gentle without weakness. Yet without doubt the purpose of the author is to share her religiosity with the reader. Unashamedly she speaks to us of her special friends, the saints, as real-life companions. She relates the Eucharistic miracles with faith and awe like a child discovering a new venue and a new wonder set before her amazed eyes.

Nevertheless, it is the final chapters of this book that ultimately arrest and command our attention. Her pain drives her into and out of the pit of despair. Reborn by the power of God as a new person, Joan McHugh completes her *Confessions*, vulnerable as Jesus on the cross, yet finally lying in tranquility on the shore of a vast sea of unsuspected suffering.

If the reader is able to enter this book with the same sympathetic and non-judgmental attitude, the reward will be great, not least of which is to suggest an inner quest of one's own. Even before its publication, I have recommended this wonderful book to many readers, as I do now to you who are about to begin the first chapter.

Fr. Anselm W. Romb, OFM Conv.

Introduction

Tommy and I celebrated a belated 25th wedding anniversary by giving each other a trip to Italy. During the planning stage, we agreed that we wanted to go without an itinerary, reservations or a schedule, without any constraints — period. For the first time in our lives we wanted to be free to follow our spirits, to go wherever we felt, to have the freedom to discover out-of-the-way places to stay. We would have ten days together, and I would stay on for a month. What a gift it was on both counts, first to share Italy with each other, then for me to have the freedom to roam around like a famous author and find some Mediterranean villa with a view where I could write my bestseller!

Every time I enter a bookstore I fantasize that someday I will be on those shelves next to Danielle Steele, *outselling* her. My subject matter would be a little different, however. I have an insatiable desire to write true-to-life accounts of the way God interacts with His people. As Christians we have Good News to share which is so compelling and awesome that the most popular books of all time can't compare with it. Yet secular authors command an enormous readership. *I want to generate a following for Jesus.*

One of my favorite scenes from the movie, "Oh God," takes place when John Denver bursts into the newspaper office with a story he wants to tell: "Please," he begs the editor, "I want to tell everyone that I have just talked to God! We have to let them know that God is alive, and that I just saw Him and He said to tell everyone that He loves them and that He wants us to believe in Him." "How could I print that?" the incredulous editor gasped, "no one would believe it and I would lose my job." Denver responded: "You do it, and leave the rest to God."

That's what I want to do — write about my experience of God and leave the rest to Him. I have been drawn by an intensity to find Him since I was a child. My life has been a search for Him and the struggles and the rewards of the search are what I want to share. Like E.T. always struggling to "phone home," I have been struggling to make contact with God. I believe, with St. Augustine, that "Our hearts are restless until they rest in Thee," and I also believe that He creates this restlessness in us, this craving which no one nor anything else can satisfy but God.

A few weeks before our departure, we bought a map of Italy and plotted our course, intending to visit some of the sites of the Eucharistic miracles which we'd recently heard and read about and in which we were both interested. In my sixteen years of Catholic education, I'd never even heard about these visible manifestations of Christ's Real Presence – but thanks to the efforts of Mother Angelica, Bob and Penny Lord and Joan Carroll Cruz, they are becoming known in the United States. Our journey became a pilgrimage in which we were privileged to view some of the sacred relics of Christ's Real Presence, authenticated by the Church but relatively unknown in the United States. Instead of aimlessly wandering around the country visiting lovely resorts, the Lord took our heart's desire to be in Italy and offered us a plan, *His plan*, for our journey. How often the words of the Psalmist have come true in my life:

> *Trust in the Lord and do good*
> *That you may dwell in the land and be safe.*
> *Take delight in the Lord,*
> *And He will grant you your heart's desires.*
>
> (Psalm 37)

How many years it has taken me to realize that God wants for us what is deepest in our own hearts, and then some. God must have designed this trip according to His will, because only He could know the depth of my devotion to the Holy Eucharist and the joy it would give me to witness different manifestations of His presence through the Eucharistic miracles. This quest to seek the living Lord, who faith tells me is physically present in the Holy Eucharist, has been with me since my childhood. It is a quest that is tied very integrally to my own spiritual growth and inner healing.

A few days before leaving for Italy, I made a holy hour at Marytown, a Franciscan Friary near my home, where there is Perpetual Adoration of the Blessed Sacrament. There, in that sacred space in the presence of Jesus, I prayed for help. I wrote in my journal that day that I felt stripped of consolation or direction. I can be walking along and suddenly fall into a dark hole inside myself. My husband or a friend or some behavior of one of my children will act as a trigger which stirs up some negative feelings. I remember my mother always being in a state of inner anguish. Was I becoming like her? *So many things seem to cause me pain: my marriage, my relationships, problems in my family. It seems I can't go two hours without feeling some pain – of rejection, anger, fear, abandonment. I don't know anymore if I'm causing the pain or others are. I feel rejections so deeply. Am I losing my mind, becoming hurt so constantly? My deepest anguish is my marriage. I love Tommy deeply, yet there is a part of me that can't love, that is cold and emotionally paralyzed. I try not to blame my husband, but sometimes some remark or behavior of his seems to draw out of me powerful negative emotions. I have bottomed out. I am truly powerless, unable to change the situation at all.*

Tommy and I met at a party given by my best friend, Kandy, *twenty eight years ago!* I had just arrived home from Italy where I had lived and worked on and off for several years. Kandy insisted I come to the party because there was someone she wanted me to meet. She had told Tom McHugh the same thing. No sooner did we meet than I watched him spend most of the evening sitting on a piano bench with my friend Louise, who I had lived and traveled with in Europe, talking and laughing and having a great old time.

Best friends Kandy and Joan graduating from The Convent of the Sacred Heart

When he asked to walk me home, I covered over my jealousy, and began a relationship with my future husband. It was only when he read the manuscript for this book that he told me the reason he spent time with Louise that night was because she was willing to sit and talk. Apparently I was flitting about like a social butterfly, rekindling old friendships while ignoring him.

When he walked me home I told him I was going to return to Italy to marry an Italian, that I was not cut out for station wagons and white picket fences. I was a woman of the world and had grown beyond what America had to offer. Each time we went to dinner, we discussed everything under the sun, including Paolo, my Italian boyfriend! Tommy was easy to talk to,

October 22, 1966

understanding, and he had so much wisdom. He was such a good new friend to have, plus he had a great sense of humor and he liked to dance. We came from similar backgrounds and he was so compassionate when I shared anything personal, saying that things happen for a reason, and that God in His providence cares for us like a Father. I fell in love.

Now, in the chapel at Marytown, it was as if all the lights went out in my life. I was hurting and lost and couldn't find my way in the dark. I turned to God for help: *I place our marriage and all my problems at Your feet, Lord. Please give me a touch of your hand, Jesus, to let me know You hear me and are with me. Some days I want to run and never come back; I have no strength left, no will, no desire, no trust, no anything. I have faith in You—period. I am full of darkness. I no longer think that I'd be one of Your chosen. I am in the crowd looking at You, talking to You in my heart, but not brave enough to be crucified with You. Jesus, help me love You and those around me. I'm afraid I've not reflected Your love to others. I've reflected selfishness, impatience, anger, judgment, criticism and pride. Please guide me—and us—in our pilgrimage to the Eucharistic shrines. Heal me, Lord, and show me how I can serve You through this trip.*

Before leaving the chapel that day, I opened Scripture to see if any passage especially moved me. I always hope the Lord will speak a word to me very clearly. He did. I opened to the following verse from Exodus 6:

> *"I am the Lord. I will free you from the forced labor of the Egyptians and will deliver you from their slavery. I will rescue you by my outstretched arm and with mighty acts of judgment. I will take you as my own people, and you shall have me as your God. You will know that I, the Lord, am your God when I free you from the labor of the Egyptians and bring you into the land which I swore to give to Abraham, Isaac and Jacob. I will give it to you as your own possession—I, the Lord!"*

I cried. I heard the Lord telling me that He is with me and will free me from the bondage I've been in by bringing me into the new land which He will give me as my own possession. Italy? The Eucharistic pilgrimage? Wholeness in myself? His will for my life? The trip would be a gift from the Lord, Himself, who will rescue me — from the darkness of unresolved pain, stored in some dark corner of my heart where it rises up periodically to hurt me and those close to me. He will help me find my true self, to integrate that part of me that I've denied and rejected, that self which can't love and is broken and full of rage. Midlife has forced truth to the surface. There is no turning back now, only hope in Jesus' promise: *"If you remain in my word, you will truly be my disciples, and you will know the truth, and the truth will set you free."* (John 8: 31-33)

The Scripture reading penetrated my layers of protection and defense and spoke to the inner child who yearns to be free. Jesus told us that he came to free the prisoners, give sight to the blind and heal the lame. *Lord, thank you for showing me that I am the prisoner who needs to be set free, I am blind and lame and in need of your touch. Heal me, Lord, I beg you.*

My heart was full of expectant faith that the Lord had something very special in store for me — for us — in Italy. My faith was rewarded and *Feast of Faith, Confessions of a Eucharistic Pilgrim,* is one of the fruits of the trip. When Tommy returned home after ten days, I began dictating my experiences into a tape recorder every night before bed. When I edited the tapes for this manuscript, I had to reconstruct the first few chapters from memory. Of the ten days we enjoyed together, only three of those are in the book. Although we experienced much together, this book recounts *my* faith journey rather than *our* journey.

While editing the tapes I was doubly blessed in remembering all the graces I had received. In Italy I was praying my heart out and the Lord answered; but only afterwards I recognized a *pattern* to the healing I was experiencing. Everything was connected, grace built on grace, all part of a design of which I was not aware while it was happening. I am sharing my journey of the heart in the hope it will witness to God's lavish love and nearness to us mortals, to His desire to walk with us, talk with us, teach us and most of all touch us with His healing presence. I pray that this book will be a blessing to everyone who reads it; that Jesus will draw you closer to His Eucharistic Heart which reaches out in deepest hunger and thirst for souls, *because He wants to fill us with Himself.*

Joan McHugh

1

Arrival in Italy

When the plane touched down at Rome's Fiumicino Airport I felt an excitement unlike anything I'd experienced on many other flights to Italy. We were in Rome, all right; both the heat and the traffic attested to it! But nothing could wipe the grin off my face. It felt wonderful to be back in Italy.

We stood in line for a cab at Rome's airport which would take us into the city where we were to pick up our rental car. Just before the trip we invested in one of the latest model Camcorders, small and easy enough to work that even someone as inexperienced as myself could operate it. We delighted in the prospect of videotaping our trip in order to share it with our family and friends.

The cab dropped us off at Harry's Bar on the Via Veneto, a short distance from the Hertz Car

Nothing *could dampen the joy
of our pilgrimage!*

Rental. While Tommy paid the cab driver the exorbitant fare of $60, I organized the luggage next to the little outdoor cafe where I would wait for him. Then he disappeared into what looked like a subway station to find the Hertz office, while I ordered a cup of *cappuccino* – in Italian.

I could understand the language well enough. I learned to speak it fluently, thirty years ago, when several of us came over after college to live and work in Florence. In those days, we regarded anyone who went to Harry's Bar as a spoiled American tourist who had no clue how really to enjoy himself in Italy. We would *never* go to Harry's Bar or anyplace like it then. Thirty years dims the memory.

Now I was sitting there quite happily, feeling only gratitude to be back in Italy sipping a cup of *cappuccino*.

Our New Video Camera Stolen

Now, sitting at Harry's Bar, I found myself stumbling over the simplest Italian words. My Italian was rusty and it was frustrating. After what seemed like an hour, Tommy swung around the corner in a little red Fiat and we piled the luggage in the car. Thank goodness he was driving because we might as well have been on the Indianapolis speedway. Traffic was a nightmare, not to mention the lack of courtesy exhibited by European drivers. While driving down the Via Salaria, I thought about the fun we'd have using the movie camera. *The new camera!* I didn't remember seeing the case among the luggage. We stopped the car and made a search. No camera. In the hurried confusion of getting out of the cab on the Via Veneto, I didn't count the bags which the cab driver had unloaded on the sidewalk because we didn't have that many and it seemed unnecessary. In the haste of paying him and dodging traffic, neither of us took note of the fact that the camera never came out of the trunk.

Causing a Scene on the Via Salaria

Tears rolled down my cheeks. I was so upset all I could do was cry. I couldn't believe it. This was like a nightmare, only it was real. It was an expensive investment, but that isn't what bothered me. It was the loss of all the movies we would have taken to record what we knew would be the trip of our lives. We drove back to Harry's Bar on the chance that it was all a big mistake, hoping the cabby might have found it on his next fare and returned it. No such luck. And to try to trace one yellow cab in a city of 3,000 of them was impossible. There was one more alternative. We could go to a camera store and buy another, hoping to come out even with a reimbursement from the insurance company. We headed straight for a nearby camera shop which had many makes and models from which to choose. I found the exact same camera—but for nearly double the price. I had paid close to $1,000 in the States for the Camcorder. In Italy they wanted almost $2,000. It was out of the question.

What a disappointment. It was outright depressing. There was only one slight consolation. I believe God allows these things to happen and that He would bring some good out of it. *I had to believe that.* So many times in my life the wrong turns or the "mistakes" have actually turned into blessings. According to St. Paul, all things do work together for the good of those who love God, and yes, I believe He can bring good out of what seems like "bad" situations. This was bad alright, it even felt evil.

Orvieto or Bust!!!

By the grace of God we found our way out of the maze of Roman traffic and headed to Orvieto, the site of one of the Eucharistic miracles. Nothing would deter us from our journey. The air conditioner in the car was broken and the temperature had to have been 100 degrees. There was a heat spell in Italy which lasted the entire month I was there. Americans are not used to that kind of heat and we found ourselves constantly stopping to buy bottled water. We never went anywhere without our bottles of water.

What a joy to be in Italy and to stroll around this delightful hill town of Orvieto. We found a hotel within easy walking distance to the Cathedral. I opened those big wooden shutters which looked out on hundreds of red-tiled roofs to let in the familiar noises of an Italian city—which were like music to my ears. Ambling along the cobblestone streets I felt so at home, and so happy to have this time together. Not to have to worry about anyone else was freeing, to say the least. We found a quaint restaurant for dinner, one of those nondescript looking places that have the best food in the world. Tommy ordered an expensive bottle of wine to celebrate our anniversary. *This was so special.* I was having fun trying to speak Italian again, and when the people sense you can understand them, *they help you so much*! We walked around after dinner, holding hands like newlyweds. It felt like a honeymoon without all the insecurity that goes along on the first honeymoon. The shops were so attractive, as was all the beautiful hand painted pottery which made you want to bring home one of everything. We would buy a special memento from Orvieto tomorrow. Although we had been to this old and charming city several times, we never knew about the miracle of the Eucharist. Now, finally here, I could barely wait another minute to see how and why the Lord had revealed Himself through a Eucharistic miracle way back in the 13th century.

Scripture Meditation

". . . I know well the plans I have in mind for you. . . plans for your welfare, not for woe; plans to give you a future full of hope. When you call me, when you go to pray to me, I will listen to you. When you look for me, you will find me. Yes, when you seek me with all your heart, you will find me with you, says the Lord, and I will change your lot; I will gather you together from all the nations and all the places to which I have banished you, says the Lord, and bring you back to the place from which I have exiled you." (Jeremiah 29: 11-16)

Dear Lord Jesus,

I believe You are leading us on our journey according to Your perfect plan for our lives. Please show me the path You have marked for me leading to the fullness of life. I want to follow You because I am like a sheep in need of a Shepherd. Lord, please save that lost and wounded person who has strayed off the path and is searching for You. Rescue me from that place of inner exile which is like a pit which I fall into sometimes. Free me, Lord, from that dark and barren place which paralyzes me and keeps me from loving, and lead me back to the protection and warmth of Your love.

2

The Miracle of Corpus Christi

The Cathedral of Orvieto is a miracle in its own right. Built over the site of two churches which for centuries were in states of crumbling disrepair, the present cathedral was built in record time after the Eucharistic miracle of 1263. We found our way through a maze of streets hoping to attend morning Mass in the cathedral. We caught sight of it at the end of a long narrow street. The early morning sun cast a golden light on the mosaic-decorated facade and the Rose window, causing the brilliant colors to sparkle like precious gems. Known as the jewel of Italian architecture, the cathedral was breathtakingly beautiful.

Thank You for Your Perfect Timing!

Once inside, we were directed to the "Chapel of the Corporal," the chapel named after the chalice cloth involved in the Eucharistic miracle. Following the left aisle to the end of the transept, we found the chapel overrun with electricians and wires. Barely aware of what we were even looking for, I felt my heart sink when the custodian told us that the miracle was usually contained in a special reliquary and only exhibited to the public twice a year: on the afternoon of Easter day and on the Feast of Corpus Christi. "But," he said, "due to the work they are doing, it will be on display for a few days." *Thank you, Lord, for Your perfect timing!* I don't know what I would have done had I not been able to see the sacred relic.

The magnificent chapel was flooded with light and there, amidst the lights and wires and tourists, was the blood-stained corporal exposed in a marble tabernacle high behind the main altar.

At Home in This Chapel

We barely knew the facts surrounding the miracle, it was all so new and there was so much information to digest. We stayed in that chapel a long time – kneeling, sitting, and studying the frescoed walls which featured episodes recounting the story of the miracle. Here we were half way across the world in a foreign country knowing no one, and yet I felt so at home. What a rich heritage we have in our Church – in our faith, our sacraments, our traditions, our saints. God loves us so much as to give us His own Son, brutally tortured and crucified for our redemption. Seeing Christ's blood stains on the linen cloth just a few feet from me brought Him to life as never before. Often during Scripture reflections in my life, I have wanted to be considered one of "His own" in this world. After preaching to the crowds, Scripture tells us that Jesus would retire with His small group of disciples, His intimates. I've always wanted to think of myself as belonging to that group. Here in the "Chapel of the Corporal" I began to taste that intimacy. I thought that just as the disciples used to gather around Jesus, so here we were, pilgrims on the journey, gathering around the tabernacle. Just as they had the privilege of being so close to Jesus in the flesh, so do we through His Eucharistic Presence, and in a special way through the miracle of this blood-stained linen cloth.

How the Eucharistic Miracle Began

The story of the Eucharistic miracle actually began in Belgium some years prior to its actual occurrence. Blessed Juliana of Liege, Belgium, a nun, had been having dreams of the moon streaked with a black band. "She saw this vision day and night. She could not get it out of her mind. Then, she had a vision from Our Lord Jesus in which He explained the meaning of the moon streaked with a black band. Our Lord explained to her that the moon represented the Christian year with all its feasts. The black band represented the one feast which was missing from the Christian calendar, one in honor of Jesus in the Blessed Sacrament.

After the apparition, she devoted the rest of her life trying to initiate a feast in the Church in honor of the Blessed Sacrament."[1] She confided her visions to a Belgian clergyman, James Pantaleon, but she died before they were able to initiate a feast in honor of our Lord's body.

The Miracle Happened during Mass

Five years after her death, her vision would come to life through a miracle of the Eucharist. The actual miracle happened in a small lake town, Bolsena, not too far from Orvieto, where a priest, Peter of Prague, was celebrating Mass at the crypt of St. Christina, a virgin martyr from that town. Peter of Prague was making a pilgrimage to Rome to pray at the tomb of his patron saint, St. Peter. In those days, it was customary to make such pilgrimages to ask for favors at the tombs of their patron saints. He was having a faith crisis and was assailed with doubts about the Real Presence of Christ in the Eucharist.

Now, while saying Mass in Bolsena, he had barely spoken the words of consecration when blood started to drip from the consecrated Host. The blood dripped over his hands on to the altar, on to the Eucharistic altar cloth known as the corporal, and on to the marble squares on which he was standing.

Showing the Pope Our Lord's Body and Blood

Confused and astonished, he first attempted to hide the blood. Instead he decided to send a messenger to Pope Urban IV who just happened to be staying in nearby Orvieto at the Papal Palace. The Pope sent word to bring the miracle to Orvieto and so Peter of Prague and a small group set out immediately. The Pope, meanwhile, grew impatient and headed for Bolsena with practically the entire town of Orvieto in pursuit. He met Peter of Prague at the Bridge of the Sun, somewhere between both towns, and when the Pope saw the sacred presence of the Lord in the bloody corporal, he went down on his knees in adoration of Him. As God would have it, the Pope was none other than James Pantaleon, the Belgian friend of Blessed Juliana of Liege to whom she confided her vision of the need for a feast in honor of Jesus in the Blessed Sacrament. Now he was Pope and in a position to turn the Lord's wish into reality.

Back in Orvieto, the Pope stood on the balcony of the Papal Palace and reverently raised the bloody corporal to show the people. He declared a miracle and said that this truly dispels the heresies of the day aimed at destroying the doctrine of Christ's Real Presence in the Eucharist.

Heresies regarding the Eucharist

The Eucharist has had its detractors throughout history, but especially during the Middle Ages. It was a very devotional era especially in regard

Detail from a painting by Raphael *in the Vatican depicting the actual occurrence of the miracle of the Eucharist*

Detail showing the blood-stained Corporal

The dried blood stains on the Corporal are still visible after 700 years

A painting on the wall of the Blessed Sacrament Chapel in the Cathedral of Orvieto showing Pope Urban IV kneeling before the sacred altar cloth containing Our Lord's Blood

"You have written well of the Sacrament of My Body," *Jesus said to St. Thomas Aquinas, then asked him what reward he wanted, to which St. Thomas replied:* "Only Yourself." *This painting is on an altar panel in Italy.*

to the Holy Eucharist and the Blessed Mother. During the twelfth and thirteenth centuries, many new rituals developed to express the deep respect of the faithful in the presence of their Eucharistic Lord. The practice of elevating the Host during the consecration of the Mass for the adoration of the faithful was instituted. This supposedly was established in reparation for the false teaching on the Real Presence. Berengarius, a clergyman, was among those who spread considerable confusion about the Eucharist as to whether the material Bread and Wine could co-exist with the spiritual Body and Blood of Christ. The words of Christ, "This is My Body," have been given many interpretations through the centuries, the following being the most common: "This bread is a sign of my body," or "This bread becomes my body when eaten," or "That which is under the visible appearances of bread is My Body." The first two are erroneous and the third contains the truth of Christ's message.

The Feast of Corpus Christi

Pope Urban IV began work immediately on a Papal Bull, *Transiturus*, which he issued on August 11, 1264, and through which he instituted The Feast of Corpus Christi, the Feast of the Body of Christ. Christ's wish, first revealed to Blessed Juliana many years earlier in Belgium, had finally become a reality.

The Pope invited St. Thomas Aquinas to write the Liturgy for the Mass. Known as "The Eucharistic or Angelic Doctor," St. Thomas was very devoted to the Blessed Sacrament and worked tirelessly to promote devotion to the Real Presence of Jesus in the Holy Eucharist. The Eucharist, in Aquinas' words, is "the greatest of the miracles of Jesus Christ." He says: "This sacrament is given under the form of food and drink. Therefore every effect which is produced for physical life by material food and drink, that is, sustenance, growth, regeneration and pleasure, all of these effects are produced by this sacrament for the spiritual life."[2] St. Thomas wrote that just as we cannot live without food, so also is the spiritual food of the Eucharist necessary, for without it we cannot maintain our spiritual life. No theologian before or since explained the doctrine of transsubstantiation better than St. Thomas Aquinas.

Jesus Appears to St. Thomas Aquinas

According to William da Tocco, a former pupil who became one of his biographers, his learning was exceeded only by his piety. He recounts that Thomas used to spend hours in prayer, and "When consecrating at Mass, he would be overcome by such intensity of devotion as to be dissolved in tears, utterly absorbed in its mysteries and nourished with its fruits." [3]

He taught at the University of Paris for many years, and his scholarly reputation and his devotion to the Eucharist earned him a challenge from the other Doctors of the Sorbonne. They put before him a problem about the nature of the mystical change in the elements of the Blessed Sacrament, and he proceeded to write, in his customary manner, a very careful and elaborately lucid statement of his own solution. "He sought for guidance in more than usually prolonged prayer and intercession; and finally, with one of those few but striking bodily gestures that mark the turning points of his life, he threw down his thesis at the foot of the crucifix on the altar, and left it lying there; as if awaiting judgment. Then he turned and came down the altar steps and buried himself once more in prayer; but the other Friars, it is said, were watching; and well they might be. For they declared afterwards that the figure of Christ had come down from the cross before their mortal eyes; and stood upon the scroll, saying, 'Thomas, thou hast written well concerning the Sacrament of My Body.' It was after this vision that the incident is said to have happened, of his being borne up miraculously in mid-air." [4]

A Final Revelation

St. Thomas wrote the liturgy for the Proper of the Mass for the Feast of Corpus Christi, and he also composed two Eucharistic hymns, much loved and sung in Church to this day: *Tantum Ergo* and *Salutaris*. Towards the end of his life, he received another revelation while he was celebrating Mass on the Feast of St. Nicholas. It so affected him that he wrote and dictated no more, leaving his great *Summa Theologiae* unfinished. "The end of my labors has come," he said, "All that I have written appears to be as so much straw after the things that have been revealed to me." [5] Barely 50 years old when he died, St. Thomas declared on his deathbed regarding the Eucharist:

> If in this world there be any knowledge of this
> Mystery keener than that of faith, I wish now to
> affirm that I believe in the Real Presence of Jesus
> Christ in this Sacrament, truly God and truly man,
> the Son of God, the Son of the Virgin Mary. This
> I believe and hold for true and certain.[6]

Kneeling in the Chapel of the Corporal in Orvieto, I felt the intensity of Jesus' desire to be close to us. *He is so burdened by our lack of faith in His Presence among us.* We know that He is present to us in different ways, not only through the Eucharist. Church documents list five ways Christ manifests Himself to us: In the assembly, in His Word, in the Sacraments, in ordained ministers and in the Eucharist where "this presence of Christ under the appearance of bread and wine is called real, not to exclude the other kinds of presence as though they were not real, but because it is real *par excellence.*" [7]

His presence in the Eucharist is listed as *par excellence.* Jesus Christ has come among us in this very special way for a reason. *He wants to impress upon us the truth of His actual physical Presence.* He wants to hide in our hearts, to nourish us, to supply us with His life which, according to St. Thomas Aquinas, will spiritually restore us.

Jesus Shares the Desires of His Heart

I remember the imagery of Jesus "hiding" in our hearts from a book I read often in high school. Written by Sister Josefa Menendez, a simple Spanish nun belonging to the Religious of the Sacred Heart of Jesus, it is a deeply moving account of the remarkable revelations she received from Our Lord. "The Way of Divine Love," was filled with revelations of Jesus' love and His thirst for souls. I still have my worn out paperback which I used to bring to our summer home at the ocean during Easter vacation. I would open it for a quick look and read into the wee hours, unable to put it down because of the spiritual riches it contained. Like reading a diary of two lovers who share deeply of their love for each other, Our Lord instructed Josefa to write down the innermost secrets of their relationship: *"Now write for My souls: I want to tell them of the poignant sorrow which filled My heart at the Last Supper. If it was bliss for Me to think of all those to whom I should be both Companion and Heavenly Food, of all who would surround Me to the end of time with adoration, reparation, and love. . .this in no wise diminished My grief at the many who would leave Me deserted in My tabernacle and who would not even believe in My Real Presence. . .Sacrileges and outrages, and all the nameless abominations to be committed against Me passed before My eyes. . . It is love for souls that keeps Me a prisoner in the Blessed Sacrament. I stay there that all may come and find the comfort they need in the tenderest of Hearts, the best of Fathers, the most faithful of Friends, who will never abandon them. The Holy Eucharist is the invention of Love. . .Yet how few souls correspond to that love which spends and consumes itself for them!"* [8]

Those words bore themselves into my heart. They strengthened my faith in His Real Presence in the Eucharist, and deepened my awareness of His hunger and thirst for souls—which is not something found in most theological text books. Jesus used to show Himself to Josefa in the Host exposed for Adoration, just as He had done to St. Margaret Mary Alacoque requesting that she establish a feast in honor of His Sacred Heart.

His Eucharistic Presence Is Unique

Kneeling in the Cathedral of Orvieto in front of the blood-stained linen cloth, I felt privileged to be so near Jesus. Through His blood I felt Him reaching out and offering Himself to us in total love—which gives everything and asks only for love in return. He poured Himself out for our salvation—literally and completely; He remains here now, showing us His commitment, His suffering, His gift, His heart, for us. As Mother Teresa says, "Through the Cross we know how much Jesus loved us then, through the Eucharist, we understand how much Jesus loves us now." But He has been abandoned and misunderstood. While we know that He is present *spiritually* in the world, His Eucharistic Presence is unique and it alone is referred to as the *Real Presence*. "This holy Sacrament, given to men by a loving God as a perpetual presence among His children, while keenly adored by the saints and by the faithful members of the Church throughout the ages, has on the other hand been doubted by many, neglected and ignored by others, received unworthily by some, and even desecrated by a few. For these reasons, and others known only to God, the Lord has seen fit at times to manifest His presence by extraordinary Eucharistic miracles." [9]

The Blood-Stained Marble Squares

We wanted to see the actual site where this Eucharistic miracle occurred, so we drove the few miles to nearby Bolsena, to the Basilica of St. Christina, where the marble stones on which the blood dripped during the consecration are kept. There are four stones, one of which is on display behind glass in a special tabernacle made for it. It was a wondrous sight to behold. In the lower right hand corner of the marble square, you can see a round red drop of blood. The centuries have not dimmed the color and it was interesting to learn that although liquid does not usually penetrate marble, when a priest attempted to chip off a piece of the marble to take as a relic, he found the blood to have completely penetrated it. There is a deacon who informs people who are interested that when people have prayed in front of the marble square, they have seen the face of Jesus and have received instantaneous cures.

We stayed at a lovely hotel overlooking Lake Bolsena, complete with patio, beach and a whole lake in which to swim. In the evening after dinner we walked around the small town, imagining what it must have looked like at the time of the miracle. We would miss the "Mysteries of Saint Christina" by one week, living tableaux presented to commemorate the feast of the patron saint of Bolsena on July 23. They were beginning to erect wooden stages in various points around the city, where the townspeople would enact scenes from the life of St. Christina, a young virgin from the town who was martyred for her faith.

Tomorrow we're off to see another Eucharistic miracle in the "City of Saint Catherine" as it is sometimes called, Siena, the home of one of the greatest saints in the history of the Church.

Scripture Meditation

"Then He took the bread, said the blessing, broke it, and gave it to them saying, 'This is My Body, which will be given for you; do this in memory of Me. And likewise the cup after they had eaten, saying, 'This cup is the new covenant of my blood, which will be shed for you.'"(Luke 22: 19-20)

Dear Lord Jesus,

Your commitment to us is so total and intimate, You have made Yourself into our food and drink so that Your Presence can fill the very marrow of our bones. Jesus I believe You are really there in the consecrated Host—Body, Blood, Soul and Divinity. During the Consecration You revealed Yourself to St. John of the Cross in such majesty and glory he feared he could not continue the Mass. Even though I cannot see you with my bodily eyes, help me see Your Real Presence with the eyes of my soul and sing with the angels, "Joy to the world, the Lord is come!"

3

The City of St. Catherine

Visiting Miniature Towns

The drive to Siena was breathtaking. The landscape was dotted with tiny hill towns perched atop small mountains. A priest friend from home urged us to stop in Montepulciano, so we detoured a bit and headed for this ancient hill town for lunch. On the way we passed through another tiny hill

Pienza was charming and full of surprises

town, Pienza, which looked so inviting we parked the car and gave ourselves a tour. Like a model town in miniature, it was inhabited by 1500 people and the streets were so narrow that with outstretched arms you could touch the walls on both sides of the street. Huge blossoming geraniums cascaded from windows and balconies, and at every street corner there was another sweeping view of the rolling Tuscan countryside. We discovered it was the boyhood home of Piccolomini, who entered the priesthood at 40 and later became Pope Pius II. Returning to his hometown as Pius II, he was so touched by the display of affection and by seeing his childhood friends among the elderly present, he commissioned the elevation of the small borgo to a model town. No wonder it was so perfectly beautiful!

Finding the Borgia Palace

Facing cathedral square was a nondescript looking building which was one of the great surprises of the trip. It was the Borgia Palace, built by Cardinal Borgia, the father of Caesar and Lucretia and the future Pope Alexander VI. *My mother's name was Sabina Borgia!* Standing in front of the Borgia Palace gave me a felt sense of oneness with my heritage, albeit famous and infamous! It made the world very small, and left me feeling so *connected* to the entire human race.

Melted Cheese Sandwiches and St. Agnes

We arrived in Montepulciano at lunchtime, just when you don't want to arrive anywhere in Italy. Everything is closed! It must have been something over 100 degrees because all we wanted to do was find a light lunch and sit in the shade. While I went to buy film, Tommy bought us two ham and cheese sandwiches at the outdoor cafe, and in less than five minutes the cheese was melting and escaping from the rolls! The convent where St. Agnes of Montepulciano lived and died was just down the street, but even that was closed for siesta. I had never heard of this saint, so while Tommy read a day old *New York Times*, I read about St. Agnes.

She entered the convent at nine, and led a life of extraordinary spirituality. She fasted on bread and water for fifteen years and was favored with many visions. In one, an angel led her under an olive tree and offered her a cup saying, *"Drink this chalice, spouse of Christ, the Lord Jesus drank it for you."* She died when she was 49 telling her weeping nuns to rejoice because she would be with Jesus and watching over them.

Her body is incorrupt and many notables came to visit her tomb including the Emperor Charles IV and St. Catherine of Siena. When she bent to kiss Agnes' foot, it lifted itself up to meet her lips! Several artists have immortalized this incident in oil paintings.

We said the Rosary on the way to Siena, something new and special for us to do together. We share so many things together in marriage, why not our prayer life? We prayed for our children, and for special concerns each of us carried in our hearts. I had a deep sense of comfort praying the Rosary with Tommy, believing that Our Lady was pleased in our united effort and would take *special* care of our requests.

The "City of St. Catherine"

It was so good to be in this town which gave birth to one of the greatest saints of all time. The tawny rose-colored buildings made it resemble a Hollywood movie set where it seemed, as if, any minute St. Catherine would emerge from her house.

How I wished she would, but that was quite impossible, seeing as she died in 1380.

We set out first to visit the Basilica of St. Francis to see the Eucharistic miracle which happened in Siena in 1730. No sooner had we set foot in this beautiful old Franciscan church, than we met Father Antonio Giannini, the custodian of the miracle. We recognized him from Bob and Penny Lord's book and once he realized our interest, he was so kind in answering our questions.

This miracle is different from the one that happened in Bolsena. It has to do with Communion Hosts which are miraculously preserved, and have been for 250 years! At first, I didn't comprehend the beauty of this miracle — until Father Giannini elaborated. But first the story.

The Miracle Story

On the eve of the Feast of the Assumption in 1730, while everyone attended a vigil ceremony at the cathedral, thieves broke into the basilica and stole the golden ciborium containing a large amount of consecrated Hosts. The theft went undetected until the next morning, when crowds came to Mass for the Feast of the Assumption.

At communion the priest opened the tabernacle and realized the ciborium was missing. Later someone found the top of the ciborium in the street which meant that sacrilege was probably involved. The traditional festivities for Our Lady's Assumption were canceled. The archbishop asked for public prayers of reparation, while a search went out all over town for the consecrated Hosts.

Three days later, a priest was praying in the nearby church of St. Mary of Provenzano, when he noticed something white protruding from the poor box attached to his kneeler. The archbishop called a meeting to inspect the Hosts, many of which were suspended in cobwebs inside the poor box. The following day, the archbishop carried the Sacred Hosts in a solemn procession back to the Church of St. Francis.

Why weren't they consumed? A good question, considering they were so revered and appreciated upon their finding. The faithful came from nearby towns to pray in thanksgiving for their return and to venerate these sacred Hosts. Perhaps the priests felt constrained to allow the public this opportunity. They also had been soiled, and until they were properly cleaned, it would not be advisable to consume them.

The Hosts Were Incorrupt!

With the passage of years, it became obvious that the Hosts were not deteriorating. Were they witnessing some sort of a miracle? The Conventual Franciscans, whose church it was, began to believe that they were witnessing a miracle of preservation. "Fifty years passed and an official investigation was conducted into the authenticity of the miracle. The minister general of the Franciscan Order, Father Carlo Vipera, examined the Hosts on April 14, 1780, and upon tasting one of them he found it fresh and incorrupt." [1]

Further tests were done repeatedly over the years. In one test the archbishop ordered a number of unconsecrated hosts to be put in a sealed container and kept in the chancery office. "Ten years later these were examined and found to be not only disfigured, but also withered. In 1850, 61 years after they were placed in a sealed box, these unconsecrated hosts were found reduced to particles of a dark yellow color, while the consecrated hosts retained their original freshness." [2]

Another commission did acid and starch tests on the Hosts. They concluded that unleavened bread which was not hermetically sealed and exposed to the activity of micro-organisms would remain intact for no more than a few years. In 1914, Professor Siro Grimaldi, professor of chemistry at the University of Siena was the chief medical examiner of the

"These Hosts are incorrupt by reason of the Real Presence of Jesus," Fr. Giannini said. *"He wants us to know that it is His Presence in the Bread which keeps them intact. Science cannot explain this."*

Pope John Paul II prays in front of the Sacred Hosts in September of 1980 when he came to Siena in honor of the 250th anniversary of this Eucharistic Miracle

Hosts. He concluded: "The holy Particles of unleavened bread represent an example of perfect preservation. . .a singular phenomenon that inverts the natural law of the conservation of organic material. It is a fact unique in the annals of science."[3] Professor Grimaldi wrote a book about the miracle entitled *A Scientific Adorer*.

Father Giannini placed the ciborium containing the miraculous Hosts in the center of the altar so I could photograph them. They were very wholesome and shiny-looking. *They looked like they were perfectly preserved*. They still retain the scent of unleavened bread. The Hosts were consecrated in 1730, and they have been venerated as the Body and Blood of Christ in the Basilica of St. Francis for over 250 years.

An *Ongoing* Miracle of Jesus' Presence

Why so special? This miracle is of great importance because it shows us that it is Jesus' sacred Presence which keeps the Hosts in existence. There is no scientific explanation possible. These Hosts are incorrupt by reason of the Real Presence of Jesus. *He wants us to know that He is really in the bread; the consecrated Hosts represent Him, His Body, Blood, Soul and Divinity*. Other "control" Hosts disintegrated in five years. These have defied the natural laws of corruption by remaining perfectly preserved. They have not discolored or disfigured in any way. This is an ongoing miracle through which Jesus wants to get our attention and convince us of His Real Presence. On the wall was a poster of Pope John Paul II kneeling in adoration of the Sacred Hosts when he came to Siena in 1980 to commemorate the 250th anniversary of the miracle. We stayed for Mass and Benediction and I wanted to stay even longer. *I wanted to set up a tent!* It was so good to be here, to be close to Jesus in this special miracle of His ongoing love for us.

Thank you Lord for the privilege of being with You here, in this place, where You have been for 250 years, waiting for people to believe. I believe, Lord.

Catherine, the Twenty-Third Child

We went back across town and spent the afternoon touring St. Catherine's home, stopping now and then to read and pray in the chapels inside. Today her home would be called an estate. Her father ran a very successful dye works and their home included the business, their twenty five children, and their spouses and in-laws! Incredible as it seems,

Catherine came along as the twenty-third child and turned the house upside down! That she was no ordinary child was attested to by the struggles her parents had trying to introduce her into society and to a rich husband. She wanted no part of either. Unlike other children, Catherine craved solitude and prayer. When she and her brother were walking home from her married sister's house one day, she had a vision of Jesus who appeared over St. Dominic's Church, a stone's throw from her house. Accompanied by Sts. Paul and John, Jesus drew her to Himself, blessing her with the sign of the cross. Starry-eyed and filled with wonder, she told her brother Stefano that if only he could have seen what she saw, he would never want to disturb her. She was six years old. When she got home and related the vision, neither her parents nor any of her twenty-four brothers and sisters believed her. That didn't stop her from pursuing a life of deep prayer from that point on. *Nothing stopped Catherine!*

To read about Catherine and her relationship with the Lord is to be caught up in a passionate love story which is more exciting than any best-selling romance novel on the market. God used her natural gifts for His benefit. "Fire is my nature" is the way she described herself. She was a firebrand alright, on fire with the love of Christ. *I love St. Catherine of Siena.*

Catherine and God Were a Real Team

Catherine listened to her dreams, cried a lot and had an insatiable desire to share her faith. *I can relate to that!* She wore out two male secretaries who took down her voluminous dictation and got angry when one of them fell asleep while she was dictating. In a century marked by social, political and religious chaos, there appeared a woman who was shot out of a spiritual cannon and made such an impact on the world that we still reap the fruits of her labors. She and St. Teresa of Avila are the two women saints who have been awarded the title of Doctor of the Church. That is quite an accomplishment considering that Catherine never went to school and couldn't read or write.

I believe God gave us Catherine to show us Himself. While other mystics dwelt in the realm of the speculative, Catherine *practiced* what she learned from God. They were quite a team. God backed her up in everything she said and did, strengthening her with visions of Himself. Sometimes He graced her with His visible presence, and at other times He was accompanied by Our Lady and certain saints. He spoke to her with words of encouragement or reproof or instructed her about some matter of faith. When she neither saw Him nor heard Him, she became disconsolate. Her longing for Him increased until she cried out: *"Lord where were You when I sought You and could not find You?"* to which the Lord replied, *"In your heart."* After that, she never sought Him in vain.[4]

God Responds to Catherine's Questions

Catherine left us a testament of their intimate communication in *The Dialogue*, a thick volume of four questions Catherine asked God and God's responses, which Catherine received while in ecstasy. "Here is the way," Jesus said in *The Dialogue*, "if you would come to perfect knowledge and enjoyment of me, eternal Life: Never leave the knowledge of yourself. Then, put down as you are in the valley of humility you will know me in yourself, and from this knowledge you will draw all that you need. . . .After the soul has come to know herself she finds humility and hatred for her selfish sensual passion, recognizing the perverse law that is bound up in her members and is always fighting against the spirit. . . . Through all the blessings she has received from me she discovers within her very self the breadth of my goodness. She humbly attributes to me her discovery of this self-knowledge, because she knows that my grace has drawn her from darkness and carried her into the light of true knowledge. . . .And just as she loves me in truth, so also she serves her neighbors in truth. Nor could she do otherwise, for love of me and love of neighbor are one and the same thing: Since love of neighbor has its source in me, the more the soul loves me, the more she loves her neighbors." [5]

Catherine was so beautiful that the Mother Superior of the Dominican convent at first refused her. Catherine *knew* she belonged in the convent because God had given her a dream, showing her specifically, through St. Dominic offering her the Dominican habit, that she was to follow the desire of her heart and enter that order. She became a Third Order Dominican.

Catherine was favored with extraordinary spiritual experiences. She was mystically betrothed to Jesus and wore a wedding ring of pearls and diamonds which she told her confessor and biographer, Raymond of Capua, that it gave her great strength especially during times of trial, and there was never a moment when it was out of her sight.

She tried to keep her suffering secret. Jesus had offered her a choice of two crowns, she said; one of them was made with gold and set with precious jewels, and the other was made with thorns, like His own. She chose the crown of thorns to wear in this world, leaving the jeweled crown for eternity.

Jesus' Wounds Lead Her to Battle

He gave her His own wounds, invisible, but physically very painful to bear. Catherine also suffered spiritually, for the confusion and disruption in the Church which was at war with Florence and other cities throughout Italy. Churches were locked and priests were forbidden to say Mass. The Pope had taken up residence in Avignon, France, and Catherine feared that unless and until Gregory XI restored the Papacy and reclaimed the chair of Peter in Rome, Catholicism itself was endangered. She wrote letters to *everyone*, the Pope especially, and in the spring of 1376 she and twenty three companions set out for Avignon to meet with him. She stayed for four months, winning Pope Gregory's confidence and trust with her simple, straightforward manner and her passionate zeal for the Gospel. It was through her efforts that he eventually returned to Rome.

Fresco in St. Catherine's Chapel in the Basilica of St. Dominic showing her mystical rapture

Catherine's style and charm was disarming. Known as the "blessed child of the people," her critics grew right along with her popularity. As word of her supernatural experiences became known, she enraged people who came after her trying to discredit her publicly to prove that she was an unbalanced fanatic. She was a prophet without honor in her own country. One morning when Catherine knelt enraptured during Mass, a wealthy noblewoman knelt next to her at the Communion rail. To prove Catherine was a fake, she stuck a long pin in the heel of Catherine's foot. The saint didn't flinch. Afterwards, when Catherine came to her senses, she felt the pain in her foot and had to be treated by a doctor.

She *Begged* to Receive Jesus Daily

St. Catherine had a very deep devotion to Jesus in the Holy Eucharist. Her spiritual experiences related to the Real Presence of Jesus in the Eucharist are inspiring as are the written words she recorded about the Holy Eucharist in *The Dialogue*. It is interesting to know that in those days, people did not go to daily Mass like they do today. The Eucharist was not as readily distributed as it is now; to receive Jesus in the Eucharist on a daily basis was almost unheard of. Catherine *begged* for the privilege of receiving Christ daily; neither the priests at her parish church of St. Dominic's nor her mother superior would allow this. She finally held sway over her confessor, Raymond of Capua, who agreed to her wishes. It is recorded that the matter was brought before Pope Gregory XI, Catherine's friend, who interceded and wrote a papal bull decreeing that she could receive communion daily!

"Catherine had visions during the consecration of the Mass, sometimes seeing Jesus dressed as a priest, repeating the words He spoke at the Last Supper. Other times, when she gazed upon the raised Host, instead of seeing the Consecrated Host, she saw the Baby Jesus in the priest's hands. When we hear some people say they do not *need* miracles of the Eucharist to believe in the Lord truly present in the consecrated Host, I can't help recall Catherine, who was strengthened in her belief in Him when she saw the Host in this miraculous form. *She did not need the miracle to believe*, but she did not refuse the help it gave her when she needed *strength*, or maybe as Mother Angelica said, *the grace to believe*."[6]

Catherine *Knew* whether a Host Was Consecrated

One day a priest tried to trick her by substituting an unconsecrated Host when he gave her communion. Catherine knew immediately and lashed out at him in anger for depriving someone who hungered for Jesus.

"Priests were touched by happenings during Holy Mass with Catherine. One reported he saw the Host go to her without him moving his arm. Other priests said they saw the Host nod to her, almost as if in recognition. There were those who could feel their arms being pulled toward her, with the Host. Raymond of Capua reported he *saw* a Host travel clear across the church to Catherine. It was as if the Lord desired her as much as she longed for Him. There was a magnet between them and the magnet was the Eucharist.

God Instructs Catherine about the Eucharist

"At the moment of receiving Communion, her face would become transfixed, as if glorified, surrounded by an aura. Catherine often went into ecstasy at that time, levitating. Her friends remained with her so they could assist her home, as even from childhood, Catherine was always left weakened after an ecstasy."[7]

God's dictation to Catherine in *The Dialogue* regarding the Holy Eucharist is a powerful confirmation of the doctrine as Christ taught it and we believe it. He tells Catherine that He, God the Father eternal, is like the Sun. From Him proceed the Holy Spirit who is fire, and the Son who is wisdom. Through the Son's wisdom, we receive light, which came into the world, the divine merging with our humanity. How do we receive this light? And to whom does He entrust it? "To my ministers in the mystic body of holy Church, so that you might have life when they give you His Body as food and His Blood as drink. I have said that this body of his is a sun. Therefore you could not be given the body without being given the blood as well; nor either the Body or the Blood without the Soul of this Word; nor the Soul or Body without the Divinity of me, God eternal. For the one cannot be separated from the other—just as the divine nature can nevermore be separated from the human nature, not by death or by any other thing past or present or future. So it is the whole divine being that you receive in that most gracious sacrament under the whiteness of bread."[8]

I Leave Behind My Imprint of Grace

God tells her that she must receive this sacrament not only with her bodily senses but with her spiritual sensitivity, by disposing her soul to receive and see and taste this sacrament with affectionate love. Then the Father uses beautiful imagery to describe the way Jesus becomes present in the soul through Holy Communion: "Dearest daughter, contemplate the marvelous state of the soul who receives this bread of life, this food of angels, as she ought. When she receives this sacrament she lives in me and I in her. Just as the fish is in the sea and the sea in the fish, so am I in the soul and the soul in me, the sea of peace. Grace lives in such a soul because, having received this bread of life in grace, she lives in grace.

When this appearance of bread has been consumed, I leave behind the imprint of my grace, just as a seal that is pressed into warm wax leaves its imprint when it is lifted off. Thus does the power of this sacrament remain there in the soul; that is, the warmth of my divine charity, the mercy of the Holy Spirit, remains there. The light of my only-begotten Son's wisdom remains there, enlightening the mind's eye. The soul is left strong, sharing in my strength and power, which make her strong and powerful against her selfish sensuality and against the devil in the world.

So you see, the imprint remains once the seal is lifted off. In other words, once the material appearances of the bread have been consumed, this true Sun returns to his orbit. Not that he had ever left it, for he is united with me. But my deep charity gave him to you as food for your salvation and for your nourishment in this life where you are pilgrim travelers, so that you would have refreshment and would not forget the blessing of the blood. I in my divine providence gave you this food, my gentle truth, to help you in your need. See, then, how bound and obligated you are to love me in return, since I have loved you so much, and because I am supreme eternal Goodness, deserving to be loved by you."[9]

Catherine Lived on the Eucharist Alone

St. Catherine had an apparition in 1372, eight years before she died, which affected her deeply for the remainder of her earthly life.

She was allowed to drink of the Blood of Jesus, from His side. She shared with Blessed Raymond that after drinking the Blood of Jesus, she couldn't eat anymore. She was neither hungry, nor could she hold anything in her stomach, other than the Sacred Species, the Body and Blood of Jesus. . . .For the seven year period prior to her death, she took no food into her body other than the Eucharist. Her fasting did not affect her energy, however. She maintained a very active life during those seven years. As a matter of fact, most of her greatest accomplishments occurred during that period. Her death had nothing to do with malnutrition, or anything connected with lack of food. She had a vision in the early part of 1380, in which the ship of the Church crushed her to the earth. She offered herself as a willing sacrifice. She was ill from this time until April 21 of that year, when she suffered a paralytic stroke from the waist down. On April 29, she went to her reward."[10]

We spent the entire afternoon in Catherine's house, not wanting to leave. Although there was much else to see and do in Siena, this woman stole our hearts. Later we visited the cathedral, which is one of the most beautiful ever built. These medieval cathedrals are awesome, but not half as awesome as some of the saints, like St. Catherine, a "cathedral of the spirit," living testimonies of God's abiding presence.

At dinner in the open square, we feasted on Italian cuisine. There were hundreds and hundreds of tourists dining at these open air restaurants, which are such a novelty and so enjoyable. Again we toasted our trip and celebrated these days of grace, walking slowly back to the hotel relishing every moment of this experience.

Scripture Meditation

"They that hope in the Lord will renew their strength, they will soar as with eagles' wings." (Is 40: 31)

Dear Lord Jesus,

You give us such reasons for hope! The ways of Your presence in the world are so obvious through the eyes of faith. You feed us with Your own Self. You remain with us by extraordinary means in the Eucharist. Jesus, please let me experience the depth of hope and trust in You that St. Catherine did, so that I, too, can inwardly soar like an eagle. Lord Jesus, I place all my hope and trust in You.

4

Eucharistic Miracles in Florence

We took a cab to the train station this morning so Tommy could catch a train to Rome. We had enjoyed our time together so much, praying and playing together, that time had literally flown and now he was on his way home. (A week of our time together is unrecorded.) Temperatures hovered around 100 degrees. Tommy walked ahead of me down the long ramp. He had on new pants which were a bit long because they were incorrectly tailored. He was perspiring and as I watched him carrying those heavy bags, I saw what a good man he is, what a good and generous and big-hearted person he is. He has put up with a lot of my stuff over the years—and with it all he never flinches; he keeps loving. He's got an indomitable spirit. Like an Oriental wife following ten paces behind, I was caught up in all these thoughts while walking down the hot ramp in the Florence train station. God has been so good to us and even though we've had some very difficult and painful struggles, this trip has reinforced the love which has been there all along, hidden sometimes behind so many responsibilities and cares which we both carry at home. Now he was leaving, and I would miss him terribly. I watched him get a seat, then waited for the train to pull out, wiping my eyes before he even left. I could tell he was sad too.

Thank goodness I had on sunglasses, because I could cry all I wanted without anyone knowing. My sadness and loneliness were compounded by the bittersweet memory of the many times I spent in this train station, thirty years ago! People called me "Signorina" then; I was 30 pounds lighter and my hair was brown. Now I was an automatic "Signora." I nursed my melancholy on a long, rambling walk through the city which I once called home.

What a Great Dream!

Under an awning at one of those charming outdoor cafes, I ordered a *cappucino* and recorded a dream I had last night. In the dream I gave my Aunt Helen a beautiful pair of earrings, rectangular-shaped, depicting scenes of Orvieto, Bolsena, Siena and Florence. They were colorful three dimensional views, so that as you looked at the earrings, you could go through them, as it were, to these places. On either side of the scenes sat two angels, one on the left and one on the right. They were perched on the corners of the earrings, just watching. My aunt loved these earrings and thanked me so much for the gift.

"*What a wonderful gift,*" she kept saying. She was deeply pleased and moved by these earrings. I thought about that dream all day long! What did it mean? My aunt Helen has been a spiritual soul mate since I was a teenager. She's my Dad's sister who used to come to New York when I was in high school and take me out to lunch. We'd go to an outdoor cafe at the Central Park Zoo where we'd watch the seals while sharing secrets of our faith. It was her enthusiasm for the saints that whetted my appetite to learn more about them. She was widely-travelled, having visited most of the Marian shrines and the birthplaces of famous saints in Europe.

Helen has been a mother, sister, friend and spiritual director to me all wrapped into one.

My Heavenly Traveling Companions

I've been recording and studying my dreams for fifteen years, and when we honor them, so to speak, by paying attention to them, they honor us by divulging all sorts of information and wisdom. The Bible is filled with examples of God communicating to His people through dreams and visions. *"Should there be a prophet among you, in visions will I reveal myself to him, in dreams will I speak to him;"* (Nb 12: 6) Each person and symbol in the dream represents some part of ourselves, and they appear in sort of a drama fashion to show us something, to throw up a question to us, to help us see where we're blocked or broken.[1] In the dream, Helen represents the me who is journeying to these sacred places and she realizes what a wonderful gift it is. That is to say, I am overjoyed at the gift of this trip—and the gift of the angels to accompany me! Were they like Raphael, the archangel who was sent to accompany Tobias on his long journey and who became a trusted friend bestowing on Tobias innumerable blessings? *"For a good angel will go with him; his journey will be successful, and he will come back safe and sound."* (Tob 5: 21) Among other things, Raphael saved Tobias from being eaten by a big fish and then he showed Tobias how to use the liver, gall and heart of the fish for medicine. He even found him a wife. What awesome powers the angels have! How consoling to know that two of them would be my travelling companions.

One of Aunt Helen's favorite saints is St. Frances of Rome who was constantly accompanied by an archangel who never left her side. Although no one else could see him, his radiance was so brilliant that she was able to read by his light at night! Many saints were privileged to see their guardian angels, those ministering spirits whom the Bible says are sent to serve us and lead us to our salvation. *"See that you do not despise one of these little ones, for I say to you that their angels in heaven always look upon the face of my heavenly Father,"* Matt (18: 10) Jesus tells us.

Angels Are Present at Mass

Stories of angels abound in Scripture and in the lives of the saints and martyrs. ". . .*He will command his angels concerning you, and with their hands they will support you, lest you dash your foot against a stone."* (Matt 4: 6) "St. Bernard tells us that angels kneel at our feet when we receive Holy Communion. And just as the Blessed Mother was present beneath the Cross, so too is she present during the Holy Sacrifice of the Mass; and according to sainted writers, angels surround them in adoring attendance."[2] From the private revelations of St. Bridget we read: "One day, when I was assisting at the Holy Sacrifice, I saw an immense number of Holy Angels descend and gather around the altar, contemplating the priest. They sang heavenly canticles that ravished my heart; Heaven itself seemed to be contemplating the great Sacrifice. And yet we poor blind and miserable creatures assist at the Mass with so little love, relish and respect!"[3]

Their Presence Is Real

There is a resurgence of interest in angels today, with many books being written about these heavenly beings. Their presence is such a gift to us; they are like invisible friends who are constantly at our side, looking out for our interests. Sometimes it's hard to believe they are really there, until we read stories which confirm their presence. One of my favorite stories involves Mother Angelica of the *Eternal Word Television Network*, who shares that when she was ten or eleven years old she went to town to do an errand for her mother, heard someone screaming, and looked around to stare into the headlights of a car. At that point, she felt two hands pick her up and swing her over a chain barricade to safety. At home her mother who had sensed danger, had been praying. Both are convinced that an angel had saved her life.

I wondered who the angels were in my dream. Were they Sts. Gabriel and Raphael, the angels whom the Portuguese explorer, Vasco da Gama, named his two ships after when he sailed to India? I would name one of the angels "Raphael" in honor of Father Joe Whalen, my good friend who teams up with St. Raphael in a healing ministry, and I decided that the other angel must be my guardian angel.

A further thought came to me about the earrings. They are a decoration, and are worn not only to beautify oneself but to please others. May it be that this journey will not only be a gift for me, but it will be a source of inspiration for others, who will visit these places through my writing.

In Search of Two Eucharistic Miracles

Using my marked up and crumpled map, I had a slight problem finding the church of Saint Ambrose, the site of two Eucharistic miracles. After a half-hour walk, which for this city is rather long, I became confused and approached two policemen for directions. After some discussion and looking at the map, they told me they didn't think it was near here. I thanked them and kept walking, determined to find it. I walked exactly two blocks and ran right into it! What a laugh I had for myself. It's an old and forgotten-looking church, tucked in the corner of a small public square.

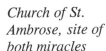

Church of St. Ambrose, site of both miracles

A man was vacuuming the church. I asked him where the Eucharistic miracle was and he said "over there," pointing to the left altar. I felt a little sad that it had fallen into such ignominy. No one was paying much attention to a Eucharistic miracle or to anything else for that matter, although I must say the church was in the process of being restored. But it was very old and decrepit. Nevertheless, I went over to the altar and started taking pictures. Actually, there were two miracles of the Eucharist which occurred here. "The first one happened on December 29, 1230 and involved a priest named Uguccione who was the chaplain of a monastery of nuns who were affiliated with the church of Saint Ambrose. After celebrating Mass one morning, the priest neglected to wipe the chalice dry, leaving a small amount of consecrated wine in the bottom of the vessel. The next morning while preparing for another Mass, he was shocked to find a quantity of coagulated blood at the bottom of the chalice. This blood is still perfectly preserved after 760 years.

"The second miracle occurred on March 24, 1595 when the altar cloth of the main altar caught fire, damaging the altar and the tabernacle. A pyx containing consecrated Hosts fell to the floor and opened on impact. Those that fell onto the carpet at the foot of the altar twisted and curled and they united together from the heat of the fire. These Hosts are still perfectly preserved after almost 400 years.

"Every year the monstrance containing the two Eucharistic relics is placed on display in the church of Saint Ambrose. At the very top is a receptacle held by a small golden angel, in which a recently consecrated Host can be placed. Beneath this, between two larger angels, is a crystal through which one can see the crystal vial and the coagulated blood of the miracle of 1230. According to the pastor of the parish the miracles are 'a strong reminder of the Real Presence of Jesus in the Eucharist.'"4

Desire to Sit at the Feet of Jesus

We know that wherever Jesus is, angels are always present. It was strangely comforting to think that they were beside Our Eucharistic Lord in this forgotten church, keeping Him company in the tabernacle. I was disappointed not to be able to see the sacred relics of Jesus' Body and Blood reserved in a special tabernacle in this old church. After taking some pictures of the tabernacle I stayed and said the Chaplet of Mercy, asking Jesus to intercede in the lives of all the people that I took with me on this trip. The man continued to vacuum and I continued to feel sad that these beautiful miracles of Christ's presence were so ignored amidst the hustle and bustle and busyness of modern day Florence. The walls of St. Ambrose are decorated with paintings by Roselli which portray a procession with the miraculous relics through the streets of Florence in 1340 when the city was afflicted with a pestilence. I was drawn to this place to search out these miracles. I have a strong desire to sit at the feet of Jesus in these places, to be with Him and to spread the word that this really happened. I feel so privileged to be here. I believe in His Real Presence and have since I was a child. It is either true or it isn't true. *If it isn't true it's the greatest hoax and deception of all time. If it is true, it is the most awesome and wonderful reality in the world.*

Nuns Taught Old Testament Roots of Eucharist

The Sacred Heart nuns taught us well—and thoroughly—showing us the Scriptural roots of the Eucharist which are found in the Old Testament. When the people were getting ready to leave Egypt they had to put the blood of the lamb on their doorposts in order to be passed over by the angel of death. In the New Testament, Jesus is the Paschal Lamb whose flesh and blood saved us and nourishes us on our journey. In the Old Testament, Moses confirmed God's covenant and promises with the blood of animals. In the New Testament, Christ confirmed His covenant with His own blood saying, *"This is my blood of the New Testament which shall be shed for you."*

Jesus' Bread of Life Discourse

Was the sadness I was feeling in this chapel similar to what Jesus felt when He taught the people about His Presence in the Bread—and many (not his disciples) walked away? In the sixth chapter of John's Gospel, Jesus gives His "Bread of Life" discourse in which He establishes Himself as our Bread. The people were not well disposed to this idea. Jesus had just multiplied the loaves and fishes before their eyes, feeding five thousand people at one sitting. This miracle stirred up the enthusiasm of the crowd like nothing else had. They saw Him as a prophet and possibly as the King they had been waiting for who would help their nation reclaim its power and independence. If He could feed that many people with a little bread and fish, He could also perform other miracles.

Work for Food That Doesn't Spoil

Scripture tells us that the crowds followed Jesus to the other side of the lake, where they approached Him the next day. He saw them coming and could read their hearts: "*I am telling you the truth: you are looking for Me because you ate the bread and had all you wanted, not because you understood my miracles. Do not work for food that spoils; instead, work for the food that lasts for eternal life.*" (John 6: 26-27)

Despite the fact that he unmasked their materialistic motives, he remains patient with them. What work did they have to do, they asked Him, to eat the food of eternal life. His unexpected answer didn't satisfy them: "*What God wants you to do is to believe in the one he sent.*" (vs. 29) They pressed him further, demanding another sign to convince them to believe him. Was the food that lasts for eternal life like the bread Moses gave his people in the desert? Jesus set them straight about that: "*What Moses gave you was not the bread from heaven; it is my Father who gives you the real bread from heaven. For the bread that God gives is he who comes down from heaven and gives life to the world.*" (vs. 35) Their interest is peaked and they ask for this bread: "*Give us this bread always.*" (vs. 34)

I Am the Living Bread

"*I am the bread of life,*" Jesus told them, "*He who comes to me will never be hungry; he who believes in me will never be thirsty.*" (vs. 35) Jesus was speaking clearly, identifying Himself as the Bread of Life, but they had trouble with this. They started grumbling and challenging his claim to this kind of divinity, questioning how he could come down from heaven because he was the son of Joseph and they knew his mother and father. Jesus understands and reiterates that his authority comes from his Father in heaven who gave Jesus power to raise people to life on the last day. He reminds them that the people who ate the manna in the desert died. That bread did not have the power that he was talking about. The living bread which Jesus was offering would give them freedom from death; it would give them eternal life. *"I am the bread of life. Your ancestors ate manna in the desert, but they died. But the bread that comes down from heaven is of such a kind that whoever eats it will not die. I am the living bread that came down from heaven. The bread that I will give is my flesh, which I give so that the world may live."* (vs.49-51)

St. Catherine of Siena and other saints report that they often saw Jesus standing in the place of the priest when they received Communion

His Literal Words Caused Arguments

Scripture tells us they argued angrily. Most of them could not make that leap of faith, they could not take Jesus literally. If Jesus had been speaking figuratively, the Jews would not have been outraged. They knew very well what He was saying; it was His literal words which caused their arguments, it was His literal words which drove many to desert Him. The saying was "too hard," Scripture tells us, they were scandalized by this talk of eating His flesh and drinking His blood, and many "walked no more with Him." They would not have been upset had he been speaking symbolically. Jesus didn't change His words, or try to rationalize His statements in order to bring them back. He let them go. And then He turned to His twelve, His intimate friends, wondering if they had enough faith in Him to believe that He was actually going to feed them with His own flesh and blood. They were not scandalized by His words, they had grown to trust Him and have confidence in what He said and did. They would remain loyal to Him—until the crucifixion. They had the faith that the others lacked—except one, Judas, who was let down because he realized that Jesus was not the kind of King he wanted to follow. Judas could not open his heart to Jesus in faith and love because he was bound up in greed and selfish ambition. He would betray Him.

Christ Meant What He Said!

Unless we take Christ's words literally, they are incoherent and deceptive. He spoke plainly, clearly and forcefully, yet many people still don't believe. Granted it is a great mystery, but then what is faith, if it is not to hold that mystery in our hearts, believing Jesus rather than ourselves? On my way back to the hotel, I was thinking about all this and imagining Christ coming to Florence right now. If He were walking down the street, saying the same things as He did and behaving in the same ways, healing the sick and challenging the self-righteous, egotistical and godless rulers, many people would walk away now, calling Him a "fanatic." The world is losing its spiritual conscience; it is losing its heart.

Scripture Meditation

"I tell you the truth, unless you eat the flesh of the son of Man and drink his blood, you have no life in you. Whoever eats my flesh and drinks my blood has eternal life, and I will raise him up at the last day. For my flesh

is real food and my blood is real drink. Whoever eats my flesh and drinks my blood remains in me and I in him. Just as the living Father sent me and I live because of the Father, so the one who feeds on me will live because of Me. This is the bread that came down from heaven; it is not like the bread that your ancestors ate but later died. The one who eats this bread will live forever. . .Because of this many of Jesus' followers turned back and would not go with Him anymore. So he asked the twelve disciples, 'And you, would you also like to leave?'" (John 6: 53-58, 66-67)

Dear Lord Jesus,

I am becoming aware of how deeply You want us to believe in Your Real Presence in the Holy Eucharist. You are performing these miracles to let us know without a shred of a doubt that it is Your Flesh and Blood in the consecrated bread and wine. Jesus, I believe but please help my unbelief. I do not want to walk away. On the contrary, I want to be Your intimate friend. When the Angel of Portugal held up the bleeding Host to the children of Fatima, he taught them to pray: "My God, I believe, I adore, I hope and I love You! I ask pardon for those who do not believe, do not adore, do not hope and do not love You."

5

The Apple of His Eye

While sipping *cappuccino* on the small roof garden of my hotel, I drank in the early morning sights and sounds of Florence, savoring every moment of being in this city that I love. It was a hazy, hot summer morning. How pretty the flowers were that bordered the roof garden, how like an oil painting were the red-tiled Florentine roofs that stretched as far as the eye could see — TV antennas and laundry lines notwithstanding — they added a note of reality to this surrealistic scene.

My life is like a colorful tapestry filled with so many beautiful gifts. Yes, there are the knots and entanglements on the back side, but in some ways the problems and pains have made the front side possible. I think my faith came out of my brokenness and my need for God. It is the greatest treasure of my life. How did I receive it? Scripture tells us that *"faith comes from hearing the message, and the message comes through preaching Christ."* (Romans 10:17) It is our salvation, and it is a pure gift. *"For it is by God's grace that you have been saved through faith. It is not the result of your own efforts, but God's gift, so that no one can boast about it."* (Ephesians 2: 8-9) Faith expresses itself by the reception of baptism. For a child it is the faith of the believing community that brings it under the influence of the love of God. Grace is, after all, a share in the divine love life of the Trinity. My community was my family, but it was my mother who passed on the gift of faith to me.

I first remember listening to the words of the "Prayer Before the Crucifix" which she read aloud to me as a child: "*Look down upon me, good and gentle Jesus, while before thy face I humbly kneel...fix deep in my heart lively sentiments of faith, hope and charity and a true contrition for my sins. . .*" I didn't even know the meaning of most of the words, yet I memorized them and imagined a kindly white-bearded Father God looking down and watching over us from His heavenly throne.

Why Did I Need This Pilgrimage?

Did I receive faith by listening to the words of that prayer, or could it have been when I was six, in a hospital in Long Branch, New Jersey, where I was diagnosed with polio and put in an oxygen tent for a month? Of the scant memories I have of my childhood, one of them is of my nightly terrors within those clear plastic walls, when I cried, wailed, screamed for God my Father to help me. He was real to me in my child's heart; in my desperation I turned to Him and begged for His intercession. Children were dying by the droves that summer. Many suffered paralysis and shrunken limbs. I walked out of the hospital a month later, perfectly healthy.

That was the beginning, as far as I can tell, of my faith life. It was also the beginning of an insatiable need for love — for intimacy, for the emotional presence of my mother and father — a presence which for many different reasons was hardly available to me. I was as unable to be open and affectionate with them as they were with me. This need led me to God, to find comfort in His Presence at Mass and in the Eucharist; that hunger and craving for love still drives me and is part of the reason for this pilgrimage.[1]

As soon as I got home from the hospital that summer, I ran into Gertrude's arms. She was the black nanny who had come to live with us and, after an initial "squaring off" between us, we became friends. She had baked a chocolate cake for my homecoming. I took a piece to eat on the front porch. It was a hazy summer afternoon. Sailboats dotted the ocean shoreline and the familiar smell of salt water suddenly felt so good. While eating a huge piece of cake, I clearly remember feeling so thankful for the sun, the ocean, our beautiful Victorian summer home, Gertrude, my parents and brother, my bike, the chocolate cake, and absolutely everything and everyone I had previously taken for granted. I felt brand new and it was a wonderful, alive feeling.

Growing Up

I grew up in an apartment in New York City in the 50's during the era of Howdy Doody, Captain Video and Elvis Presley. My parents sent me to *The Convent of the Sacred Heart*, a private Catholic grade and high school for girls, which was one of the greatest gifts of my life. Our family spent summers at the Jersey Shore and enjoyed privileges which some people never have. "Joanie, your wish is my command," my Dad always teased, then he'd brag to others that I was "the apple of his eye." My "wishes" could melt his soft heart and often did when I made them known. On the way home from school everyday I passed a pet shop which had the cutest little black and white Marmoset monkey in the window. I wanted it more than anything in the world and when I told him about it, he offered to take a walk up the street to have a look at it. That was as good as getting it! We left the pet shop with the monkey and a cage and over the next few years I practically turned the little monkey into a human being. My mother made diapers for him and I "walked" him up and down 86th Street in my old doll carriage. "Chi Chi" was the hit of the apartment building and the whole neighborhood!

The author and two friends who lived next door

Despite the special advantages I had, growing up was painful. To all eyes, my life appeared idyllic. No one really knew what went on behind the scenes of my life. No one knew because I tried to deny the problems and pain resulting from the diseases of alcoholism and mental illness in our family.

My Mom and Dad

My parents were very special people, each enormously gifted in different ways. Their marriage was not a happy one and I grew up trying to infuse into the family the love that was absent between my mom and dad. I felt responsible for the unhappiness, and threw myself into the breach, as it were, to take care of their needs, hoping that if they were happy, we could be a normal family. As a child and adolescent I all but raised myself, often trying to parent my own parents.

When my mother, a gifted pianist, was engaged to my dad she was invited to play on the same stage at Carnegie Hall with Paderewski who was then reputed to be the greatest pianist in the world. She gave up the piano after she was married to raise my brother and myself, and resumed playing years later, but never realized her dream of becoming a concert pianist. My mother was sick a great deal, suffering from severe depressions which led to periods of insanity for which she was given shock treatments. One afternoon I came home from school and found everything in my room jammed into my walk-in closet. *Everything.* I truly felt sorry for my mom and tried to help her, while at the same time I was angry at her for being the way she was. Like a squirrel storing nuts for the winter, I quietly stored up resentments and distanced myself from her. My father, on

My mom, Sabina Borgia Carter

the other hand, was outgoing and enthusiastic. A poor boy who grew up in Harlem playing baseball on the street with sawed-off broom handles, he played on the same high school team with Lou Gehrig, was a friend of Babe Ruth and was drafted to the Cincinnati Reds. They rarely played him so he quit and became a successful trial lawyer in New York City. *The New York Daily News* and *Elizabeth Arden* were two of his clients. Miss Arden was a very gracious woman who used to invite my brother Howie and me up to her pink 5th Avenue apartment for afternoon tea. We dutifully went (I wore white gloves) and politely sipped tea and munched on fruit cakes. I stashed mine in a napkin which I hid in my purse when she left the room. My brother forced himself to eat the fruit cakes which he promptly threw up when we got home!

My dad and I going on a Sunday morning outing in 98 Tango

My dad, J. Howard Carter

My Dad Taught Me To Fly

One year Daddy took up flying, bought a plane and invited me to be his co-pilot. On a Saturday morning he'd say to me, "Joanie, want to fly to Portland, Maine for lunch?" Of course I'd go, and we'd first have to check out where the old ball field was where he spent a summer when he was just a little older than I was. I flew with him so much that when I went to take official instructions one summer, my instructor was surprised by how much I knew. He checked me out to solo after seven hours, and I thought I had died and gone to heaven. I had just turned sixteen and had barely gotten my driver's license; why not get a pilot's license, too? I gave myself a tour of the beach and my house, the tennis club and all my friends houses, then flew to the golf club where I estimated what hole my dad would be playing. I found him and buzzed low over him and his excited friends, waggling my wings like crazy. He knew it was me because it was his plane, and I knew by the way he was waving his towel that he realized I was soloing. It was one of the peak moments of my life.

We had many good times together which I cherished. Daddy lived by his own routine and was available as long as I could adapt myself to his schedule, to spend time together. He was usually unavailable to do normal father-daughter things because he was out golfing or flying or drinking, so I learned to adapt my needs to his schedule, doing things to suit him and his moods. *I became his caretaker!*

Hurtful Patterns of Behavior

I didn't know then that these role reversals hurt me and that I was setting up patterns of behavior in myself which helped me then, but which would hurt me later in life. I began a habit of hiding and burying my feelings and problems deep inside of myself, where I thought they would disappear. People who knew me as an athlete and one of the class leaders, would never have guessed there was another side to me, a sad, hurting, lonely, angry and fearful adolescent who often felt inferior and cried herself to sleep at night. No one knew that I was living inside glass walls, through which I could see others but they couldn't see me.[2]

Jesus Makes Incredible Claims

No one saw me, except God. My faith was nourished by the Sacred Heart nuns who fed us a diet of sound Catholic theology combined with a study of Scripture, the sacraments and prayer. They made God real, especially through their teaching about the Mass and the Eucharist. Reading Scripture late at night in my room stimulated my spiritual hunger, especially for the Eucharist. The claims Jesus made were incredible. He was either a lunatic and a liar—*or He had to be telling the truth.* No other prophets made the claims He did, then backed up their promises with their own death and resurrection. Only God could say and do the things which Jesus Christ did and said.

The Eucharist, an Awesome Reality

I remember thinking that if His words are true, if Jesus really is "The Bread of Life," and if anyone who comes to Him will never be hungry or thirsty, then why aren't people flocking to Mass and Communion daily? Why aren't our churches bulging with people eager to touch the hem of His garment, so to speak, to draw close to Him in the miracle of His Real Presence under the appearance of bread and wine? The Son of God is making Himself available to us in the flesh on our altars where He remains in our tabernacles, present in our world just like He was when He walked the earth. *What a miracle, what a gift, what an awesome reality*!

My hunger for the abundance of life and joy Jesus promised His followers led me to daily Mass and Communion during my high school years, a practice which I still keep. God knew how needy I was, what an ache I had inside of me for love, an ache that no one or nothing else could fill but God Himself. During those intimate moments after Communion, I shared the secrets of my heart with Jesus, pouring out my problems to Him. The nuns taught us: *"Talk to Him like a friend. Nothing is too little or too big to ask Him. Give Him your total trust. But be sure that you really want what you ask Him for, because when you ask in faith, you probably will receive it."* Jesus Himself tells us we can literally move mountains if we ask Him in faith: *"Therefore I tell you, all that you ask for in prayer, believe that you will receive it and it shall be yours."* (Mark 11: 24)

My Prayers Answered

I asked and I received. During my junior year in high school I asked His help to pass an impossible final English exam. I needed a miracle to get a passing mark of 75. I told Him that if He passed me, I would sacrifice my sleep and walk two miles to daily Mass the following July. I got a 75 exactly!

That July I walked to Mass. I sat up front on the right and can still hear the electric fans whirring overhead. What was it that made me feel so good about being in that summer church, so centered, so connected to life, so hopeful, so loved, so special, so filled? No matter what was going on at home or with my friends, being with Jesus at Mass and Communion made everything okay.

A Close Encounter with the Lord

The following fall of senior year I hurt my knee during an "away" basketball game and had to sit out the rest of the game. On the way to the water cooler, I saw the chapel and decided to go in for a visit. There, in the last pew, I looked up at the crucifix, then to the tabernacle, while tears trickled down my cheeks. I couldn't hide from God. I opened my heart to Jesus and out came all the pent up pain and anguish which I kept so carefully hidden. He took the brunt of all my inner turmoil. I often felt embarrassed and ashamed of myself and my family. In His presence, He drew the truth from me, He lanced the boil of negative feelings which were eating me up on the inside. Out came the poison of shame and anger, guilt and disappointment and loneliness. He was gently loving the real me into life so that I could break out of my self-imposed silence and come out of hiding. He was teaching me to take Him at His word and trust Him, that He would meet all my needs. I knew sitting in that chapel that the intimacy of that mysterious union with Jesus was filling me. By drawing close to Him in the Eucharist I would receive nourishment from His own divine life which would pour itself into my empty heart. After a few minutes of carrying on a rather emotional conversation with Him, I walked out of the chapel feeling brand new. I had gone in with a heavy heart and came out changed. On the way back to the gym I realized that *I had just carried on a conversation with the Son of God and that He was a personal friend of mine!* Some of that joy Jesus promised began to bubble up inside of me. I felt that "*ah hah*" feeling which accompanies those special spirit-filled moments which I believe are nothing less than close encounters with the living God.

I have felt God's joy so much in my life. I feel it every time I reflect on my path in life and on the gift of faith that was passed on to me like a life raft tossed to a drowning swimmer. It was a gift which I did nothing to deserve, but which was mine for the asking.

Who Am I?

I struggled with an inferiority complex and was always trying to measure up in order to succeed. My need for recognition and approval drove me to prove how good I was, academically, socially and athletically. I seemed to know that material possessions and money were things outside of us and really had very little to do with our identity. My self-esteem was not measured so much by what I had as by what I did.

Like E. T. trying to "phone home" because he was out of his element, in his heart he knew who he was and where he belonged. In a quiet corner of my heart, I knew that my own identity was grounded in my relationship with God. I believed I was important because God thought me worthwhile enough to send His Son to earth to die on a cross for me. Mass and Communion were my connections to my spiritual home. Meeting Jesus in the Eucharist gave me a sense of belonging and completeness. Like the first apostles who cried out, *"We have found the Lord!"* I knew that I was

Processing into our convent chapel on the Feast of the Sacred Heart singing "Jesus be our king and leader, Grant us in Thy toils a part; Are we not Thy chosen soldiers, Children of Thy Sacred Heart"

important in relation to Him. He loved me for me, with no strings attached. I didn't have to win a tennis tournament, get honors in an exam, belong to a certain group of friends, or be invited to the best parties in order to matter. Unlike anyone else in life, He loved me unconditionally, and He began changing me from a "nobody" into a somebody.

The Lifelines of Faith and the Eucharist

I don't know how I would have fared on the sea of life without faith and in particular without the Eucharist. Like beacons of light, they have steered my ship through some very stormy seas into safe harbors. As a teenager, I was adrift on a rowboat in a very rough sea. I was alone, so to speak, without much parental direction, needing emotional nurturing, and vulnerable to the elements which at any moment could have destroyed me. I desperately needed an anchor and Someone to steer me and accompany me on the journey. God threw me the rope of faith when I was young, and when I grabbed on to this gift, I met Jesus who literally saved my life. He led me and continues to lead me on a healing journey, closer to His will. I used to think I would have to go off to Africa and become a nun to do His will. What a relief to learn that His will for our life has to do with whatever will bring us the most joy, the most abundance, through the use of our God-given gifts. Like the unfolding of petals on a rose, His will opens up layers of truth and love and "abundance" in my life, something which the world cannot give.

Empty Promises of the World

By the grace of God, the thirst in my soul led me to rely on my faith to seek the solution to my problems. "*Come to me,*" Christ urges us, "*If anyone thirsts, let him come to me; let him drink who believes in me. Scripture has it 'From within him rivers of living water shall flow.'*" (John 7: 37) The world offers to slake our thirst but the promises of the world are empty and cannot match the gifts we receive through faith. Imagine having to cross a desert where there is no water. But a friend gives you a flask of water which you can carry with you and which will never run out. That is the gift Jesus gives us for believing in Him!

Yet our thirst and hunger drive us to try to fill ourselves with so many things we think will satisfy us: sex, drugs and alcohol, sports, work, power, prestige. The list is endless. I shudder when I think of the choices I was spared, and of the darkness and destruction which surrounded those choices. To fill our craving for love, we try to fill ourselves with things and behaviors which ultimately give us the opposite of what they promise. Promising us fulfillment and freedom, these addictions lie to us because they ultimately enslave us by making us their prisoners, robbing us of our self respect and freedom. "To be alive is to be addicted, and to be alive and addicted is to stand in need of grace."[3]

Faith Will Never Disappoint Us

Faith will never disappoint us. Jesus is ". . .*the way, the truth and the life.*" To befriend Him is to walk as a child of the light in a world of darkness. My experience tells me that He is true to His promises to give us more that we can ask or imagine, if only we will look to Him. His love for us, proved by the sacrifice of His life on the Cross and embodied in the fruit of that sacrifice, His physical presence among us in the Eucharist, is all that we need. From my adult vantage point, I can see how His love took so many shapes and forms: He was my Teacher, Counselor, Mother and Father, Friend, Companion, Doctor, Lawyer, Advisor, Lover and Servant. At every turn He was there, showing me the way, leading me to the right people, comforting me and drying my tears, putting joy in the place of sorrow, helping me be true to myself, teaching me about truthfulness and forgiveness.

The most special gift He gave and the one I needed most was His *presence*. My need to belong, to connect, to relate to Someone drove me to be with Him every morning at Mass. He filled the craving inside of me for love; He filled the emptiness, giving me a listening ear and a loving heart. My faith and my relationship with Jesus gave me a secret inner life which, I recognize now, was a source of deep consolation and strength. In the midst of the most painful situations at home, I was able to handle almost anything because I was so nourished and supported by receiving Him in the Eucharist.

Jesus always led me towards life and to people who reflected His love to me. He gave me the gift of eventually being able to see my parents for the people they were on the inside, people who themselves were wounded and needing love. Then He gave me the opportunity to show my love and forgiveness of each of them before they died.

A New Me

The life and light that Jesus offers through the gift of Himself in the Eucharist is slowly strengthening me to love and forgive that broken and needy child inside of me. "*Love your neighbor as yourself,*" He commands us. If we were a bank we couldn't make loans to people if we didn't have any money in our vaults. And neither can we love others if we don't first love ourselves. His love is penetrating the layers of defenses and burning away all that is false and sinful in me, while He calls me forth, like Jairus' daughter, who was only asleep, not dead. He is empowering me to lay aside my facades which I carefully constructed to please others so as to be accepted. In their place my real self is emerging, the part that I always kept hidden and out of sight. It's a wonder I didn't die from all the hurt and anger I made myself carry. I tried to get rid of it by blaming and projecting faults onto others, especially my parents. Now I see the violence I did to myself by denying my own reality. "*Put away the old self of your former way of life*, St. Paul tells the Ephesians, "*and put on the new self, created in God's way in righteousness and holiness of truth.*" (Ephesians 4: 22-24)

The Apple of His Eye

My Dad's praises echo in my heart: "Joanie is the apple of my eye," "Your wish is my command." How I wish I appreciated him more when he was alive. What a gift he gave me, sowing the seeds of his love in my adolescent heart, in whatever frail and human ways he did it. I caught snatches of my own goodness through the love reflected back to me in his eyes. My parents carved a space in my heart to embrace faith and to receive the love of Jesus who *could* satisfy my heart's desires.

Now Jesus is teaching me that we are the apple of His Father's eye, that we are precious to Him and His Blessed Mother who love us unconditionally. What more could anyone ask for? We are the children of a King and a Queen who live in a royal palace and have everything we want or need to make us happy. We are spoiled with gifts befitting royalty. "*Keep me as the apple of your eye; hide me in the shadow of your wings, from the wicked who use violence against me.*" Psalm 17

The noon bells awakened me from my reverie. The Holy Spirit stirred up such a fullness and gratitude for God's providential gifts in my life, *and for His presence. His presence is the abundance He promised us!* His life in us empowers us and nourishes us with peace and joy which is not of this world.

Trying To Bridge Two Worlds

While window shopping I was observing myself trying to bridge two worlds, the spiritual and the material. I'm drawn to both of them. Sometimes I can block out the world and the shops and all the material things. I wondered on and off throughout the day, "Could I give all this up? Could I give up looking nice and having my hair done and wearing attractive clothes? Could I really do without all these things?" Just how simple is my life and just how detached am I from things? Jesus calls us to sanctity and our response must reveal the things that keep us from being close to Him. I have to ask myself, "Are material things keeping me from being close to Jesus, from serving Him?" I don't know. I remember reading that St. Teresa of Avila had been in the convent for some years when she was invited to a wealthy woman's home for tea. Teresa found herself drawn to all the beautiful material things in her home. She was on a seesaw of conflicting desires for eighteen years until the Lord gave her the grace to let go completely. Perhaps Jesus is asking me to look at what is depriving me, what is keeping me from Him, from His will. As I go from store to store buying gifts and looking at all the beautiful things, that question is in the forefront of my mind and is never resolved.

This Must Be God's Will!

I took some time to write postcards and have dinner at a little outdoor cafe which was in full view of Piazza Della Signoria. When I lived in Florence, we used to come to this square in the Spring to sit in the bleachers and watch "Calcio in Costume," a yearly soccer game played in the mud that was very dangerous. The players dressed in Medieval costumes; it was a colorful and romantic spectacle highlighted by trumpet flourishes and emotional involvement by the spectators to an extent that I've never seen before or since. Now, it was quiet here. The evening sun was setting and cast a golden glow on the Palazzo Vecchio and Uffizi Gallery. A gentle breeze brought some relief from the sweltering heat, and bells in one of nearby churches sounded for all the world to hear. It was poetically beautiful. I felt so at peace. This trip *feels* right. I miss my family and think of them constantly, but deep down I'm so content to be here. *This must be God's will!*

Tomorrow I plan to take the early morning train to Bologna to see another Eucharistic miracle. I hadn't planned on doing this but when I was reading about it the other night, my spirit jumped for joy. I'm learning to trust those enthusiastic impulses as signals from the Holy Spirit!

Scripture Meditation

"So Jesus stopped and ordered the blind man brought to him. When he came near, Jesus asked him, What do you want me to do for you? Sir, I want to see again. Then see! Your faith has made you well. At once he was able to see, and he followed Jesus, giving thanks to God. When the crowd saw it, they all praised God." (Luke 18: 41-43)

Dear Lord Jesus,

I praise and thank you every day of my life for the gift of faith. Through faith you give me light to see where I am and where I'm going in relation to You, the source of Life and Light. Through faith You lead me to truth for my life and You heal my brokenness. You are always standing at our door knocking, hoping we will open our hearts to let You enter. When we do, You never stop gifting us with everything we need to make us happy—and holy.

6

911–A Call for Help

Thick green velvet drapes sealed my hotel room in darkness — so that when the alarm sounded at 7 A.M., I turned it off thinking it was the middle of the night. A wake-up call jarred me into facing reality and the light of day. It was so hard to get out of bed!

After a quick cup of *cappuccino*, I took a taxi to the train station and discovered I was an hour early for the train to Bologna. I had gotten mixed up and thought the train was at 7:45 instead of 8:45. Another train for Bologna was just about to leave so I decided to grab it, and enjoyed the hour-long ride in a private air-conditioned compartment.

Recording an Important Dream

I used the time to record last night's dream, an important one involving a smoldering fire in the basement of my house. In the dream, I was living in Techny Towers, the beautiful old Gothic-style headquarters of the Divine Word Missionaries which was also my home. I noticed that black smoke was pouring out of hole under the staircase. Frightened, I smashed the glass of the fire alarms on either side of the front door, but nothing happened. Then I dialed 911. The fire department came and hosed down the house. Had I not seen the black smoke pouring out of the hole, the entire building would have burned.

What did it mean? It suggests that my home, which is to say myself, is in danger of being consumed and destroyed by smoldering embers in my basement. Is this trip bringing up the pain that has been smoldering in me for so long? Will it put me back on my feet spiritually by giving me light to replace a lot of the darkness I've been in, especially during the last few years?

Unresolved Marriage Problems

Recent past events have caused me so much heartache that at times I've thought of Job and wondered if I was being similarly tried. About a year ago I went on a weekend retreat and soon after I arrived, sat on the bed feeling weighed down by depression and an inability to resolve a lot of emotional problems, especially in my marriage. I wanted peace desperately and was always trying to find ways to resolve the pain I experienced in my relationship with my husband. Kneeling beside the bed, I prayed and asked the Lord to guide me during the retreat. "Please intervene in my life and give me Your light and rescue me from this pit of darkness and depression that I fall into all the time." I opened the Bible to this paragraph:

> *"One day, when the sons of God came to present themselves before the Lord, Satan also came among them. And the Lord said to Satan, "Whence do you come?" Then Satan answered the Lord and said, "From roaming the earth and patrolling it." And the Lord said to Satan, "Have you noticed my servant Job, and that there is no one on earth like him, blameless and upright, fearing God and avoiding evil?" But Satan answered the Lord and said, "Is it for nothing that Job is God-fearing? Have you not surrounded him and his family and all that he has with your protection? You have blessed the work of his hands, and his livestock are spread over the land. But now put forth your hand and touch anything that he has and surely he will blaspheme you to your face." And the Lord said to Satan, "Behold, all that he has is in your power; only do not lay a hand upon his person." So Satan went forth from the presence of the Lord. (Job 1: 6-12)*

Is the darkness and pain in my life part of the trials Satan is inflicting and will there be even more trials and if so, how will I react? The trials I had been experiencing involved every area of my life — my family, my marriage, and my ministry.

I Repressed Pain Growing Up

Perhaps the smoldering embers in the basement of my dream were all the negative feelings I was experiencing, which periodically overwhelmed me. In counseling I was just beginning to get in touch with the rage I carried deep inside of me, left over from the wounds of growing up in a family suffering from alcoholism and mental illness. Like it or not, I was a carrier of both my mother and father's negative patterns of behavior, which caused me a great deal of pain. My mother suffered from schizophrenia and severe depression for which she had to be hospitalized and given shock treatments. She was a sensitive artist who didn't know how to deal with pain; she stored it inside herself until it consumed her. My mother was a victim of her own wounds who didn't know how to help herself. My father was an alcoholic like his father before him, and although I rarely saw him out of control, his behavior was abusive, especially towards my mother. He projected all his pain on my mother, and what he didn't project, he consumed with alcohol. Neither of my parents faced pain in their lives; my mother repressed it and my father numbed it with alcohol.

Carl Schurz Park, New York City, 1944

I believe we are carriers of our parents' traits and patterns of behavior, good and bad. I am most like my mother when I behave as a victim, feeling sorry for myself and hiding inside my pain. And I am most like my father when I project my pain onto others, especially my husband, blaming him for faults or behaviors which I really can't tolerate in myself.

I absorbed all of the above. I survived by hiding, pretending, denying, taking care of others, and adapting to please others. Because things were so emotionally out of control at home, I compensated by trying to control my environment and other people. I sought approval and tried to do things as perfectly as possible to prove my worth. While these mechanisms worked well for me growing up, they began to work against me towards mid-life. I didn't know that I was doing violence to myself all those years by ignoring and silencing my real self. My behavior robbed me of my childhood.

Consequences of Conditional Love

Since we gain our self-image through the reflection of our parents' love, if that love is missing or damaged, we will suffer the consequences. Father John Powell S.J., explains it so well: "Our basic endowment of self-appreciation is largely the gift of our parents. However, if we have perceived from them — as all of us have to some extent — that their love for us was only conditional, that it was turned on only when we met their conditions and turned off when we failed to meet them, that their love was not based on what we are but conditioned on our performance, we can only conclude that our value is somehow outside ourselves. There is no cause within for true self-love, self-esteem, self-appreciation. There is no occasion for celebration.

When worthiness of love becomes a matter of passing tests and fulfilling conditions, we begin to experience more failure than success. In the experience of repeated failure, there is conflict, fear, frustration, pain, and ultimately some form of self-hatred. So we spend the rest of our lives trying to escape this pain through one of the devices described above. (Defense mechanisms) Or we try to assume an appearance that will please others and gain us loving acceptance. We give up on being ourselves and try to be someone else, someone who will be worthy of recognition and love."[1]

Traumatic Experiences

During childhood and adolescence I experienced some traumatic happenings. One involved a beating I received from my father when I was still in a crib. He probably had a tough day in court and one too many scotches after he got home one night; nevertheless, he took out his anger on me with a leather strap while my mother kept screaming, *Howard, don't.* My mother didn't do anything to stop him and I froze in fear and pain. That night I sealed off my heart—promising myself that I would never let him hurt me again. I also felt betrayed by my mother and vowed to punish her for abandoning me. I was trapped and wanted to run away—feelings that have recurred often throughout my life. Another incident happened when I was a teenager and involved a friend of my father who sexually abused me. After both of those experiences, I must have blamed myself, thinking that these things happened because I was bad; that they were my fault and they proved what a "good-for-nothing" I was. Deep down I hated myself and believed that if anyone really knew me on the inside they would see how defective I was and leave me.

Buried Emotions Are Like Rejected People!

I never thought of my childhood beating or the sexual abuse incident until several years ago. On retreat and in counseling, I brought those

"The Kingdom of God belongs to such as these."
Spring Lake, New Jersey
1946

experiences to prayer and through a healing of memories, the festering boil was lanced. Out came the bottled up hurts which were still there after many years. On one retreat I was resting on the bed and imagining myself as a five year old child at the beach, building sand castles at the water's edge. When I saw that child — myself — in my imagination, I mourned her loss — I mourned the loss of her spontaneity, playfulness, freedom, her open and carefree little self playing with abandon. I cried so much and thought I had wasted the afternoon. My spiritual director told me later that the Lord had been speaking to me from memory. He was showing her to me because He mourned her loss too — He wanted me to reclaim her! That little girl with pigtails was me, the real me that I had submerged out of fear of not being loved. In order to get in touch with our wounded inner child, we have to go back and re-experience the emotions that were blocked. Unless and until those feelings are unlocked and released from our unconscious, our inner child will be stunted and paralyzed. "Buried emotions are like rejected people; they make us pay a high price for having rejected them. Hell hath no fury like that of a scorned emotion."[2] Traumas themselves will not make us emotionally ill, but the inability to share the trauma will. Perhaps my mother suffered similar or worse traumas in her childhood and she stored the shame, hurt and fear deep inside herself. When the pain became more than she could bear, her mind left her. My mother never went on retreats or had counseling. In fact she barely left her apartment.

Jesus Want Us To Be Reborn

The opportunity that I've been given is a gift from heaven. By opening up those memories and hurts and bringing them to Jesus, He can heal us and close up the wound. This is the whole point of inner healing. Our broken, false selves must be reshaped into the original vessel which God created. Jesus tells us that we will have to be "born again." He didn't mean physically, He meant emotionally and spiritually. Jesus called the children to Him and said, *"The kingdom of God belongs to such as these. . . whoever does not receive the Kingdom of God like a child will never enter it."* (Luke 18:16) He wants us to be the true children of light and love He created; not children who hide and pretend and defend themselves as if they were fugitives. God wants to gift us and teach us the secrets of His heart. He wants to bless us with His choicest gifts. *"Heavenly Father, it was you who created my inmost self, and put me together in my mother's womb; for all these mysteries I thank you: for the wonder of myself, for the wonder of your works." (Psalm 139:13-14).*[3]

I Need Emotional Root Canals!

I live on two levels. On one, I have the gratitude and peace that comes through faith, from the deep knowing of who I am and where I'm going. My faith has carved a path for me through life. The Lord has let His face shine upon me, and has given me such an assurance of His presence in this world and His love of me that my spirit periodically rises up inside of me like a gusher, spraying everyone nearby. His Spirit propels me to write and organize projects which witness to His presence in our lives. I yearn to be "one of His own" in this world and ask Him for this gift constantly. My desire to be close to the Lord and to make Him real in the hearts of people is both a gift and a burden. A gift because it gives me my *raison d'etre*, my meaning, and nourishes my soul. A burden because He calls me to be perfect, to be whole, and I have to walk through the purifying fires which burn away all the ego defenses I've so carefully erected since childhood.

Need for an Inner House Cleaning!

It is on this level, mostly hidden from view, where I've suffered. If I am to serve the Lord, I have to be willing to be completely broken and re-shaped according to the His image of the child He created. Emptied. Stripped of defenses, pretense and egocentric expectations. Cleansed of all the "smoldering embers" which, if left unchecked, will burn my house down! I must allow Him to chisel away the masks and the false self I've constructed. That's the pain—the dismantling of the false self. The letting go of attachments—addictions—of unhealthy patterns of thinking and acting is so difficult because I first have to name them. My habitual pattern has been to deny that the problem has to do with me. It is much easier to project my feelings onto others and blame them for my misery. To be "one of His own" is to be like Jesus—free to love and be loved. I have a long way to go to be free from dark inner forces of anger, shame, resentment, fear, self-righteousness, self pity and especially a critical and judgmental spirit. All these emotions tie me up and prevent me from loving and from receiving love. John Bradshaw teaches that to get to the truth of ourself—to discover our inner child—we have to find the source of our original pain. The more hurtful our circumstances, the more we shut down emotionally.

We think we are preventing pain by doing that. In reality, we are locking it in.

Tried to Blot Myself Out

I've spent years locking myself in. The "prisoner" is the part of myself that has been the martyr, so to speak, absorbing the negative feelings which the outer me refuses to admit. Hidden from view, this me prefers to be the victim, to dwell in the darkness of my own wounds where I become isolated from others as well as from myself. As a child I probably thought that hiding pain or problems would make them disappear. Later, I confused the concept of denying self and taking up our cross with being a martyr by literally denying and squelching myself. By absorbing whatever was painful or unpleasant, I thought I was being heroic in the Christian sense of the word. I was using God to "take" my problems when in reality I was stuffing them deep inside my unconscious where they have been smoldering ever since.

Jesus never meant that we should repress and squelch ourselves, blot ourselves out, as it were, in the name of "dying to self." The self He asks us to die to is the false self, the ego self. Jesus tells us we will not find our life until we lose it: *"If anyone wishes to come after me, he must deny himself and take up his cross daily and follow me. For whoever wishes to save his life will lose it, but whoever loses his life for my sake will save it. What profit is there for one to gain the whole world yet lose or forfeit himself?"* (Luke 9: 23-26) When we die to that (old) self, we will find life. As we are healed and grow closer to God and to our own truth, we can choose to "lay down our life" for the Lord. We can't give up or die to what we don't have.[4]

Satan Can Turn the Screws

Where does Satan enter? Father Bob DeGrandis says it well: "Satan attacks in three ways: through fear (particularly fear of the future), through our emotions (to keep us centered in ourselves), and through guilt, real or imagined (particularly over past sinfulness). Satan will use any way that he can to keep us out of the present moment where God is, and cause us to project into the future or to be overwhelmed by the past."[5] When something upsetting happens in my life, it can stir up some of the emotions (and the wounds connected to them) which if I don't immediately bring them to prayer and cover them in the Blood of Jesus, Satan can use them to torment me. This most often happens in my relationships, especially my marriage. Some behavior or saying of my husband will trigger a powerful emotion in me, which usually has a "history" to it. It remembers the original trauma and his remark opens up the whole can of worms. This most often happens when Tommy makes a joke out of something. His "Irish wit" sometimes enrages me, because of the many years I witnessed my dad making fun of my mother in public. The memory of her pain is stored deep inside of me and it rises to the surface even though my husband's intent is different from my father's. At this point, I have a choice.

Bring the Pain to Jesus

If I bring this pain to Jesus immediately and lay it at the foot of His cross I can usually let go of it and leave it with Him. But if I don't do this, I begin to anguish over this remark. The anguish turns to rage and before long to hate and then to a desire to run away. It probably touches the unhealed pain left over from all the abuse—of myself and my mother. That triggers fear and I want to bolt. I've struggled with oppression, despair, wanting to run away, disgust, repulsion, confusion, and fear. When Satan gets hold of these, it can be tormenting.

Jesus Mends Our Brokenness

When we give our pains and problems to Jesus, He always answers us and brings us to the next step on our path. He has been leading me mostly through dreams, showing me where the darkness and brokenness is so that I can give it to Him for healing. I know in the deep of my spirit that pain is a gift, that when we unite our suffering to Jesus on the Cross, He carries it for us, He redeems us through suffering. His death has won us the victory of life and love and hope and healing. Can we walk the way of Calvary with Him, can we hold the tension of suffering until, in His perfect timing, He shows us the cancer of sins that are eating our soul, robbing us of His love and truth and joy? Can we trust enough to walk His way, to listen for His direction, to wait on His will for our lives? What is His will for our lives? How do we find it? Thomas Merton reaffirms the need to connect with our inner true self:

> "Finding our heart and recovering this awareness of our inmost identity implies the recognition that our external,

everyday self is to a great extent a mask and a fabrication. It is not our true self. And indeed our true self is not easy to find. It is hidden in obscurity and "nothingness" at the center where we are in direct dependence on God."[6]

Merton writes that to the extent that we find ourselves, we find God. God's will is not "out there" someplace, but buried in the truth of our own soul. As we grow closer to the Lord, He penetrates all the layers of dirt and hurt which cover up our truths, our gifts, our love, our selves!

"There is only one problem on which all my existence, my peace, my happiness depend: to discover myself in discovering God. If I find Him I will find myself and if I find my true self I will find Him."[7]

To Yield to the Potter's Touch

I pray for the grace and strength to allow God's love to penetrate my layers of darkness and sin. I pray for the trust to yield to the Potter's touch, so that I can be broken and reshaped in His image and according to His truth. God's truth for us is really our own truth, hidden like a pearl in the heart of the oyster. If only we could see ourselves as He sees us, so alive, so filled with unique gifts, so loved.

The beautiful Tuscan countryside was an uplifting sight. I was glad to be alone in the compartment because I could reflect and meditate on all these things without anyone staring at me. Why I was going to Bologna I wasn't exactly sure. But that's part of the gift of this trip—the freedom to follow the Holy Spirit when and where He leads me. While reading about a Eucharistic miracle involving a little child in Bologna, as well as the powerful intercessory powers of St. Catherine of Bologna, I decided I wanted to search out these two people. The fact that both of their bodies are incorrupt further whetted my appetite. I want to get a close-up view of them and understand what the Lord wants to tell us through the miracle of their preservation and through their teachings. They must be very special people.

Scripture Meditation

"I solemnly assure you, unless a grain of wheat falls to the earth and dies, it remains just a grain of wheat. But if it dies, it produces much fruit. The man who loves his life loses it, while the man who hates his life in this

world preserves it to life eternal. If anyone would serve me, let him follow me; where I am, there will my servant be. If anyone serves me, him the Father will honor." (John 12: 24-26)

Dear Lord Jesus,

Please give me the grace to see areas where I need to die to my ego, to recognize defense mechanisms which isolate me from my inner child and from others. I need courage, Lord, to let go of that controlling self which is born of fear and thrives on power. Jesus, I want to become the true self you have called me to be. Please Lord, show me how to unearth my inner child, who like Jairus' daughter, is asleep not dead. Touch me, Jesus, and make me whole.

7

Two New Friends

Bologna was a bustling metropolis where I suddenly felt very alone and unsure of myself. What was my urgency in coming here? I had never heard of the two people I was going to see, and wondered about my desire to visit them. It must be the Holy Spirit, I reasoned, because in my heart I felt a determination and an intensity which nothing would deter. I prayed that the taxi driver would know how to get to the Church of St. Sigismondo because all I knew was that it was near the University of Bologna. *"Relax, Joan, and go with the Spirit."* This would be an adventure!

The Child Involved in the Miracle

The church was empty except for the glass-enclosed body of Blessed Imelda Lambertini, a child beautifully dressed in a white First Communion outfit. "A very devoted, prayerful little child from one of the most prominent families in Bologna, her parents, the Count and Countess Lambertini were well known for their generosity to the Church and their service to the State. The Count had served as governor of Perugia and ambassador of the republic of Venice. The family had even given the Church a Pope, Benedict XIV, born Prosper Lambertini."[1]

As a child growing up in a close knit Christian family, Imelda accompanied her mother to daily Mass. At nine her parents allowed her to enter the Dominican monastery, Santa Maria Maddelena, in order to be educated by the nuns and where she took part in all community affairs except the Eucharist and midnight prayers. Her longing to receive Jesus in the Eucharist was apparent to the community, but in the 14th century, children had to wait until they were 12 to make their First Communion.

A Eucharistic Miracle

One day when some of her Sisters received communion she was overheard to say: "How can anyone receive Jesus in his heart and not die?" Then a Eucharistic miracle took place. On the vigil of the Feast of the Ascension in 1333, Blessed Imelda remained in church after Mass, quietly weeping with desire for Jesus in the Eucharist. A brilliant white Host appeared over Imelda's head and remained suspended in the air. The fragrance of the Host attracted the Sisters who observed this awesome sight upon reentering the chapel. They saw the Host suspended over the child's head who was in ecstasy in front of the tabernacle. A priest was summoned. As soon as he saw what was going on, he ran to get a paten. Then the Host, still suspended over her head, descended onto the paten. The priest took this as a sign that Imelda was to be given her First Holy Communion. When he gave her communion, she swooned and went into a rapture and died. Her First Communion was to be her last. The date was May 12, 1333. Imelda was 11 years old.

She was beatified by Pope Leo XIII on December 20, 1826. Some years later, Pope Pius X named Blessed Imelda the Protectress of First Holy Communicants.

This Child Founded a Community!

"The Lord had a very definite example He wanted to set by the devotion this young creature had for Him in His precious Body and Blood. In St. Mark's Gospel, 10: 14-15, Jesus tells us: *"Let the children come to Me and do not hinder them. It is to just such as these that the kingdom of God belongs. I assure you that whoever does not accept the reign of God like a little child shall not take part in it."* The pure faith of this child was so strong that Our Lord Jesus put aside the laws of nature to reward her, and instruct us.

"Devotion to this little blessed person began almost immediately after her death. Many devotional booklets were written about her, especially in connection with the Eucharist. Wherever a great devotion to the Eucharist arose, or heresy denying the Eucharist, prayers for the intercession of Imelda followed. In 1922 a Dominican community of nuns was instituted, called The Dominican Sisters of Blessed Imelda. Their charism is to spread the Eucharistic spirit by means of Perpetual Adoration to the Blessed Sacrament, and give moral, intellectual and religious aid to young people. The community also does missionary work in Brazil."[2] This child's body which is venerated in the parish church of Saint Sigesmondo is only a wax replica, not her incorrupt body as I had thought. In fact, her bones are visible below the wax reproduction of her.

Blessed Imelda Lambertini

I stayed in the church to ask for her special blessing upon my own children—that their paths in life will be blessed by the light and the love of the Lord, and their hearts opened wider and deeper to receive the gifts the Lord has for them, especially the Holy Eucharist.

Searching for St. Catherine of Bologna

The sacristan who was watching me take photos offered me postcards and literature about Blessed Imelda Lambertini, which I gratefully accepted. He was also very helpful in telling me where to go for my next stop—which was clear across town—in search of St. Catherine of Bologna. I did find a bus, but had to keep asking for directions to the church at the other end. Each person had a different answer! Some had never heard of St. Catherine of Bologna, not to mention her incorrupt body. I stopped in a bookstore hoping to find some literature on St. Catherine of Bologna, but they had never even heard of her in the bookstore. I wondered again why I was putting myself through this. By now I had such a strong desire to find this saint I knew I would stop at nothing until I found her. I stopped in the Grand Hotel of Rome where two portieres directed me with a hand made map. Wending my way through a maze of narrow back streets, I felt led to stop in another church. It was a good thing, because the sacristan there knew where The Church of Corpus Domini was, which I never would have found with the directions I had.

I Found Her Seated and Incorrupt!

An unpretentious doorway led into the beautiful Church of the Body of Christ. During World War II the entire church was destroyed except for

After her death, St. Catherine of Bologna appeared three times to a nun in the Monastery of Corpus Domini requesting that a small chapel be built for her. She has received thousands of visitors here

St. Catherine has a worldwide ministry of intercession, leading to miracles for many who pray to her

the small chapel to the left of the main church, which is the sanctuary of the Saint. A most ornate room, it is resplendent with sparkling sterling silver heart reliquaries which adorn the walls. Seated under a golden canopy between two life-size angels is a glass-enclosed St. Catherine of Bologna, hands reverently folded as if she were presiding at a meeting! She has been there since the 14th century and actively helping people, attested to by the hundreds of heart reliquaries, framed photographs and various *objets d'art* which adorn the room, all donated in thanksgiving for favors received.

Many Saints Are Incorrupt

Unlike Blessed Imelda who was wax-covered, St. Catherine of Bologna is incorrupt, that is to say, her body and organs are intact, even after the passage of centuries, without the use of any preservatives. According to extensive research done by Joan Carroll Cruz, there are three types of preserved bodies: the deliberately preserved, such as mummies, the accidentally preserved, such as bodies found in caves in hot, dry climates or in dry, cold mountain air, and the incorruptibles, whose bodies unlike the first two classes are, "neither dry nor rigid, but quite moist and flexible, even after the passage of centuries. Moreover, their preservations have been accomplished under conditions which would naturally foster and encourage putrefaction, and they have survived circumstances which would have unquestionably necessitated and resulted in the destruction of the others."[3]

There are hundreds of cases of incorrupt bodies of Saints, the more famous of them being St. Teresa of Avila, St. Catherine Laboure, St. John of the Cross, and St. Francis Xavier as well as a host of others. The latter two are especially remarkable because attempts were made to hasten their speedy disintegration by putting lime in their coffins, which should have caused immediate decay. Instead, they both remained preserved and to this day, St. John of the Cross' body is flexible, supple and totally recognizable.

"St. Madeline Sophie Barat remained perfectly preserved for twenty-eight years although she was found in damp and mildewed garments in a casket which was in a state of advanced disintegration. Nine months after her death, St. Teresa of Avila was found in a coffin, the top of which had rotted away, permitting damp earth to cover her body. Although her remains were clothed in dirty and rotten fragments of fabric, her body was not only fresh and perfectly intact after its cleansing, but was mysteriously fragrant as well."4

Her Life and Many Gifts

Adjacent to St. Catherine of Bologna's room was the cloister of the Poor Clare nuns who lived in the monastery of The Body of Christ, where I went in search of more information. St. Catherine of Bologna was a very gifted and wonderfully talented person who turned down many suitors and entered the convent as a teenager, where she put her artistic, musical and literary talents at the disposal of the Lord. She came from a noble and artistic family and was extremely learned. Due to her virtues and gifts many people tried to talk her out of the convent. She struggled a great deal with her call and prayed unceasingly one night for the Lord's will. Apparently He made it quite clear that He wanted her in the convent. Her life is marked by many visitations from the Lord, ecstasies and miracles. One of her visions is remarkable and is often represented in art. It is best described in the Saint's own words. Writing of herself in the third person she says: "She asked permission of her mistress to pass the night of Christmas in the church of the monastery and she obtained it. She went there as soon as she could, with the intention of reciting a thousand Ave Marias in honor of our most Blessed Lady: and this she really did with all the attention and fervor of which she was capable, and she was occupied in this way till midnight, the hour when it is believed our Savior was born. At this very hour she saw our Blessed Lady appear, holding in her arms the Infant Jesus, swathed in linen bands as new-born infants commonly are. This kind mother came to her and gave her Son to her. I leave you to picture the joy of this poor creature when she found herself holding the Son of the eternal Father in her arms. Trembling with respect, but still more overcome with joy, she took the liberty of caressing Him, of pressing Him against her heart and of bringing His face to her lips. When the poor creature we speak of dared to move her lips towards the Divine Infant's mouth, He disappeared, leaving her, however, filled with joy."5

Catherine Deals with Satan

St. Catherine was also subject to visions of a Satanic origin, which she learned to distinguish from the others. When a vision or an ecstasy would be from the Lord, it would be preceded by a deep sense of humility within herself; "She would inwardly bow her spirit or outwardly bow her head, or else she would be aware that the origin of her faults, past, present or future, was in herself and she considered herself as the cause of the faults of her neighbors, for whom she felt deep charity. Jesus would then enter her soul like a radiant sunshine and bring her profound peace. The devil constantly sought to instil into her mind blasphemous thoughts and doubts, especially about the Real Presence of Jesus in the Blessed Sacrament. She suffered miserably under these trials, until Jesus, Himself, came to teach her the whole doctrine. Her doubts vanished. Among other things He taught that the effects of the Sacrament are the same regardless of one's feelings."[6]

St. Catherine wrote about her spiritual battles with Satan, and in 1438 published, "The Weapons Necessary for the Spiritual Fight" which soon spread all over Italy. Catherine taught her nuns about Satan's snares out of her own experience: "Sometimes he inspires souls with an inordinate zeal for a certain virtue or some special pious exercise, so that they will be motivated in its practice by passion; or again, he permits them to become discouraged so that they will neglect everything because they are wearied and disgusted. . . .For a long time she herself was troubled with the temptation to sleep during the spiritual exercises. Once when she was again heroically struggling against it during holy Mass, God almighty permitted her to hear the angelic choirs singing after the elevation. From then on the temptation was overcome, and she was even able to devote hours to prayer during the night."[7]

Jesus Sews on the Severed Foot

While talking to the nun in the cloister, a woman who was buying postcards told me of her devotion to St. Catherine and she pointed to a very old painting of Christ on the Cross, which she said is the original one through which Christ spoke to St. Catherine. I treasured a small biography which she gave me because it was all I had on St. Catherine of Bologna. One of the incidents recorded there shows how close the Lord was to the nuns. One of the nuns was working in the garden and apparently had an accident with a hoe and cut her foot off by mistake. Her screams brought all the nuns running, including St. Catherine, who knelt next to her not knowing what to do. She looked up to the Lord and said, "*Lord, help us. What shall we do?*" She put the foot back onto her leg in the same place where it had been cut and the Lord sewed it all back together miraculously and instantly before everyone's eyes.

Catherine's Miracles

The woman buying postcards told me that there have been many miracles attributed to St. Catherine of Bologna, both during her life and in her death. The saint is extremely powerful, she said, and she herself has had so many prayers answered. Apparently, when she died they buried her, putting her body directly into the ground without a casket. A sweet fragrance emitted from the grave and soon filled the cemetery. Eighteen days after her interment, miracles began to happen at the gravesite. They decided to dig her up and there was such a sweet aroma that came from her body. Instead of decaying, there was light emanating from her, and she just glowed and smelled so sweet. They decided not to bury her, but to leave her in their midst instead. They didn't even elect a new superior for a year because they felt St. Catherine's presence so strongly.

Some years after her death, she appeared to a member of the community and requested that her body be kept in a seated position in a small chapel next to the main church. *St. Catherine then put herself in this position, making it very easy for them to comply with her wishes!* Seated there for more than 500 years, she is completely intact and the only questions might be why her face and hands have darkened. Some say it is due to the burning wax of the votive candles. St. Catherine has interceded in the lives of many people, healing and freeing them from severe illnesses. Helplessly ill people in every kind of condition — blind, crippled, burn victims, and even dead people, were cured and brought to life through her intercession. Callous sinners were led to repentance because St. Catherine would appear to them. People come from all over the world to venerate her.

"St. Catherine, Help Me Fight Darkness"

Before leaving I knelt close to the seated Saint and spoke to her like a friend. It was kind of "wonder-ful" to have her there to see and talk to; perhaps that is why God allows these miracles of preservation so that we can experience this kind of closeness with our much-loved Saints. I knew from my spirit that our meeting had been intended. Tears rolled down my cheeks. What in the world was I doing here in this cloistered convent, trying to draw close to this holy woman from the 14th century who was so totally devoted to Jesus and so used by Him in life and death? Known as Patroness of Artists, I was so moved by the depth of her faith, by the way she put her many gifts at His disposal, by the intensity of her life and her courage to fight spiritual battles. *Please pass on some of your strength and love to me, St. Catherine. Help me grow in the desire to serve the Lord so totally and with such love. Help me find the weapons you used to fight oppression and darkness and to keep Satan at a distance. Despite your struggles and doubts, you hung in there, and the Lord rewarded your fidelity. Please stay near me and help me, especially during the dark times.*

My Meeting with Her Was Providential

The nuns were locking up at noon and I was politely ushered to the front door. Had I taken the later train to Bologna that morning as originally planned, I would have missed seeing St. Catherine. The timing had to have been the Lord's. *Just one more example of the way the 'accidents' in our lives are not accidents at all, but providential. There are no coincidences in God's kingdom! Thank you, Lord, for making the arrangements for me and for orchestrating everything according to Your plan for my life — down to the smallest details. I pray that I always follow Your plan and not mine. As of today, right now, I have a sense that I'm right where I belong.*

The 100 degree noonday heat was oppressive. I found a shady outdoor restaurant under an arcade facing cathedral square and just sat for awhile, letting the experience of the morning wash over me like beautiful music. "Meeting" St. Catherine had been an unexpected gift. I was so drawn to her and felt as if I had a new best friend. I need her tenacity in embracing God's will. I'm not exactly sure what God's will for my life is right now, but this trip must be His doing because I have so much enthusiasm to see the miracles of the Eucharist and seek out these Saints. She has much to teach me. St. Catherine practiced three precepts all her life which she tried to pass on to her sisters: "the first was always to speak well of others, the second was to practice constant humility, and the third was never to meddle in matters which were no business of hers. While she was strict beyond measure with herself, she was most tender to the weaknesses of other people."[8]

The Saints Are Teaching Me Humility

God knows how deeply I need to learn these lessons. Is He showing me where I am in my spiritual reality and where I need to go, and the great distance between those two? How to bridge the gap I'm not sure. I've read enough to know that the real beginning of spiritual life is the gift of humility and maybe, in a small way, I'm getting more humility through this trip. A statement attributed to St. Maximilian Kolbe reminds me of this: *Humility is the foundation of all the virtues.* Why? Perhaps because humility grounds us in the truth of ourselves. Humility comes from the latin, "Humus" which means 'of the earth' or 'grounded.' The nuns always taught us that humility was the Lord's favorite virtue.

My eyes are being opened more completely to who I really am and what is separating me from God. Perhaps in the deep of my spirit I came on this trip knowing that this was my 911—this was my way to find the peace I so desperately want. Evidently the way I was going about it at home was leading to a burning house.

Are these medieval saints relevant for today? Definitely yes! Their faith-filled lives are testimonies of God's powerful presence in this world. They are truly heroes and heroines of Christianity who have modeled holiness by living lives of heroic faith. In Revelations we read that the saints take our prayers and set them on fire before God's throne: "*Another angel came in holding a censer of gold. He took his place at the altar of incense to deposit on the altar of gold in front of the throne, together with the prayers of all God's holy ones. From the angel's hand the smoke of the incense went up before God, and with it the prayers of God's people. Then the angel took the censer, filled it with live coals from the altar, and hurled it down to earth.*" (Revelations 8: 3-5)

My legs could barely carry me back to the hotel from the Florence train station, I was so tired. I stopped in the little restaurant where Tommy and I dined the other night and found our waiter, Giuliano. How good it was to see a familiar face. Veal alla Milanese with a little side dish of spaghetti was becoming my habitual dinner, which I ordered every night! Tommy phoned later and sounded glad to be home. I was eager for any and all news from home, good and bad. Not much bad really, except that the dishwasher broke down. So what's new! Even though I do miss him, I feel as if I'm on a mission and I'm glad I'm here. "Glad" isn't the word. "Joyous" would be more like it!

Scripture Meditation

"*I solemnly assure you, whoever says to this mountain, 'Be lifted up and thrown into the sea,' and has no inner doubts but believes that what he says will happen, shall have it done for him. I give you my word, if you are ready to believe that you will receive whatever you ask for in prayer, it shall be done for you."* (Luke 11: 22-24)

Dear Lord Jesus,

Your saints are beautiful models of trust who took You at Your word. We who follow them have the benefit of seeing how You honor their faith by "letting it be done for them" even in heaven, where they have great intercessory powers. Thank you Jesus for "leaving them behind" to guide and inspire us on our kingdom journey. I believe You will hear and answer me as You did them. Please strengthen my faith, Lord, and help me to trust You with all my heart.

8

Day of the Bells

My clock and watch didn't agree with each other this morning, which threw me into a terrible panic! I jumped out of bed and raced around like a crazed person, fearful of missing Mass and my last morning in Florence. Ready in three minutes flat, it occurred to me to call downstairs to see what time it was. What a relief! It was only 9:10 A.M. I could at least collect myself and have a last cup of *cappuccino* on the roof garden before Mass.

The Church of Orsanmichele was only a few blocks walk from my hotel. Originally constructed as an open arcade to store wheat in the Middle Ages, in time it was walled in to serve as a granary, then superb arched portals were constructed so delicately wrought that they convey the effect of stone lace. Niches on all four sides of the building contain statues of saints. When it became a church I'm not sure, but it is one of my favorites in Florence, probably because of its small size and extreme simplicity. I delight in the fact that Jesus is so accessible in the midst of the workaday world of Florentine people, hidden as He is in the tabernacle of this unassuming building, surrounded by shops and traffic-laden streets.

Why So Vulnerable, Lord?

During Mass I began to feel vulnerable. Was it due to this being my last day in Florence? Or was it because the man next to me took my hands at the kiss of peace and said "Peace, Signora" so lovingly that I felt the presence of Jesus? He made me cry. I was halfway across the world all by myself and yet I felt so at home. The postcards that I've been writing for the last two days have somehow connected me to all the people I love back home. What gifts they are to me! I was writing to some friends about a mission that I feel like I'm on but I don't know what it is. I have a hunger to seek out the presence of Jesus in these miracles of the Eucharist. At the same time I'm finding parts of myself in need of healing. I'm reaching out like the lady in Scripture for the hem of Jesus' garment; His power is melting and changing me. Can we come closer to the Light without seeing our own darkness and without being healed? St. Francis de Sales explains it beautifully: "As mountain hares become white in winter because they neither see nor eat anything but snow, so by adoring and feeding on beauty, purity and goodness itself in the Eucharist you will become altogether beautiful, pure, and good."[1]

A Concert of Bells

After Mass I stayed awhile to pray. The church bells began to peal so loudly their sound reached into my soul and touched every spiritual nerve inside of me, causing me to feel pain and joy at the same time. The Lord was ministering to me so deeply through these bells that all I could do was sit there and cry. This symphony of sound continued for at least an hour. Once outside, I realized all the bells in Florence were chiming. I leaned against a building to listen. Again the tears flowed. Memories of the sacred traditions of our Church which have touched every phase of my life flooded me with gratitude. The bells sounded the song of faith, praising and thanking God for His loving presence in His church, in His people, in Scripture, in the Sacraments and especially in the Holy Eucharist. They spoke for my heart, which was full to overflowing.

I resisted the moment of final departure from Florence as long as I could. It was getting late and I had to get my car from the garage on the other side of town. Enroute I passed the Excelsior Hotel, an unaffordable "tourist trap" when I lived in Florence, but now it was affordable and represented a touch of home. It was lunchtime and I thought I'd treat myself to a sandwich on the roof garden while having a last look at city. The roof garden was closed but I was enticed into the dining room for a sumptuous buffet. Strains of classical opera wafted through the room. This would be too hard to turn down!

Splurging at the Excelsior

Something felt right about being here—splurging. It reminded me of the first class places I've been in my life. While I was growing up my dad made sure that we always had the best; that we go to the best schools, eat at the best restaurants, stay at the best hotels, even buy the best shoes: "*If you buy a pair of shoes, don't buy cheap ones because you'll only have to buy them again. If you can afford it, buy the best you can buy.*" His value system seeped into me by osmosis. These are the kinds of restaurants he took me to in New York—the Oak Room in the Plaza, Le Pavillon, the 21 Club, to name a few. As a child my Dad was so poor he never had the fifteen cents carfare to ride a street car. When he started earning money, he eventually made enough to enjoy some of the finer things of life, which he did unabashedly at times. He appreciated what money could buy and passed that on to me, but he never let money go to his head. He was always grateful for being able to enjoy the fruits of his labors, and so I always had a sense of the giftedness of being able to have or do nice things.

Now I missed him terribly. The one year anniversary of his death was two days ago. I offered my Mass and Communion for him and prayed in thanksgiving for his life, then cried plentiful tears at the permanence of our separation. I decided to stay for lunch in this elegant, air-conditioned dining room, where I would silently commune with my dad! This is typical of a place we would have enjoyed together.

The Ponte Vecchio

Communing with My Dad

I thought back to the many times we celebrated something together. Daddy enjoyed himself wherever he was. He celebrated life. I didn't always understand or appreciate that part of my dad, but now I do. He caught me up in his celebration of life. He had an enthusiasm, a childlike wonder and an adventurousness that most people don't have. We became friends through that and now here I was continuing the tradition of enjoying and appreciating life's gifts. His *joie de vivre* lives on in me. For so long I had a hidden animosity towards him and my mother for all the hurts and abuses which went on behind the closed doors of our dysfunctional family life. God is mercifully healing all those negatives and replacing the pain of those repressed memories with new eyes of gratitude

for the love and beauty in my parents. Their gifts were always there, but my vision was obscured by the pain and by my own defenses which kept me at arm's length from both my mother and my father.

My Dad never *knew* I held him at arm's length—I always kept up the front of an adoring, loving daughter. We kept at a safe emotional distance from one another, tolerating each other's differences without ever really coming out and saying what was really on our minds and in our hearts. For many years we were like ships passing in the night. Daddy usually phoned once a week, and I still remember the strain of those superficial conversations—about the weather, our health, politics, his golf game, improvements we

*My Dad and I dancing
at my wedding*

were making on the house and so forth. Underneath I was angry at him for so many things. My list of grievances was a mile high, for all the things he did — and didn't — do, for the way he treated my mother, for the way he used me to meet his needs.

At a retreat in New Orleans about a year and a half before Daddy died, I went to Confession and told the priest I felt as if I had Saran Wrap around my heart. I couldn't enter into the joyful praise and spirit of love and thanksgiving of the retreat. I was numb. The priest's gentle questions about my early life and growing up opened a storehouse of pain and hurt. He asked me if I could forgive my Dad for his alcoholism, for all the times and ways he didn't love me or my mom. Before I left the Confessional, I *willed* to forgive my Dad and asked Jesus to melt my frozen heart.

Repressed Memories Surface

That was the beginning of a new relationship with my dad. It opened the door to a long process of healing which is ongoing as I write this, three years after his death. I prayed for strength to really let go of the blame and hurts so they wouldn't eat at me anymore and so I could freely love my dad. The Lord hears and answers every prayer, but the process of healing is painful. If we have a splinter buried in our finger, we have to suffer some pain while it is being taken out. The skin has to be broken, the needle inserted — sometimes pretty deep — so the foreign object can be pulled out. So it is with inner healing. Every time I walked into the New York apartment to take care of my dad during the last year and a half of his life, new pain surfaced. *There was so much pain.* Repressed memories were stirred up and kept me awake at night. Sleeping in my own bed in the same apartment where I grew up, I became the little girl again, silently suffering just as I used to do when I lived there. The feelings which I so carefully hid and tried to banish, were buried alive as it were, and they never died. Now, they were tormenting me.

Some memories revolved around personal hurts I suffered in relationship to my dad and some concerned hurts that happened between my mom and dad. *I swallowed everything.* Broken promises and my Dad's lack of emotional presence hurt the most. He always bragged that he was home every night and not out drinking and carousing like other men he knew. *Just because he was home every night didn't mean that he was there for me.* He lived by his own schedule and routine which suited his own needs. If the Pope wanted to pay him a visit, it would have to be according to my dad's schedule. I grew up believing that I didn't have needs, or if I did, they were secondary and unimportant compared to my parents' needs. Discounting my need for my dad's affection and *presence*, I made him into a hero and became his adoring audience. Fearing rejection and abandonment, I nurtured him emotionally to the point where everything I did in life was geared to win his approval and give him pleasure. When something hurtful happened — such as the time he got dressed on Christmas morning and announced that it was too nice a day to stay indoors, he'd be at the golf club and would see us later — the letdown and loneliness was devastating, yet I never admitted to any suffering. My craving for a happy family who loved and laughed and enjoyed each other was at the core of my pain.

A Deep Wound

The deepest wound was the lack of love between my parents. I believe I absorbed their unspoken rage, thinking that if I carried it for them, they would stay together and become happy. I also developed a rage of my own, fed by my dad's verbal abuse and abandonment of my mom. She was often hospitalized, sometimes for physical ills, sometimes for psychological, and sometimes for both. One night when the ambulance attendants came to the apartment to take her to the hospital, they were trying to make her lie back on the stretcher. She had emphysema and had to be propped up in bed with at least five or six pillows. *They were pushing her down on the stretcher.* From the living room I heard her frightened cries and ran into the bedroom, screaming at the attendants to listen to her. She couldn't lie flat because it would cut off her air. I became hysterical. Startled, they finally listened to me and wheeled her to the foyer all propped up on pillows. I stayed with her to reassure her, while my dad sat in his chair in the living room calmly sipping his scotch and giving me the responsibility for caring for her. *I was doing a good job and could take care of admitting her, he'd be along later.* I felt as if someone just stabbed me in the heart. I didn't show any feeling because I was trying to protect my mom from feeling abandoned. So I behaved in a very matter-of-fact way, assuring my mom that I'd stay with her. I remember telling her that I would sleep in her room because I knew how frightened and insecure she was. I was doing what my dad should have been doing for my mom. Sometime in my childhood I accepted responsibility for their happiness, and decided I'd suffer whatever I had to in order to bring that about. My codependence rendered me powerless and blinded me to my dad's sin. Those memories and feelings surfaced in the New York apartment. There was no other choice but to feel the depth of those emotions and then bring them to the Cross to be redeemed by the love of Jesus.

Bringing the Pain to Jesus

When I returned home after spending a week with my dad in New York, I went to Marytown to pray in front of the Blessed Sacrament. I was reflecting on all these things and asked Jesus to remove all the buried angers, resentments and pains I've so carefully stored and secretly held against my dad. By hiding our pain we also hide the ability to heal. I wanted healing for myself and for him. I had been praying for my dad's conversion ever since I could remember. His lack of faith always pained me. On top of that he had cancer now and was going to die soon. I wanted him to open his heart to receive the gift of faith more than I wanted anything. I knew I had to forgive my dad in order to receive the fullness of blessing the Lord had for the both of us. I closed my eyes and watched as my imagination presented me with a beautiful scene of Jesus and I digging these up mounds and mounds of buried wounds in my backyard. As a child, my only way to deal with painful situations in my family was to deny them power. I truly thought that if I buried negative feelings, they would disappear. I believe I began burying these feelings in the womb. There is so much research today that supports the fact that babies absorb the emotional life of the mother. The womb is the spiritual environment in which a baby lives—and absorbs—the unresolved rage or grief of the mother. I believe that my pattern of behavior was set in motion even before I was born. I entered a womb in which there had been four miscarriages. I think I wanted to take my mother's pain and unresolved grief so that I wouldn't die like my brothers and sisters and so that she would be happy. In prayer I asked Jesus to go to the womb with me so that I could give *Him* the burden I had been carrying for 50 years.

The scene shifted to the kitchen in the apartment where I grew up. My favorite childhood toy was a bathinette in which I would give my dolls baths. I would hook a small hose to the faucet in the sink, and out would come warm water which I would sponge all over my dolls. While I was delighting in the memory of this, I saw myself as a tiny baby. Jesus came into the apartment and lovingly picked me up and put me in the bathinette. Then he gave me a bath with warm, sudsy water. The sensation of the warm water combined with His touch was wonderful. His caresses filled me with liquid love. I could feel the love He had for me and I seemed to understand that this love had not been given to me by my parents. In a way, He was re-birthing me and baptizing me with His love, replacing all those dark emotions with His healing presence.

In the car on the way home from Marytown, I was thinking about how deeply I have been loved all through my life. Despite all the childhood wounds, I have been so blessed to be loved by so many different people in my lifetime, especially my husband and children. I cried for my dad to be bathed in love as I have been. He has never known Jesus' love. As a little child, he was neglected and he buried his angers too. He used to tell the story of having to wait his turn behind his two older brothers for a two minute ride on an old bike they found in a junkyard. The tires were long gone but they somehow managed to ride on the rims. My dad had to run alongside as they took their turns, fearing he'd miss his chance for a ride. My dad ran hard all his life to find love, and now I begged Jesus to bathe Daddy, to let him open his heart and feel the love of Jesus for him.

Forgiveness Releases Love

Another time I was praying for my dad and asked God to take away his spiritual blindness so that he could see Jesus. I opened Scripture to a reading which spoke to my soul. I wept. I read the words which were addressed to me personally. I understood that the spiritual blindness which I thought was my father's was mine. Since childhood, I have been looking to others to give me what I didn't receive from my mother and father. When others didn't give me what I needed, I blamed them. My husband took the brunt of my unresolved anger against my father which I projected onto him. So I ran around angry and blaming and seeing the bad in everyone, especially my husband. My anger at my father bound the both of us, so that love couldn't really pass between us. And it put up a wall in our marriage, because I often silently blamed my husband for behavior of his which opened me to the repressed pain of my childhood. By deciding to forgive my father, the Lord was showing me the root of the problem in myself. Not only was He calling me to forgive my dad, but also to forgive myself. Forgiveness would take down the walls—in my relationship with my father and with my husband.

As the throat cancer that Daddy was suffering from progressed, so did our relationship. I asked his forgiveness for withholding myself from him for so many years and he told me there was nothing to forgive saying, "Joanie you have been the most wonderful daughter any father could ask for and you've done nothing but make me happy." I held him in my arms like a child and shared with him and loved him with such warmth. I thanked him for all the ways he had loved me, for all his attempts to stay in touch and to be present for all the little and big occasions of my life. I couldn't get the words out about how I forgave him. That would have to come later. He languished between life and death for a long time. He suffered with a gentleness and a strength that came from his core. In his helplessness, he was beautiful. I had never seen him so vulnerable. Like a child, so open, so gentle, so trusting, when anyone helped him in any way he responded with such gratitude. Love for my father melted my frozen heart and opened my eyes to see his gifts, hidden by my own spiritual blindness. What a privilege it was to care for my dad during the last year and a half of his life. Together we embraced love in each other, love that was there all along just waiting to be expressed.

To Phone Or Not To Phone Paolo?

Just before leaving the Excelsior I struggled with whether or not to phone my old boyfriend. He was a wonderful young Italian lawyer whom I fell in love with when I lived in Florence thirty years ago. *I was almost engaged to him!* When I returned home and began dating Tommy, I realized that I had to let go of Paolo, as difficult as it would be. I knew that I wanted to marry Tommy and I would have to sever my relationship with Paolo. I went on a weekend retreat to the Cenacle in Mt. Kisco, New York, and agonized over the "Dear Paolo" letter I had to write. I wrote pages and pages, filling up an entire notebook the nuns had provided for the retreatants, trying to make him understand my decision. It was one of the hardest things I've ever had to do.

I played out the phone call in my mind. *"Hello, Paolo, this is Joan, your American girlfriend from thirty years ago."* If he answered he might slam the phone down, or ask me why I never returned his letters on my final trip back to the States. Then again, I might get his wife and what would I say to her? Bad idea, I decided to forget it.

Heading out of Florence on the *autostrada*, I felt that vulnerability again. Here I was in the middle of nowhere, so to speak, off on my own. I thought of my children and my husband and what they were doing. What on earth am I doing? Why am I doing this? Where am I going? What am I searching for? I felt alone, but not lonely. This was somehow right. I prayed the Chaplet of Divine Mercy for everyone who came to mind.

Can I Be Me and Be Loved by God?

I had planned to spend a night or two in an out-of-the-way villa which I had read about and which attracted the contemplative in me. The Eucharistic miracles that I've seen so far have touched me deeply. I've become more acquainted with St. Catherine of Siena, St. Catherine of Bologna and Blessed Imelda Lambertini, who were so devoted to our Eucharistic Lord. In the deep of my spirit I'm wondering where I fit into the picture. While I've recorded my thoughts at the end of every day, I've also held back; I've kept certain things private. There's a battle going on in me which has to do with who I am as a person in God's eyes. Can I really be who God wants me to be and will that entail giving up all the material things and pleasures of life as I've known them, like having lunch at the Excelsior today? I don't know if I have the heroics in me that these saints have. I do love the Lord a great deal and I want to be His follower, but I don't know how to give everything up and be His follower. Can I be His follower and not give everything up? I do know that some of Jesus' best friends had money — Lazarus, Martha and Mary, to name a few. In fact, He was often at their house. Lazarus was the wealthiest landowner in Judea and had a house the size of a palace. They had great big government dinners there. He entertained lavishly and yet he was Jesus' closest friend. I don't know if I'm playing games with myself, if I want my cake and eat it too. I'm struggling with this and I would like to think that I have the heroics of a St. Catherine of Siena. I don't know if I could stay in my room all day and fast and pray or shave my head to show my commitment to Jesus. St. Catherine did penances in the form of bodily mortifications; she resisted terrible temptations, driving away demons that would come at her offering her beautiful nightgowns and giving her sexual fantasies. Even a young man appeared to her, enticing her to be with him. God graced her with incredible strength to fight these trials, but she had great sacrifice in her and a strong will to be united with Jesus. She had so much will that she became His spokesperson for the 14th century. One uneducated woman did more for the Church in the 14th century than hundreds did in the following centuries.

Healing Perspectives

This all leaves me with a question. Somehow I feel that we all have our gifts and our invitations from the Lord to follow Him on certain paths that He's marked for us. I think so far on this trip that this is the path that He's marked for me — to come away like this, perhaps to get perspective, perhaps to experience more healing so that I can be freer to love, to gain more insight on what's keeping me from Him, and also to get more perspective on the gifts of my life which I've either taken for granted or ignored. One example would be how periodically I suffer feeling so alone and abandoned by friends, so unnoticed by friends who were supposedly close to me and yet when I come here it's just the reverse. I think of so many people whom I love and who love me and I'm just filled with gratitude for the gift of these people in my life. How could I think that I don't have friends? Deep inside of me there's a wound of emotional abandonment and it keeps surfacing because God wants to heal it. This trip is healing that wound. I'm deeply grateful for the gifts that surround me — my family, my husband and children, special friends and relatives, priests and nuns, the varied experiences of my life, the places I've been, the people I've met, the experiences I've had which have carved out places of love and hope and joy and sorrow inside of me. The carved-out sorrowful places give me compassion and help me reach out to people in need or who are searching.

Tonight I sat at dinner in an open air dining room. Italian music was playing and the view of the twinkling lights in the surrounding mountains was spectacular. The cicadas were in full song, flowers were blooming all around and some German people were laughing and having a great time.

My Own "Room with a View"

God is giving me my own "Room with a View" here. He's giving me the time and the space to find Him, like the words of the song, "To follow Him more nearly, to see Him more clearly, to love Him more dearly."[2] I feel so cared for by my loving Father in heaven and our Blessed Mother and realize every detail of my life has been planned, right down to this moment. I don't know what's ahead, but I know that this time is a gift. I pray that it will help me hear His voice and discern His will for me. I want to serve Him.

Today began with bells and is ending with bells. Church bells in the surrounding hills sound different chimes. It occurred to me that the "Sound of Music" could have been written right here and the verse, "the hills are alive with the sound of music," keeps going through my mind. They were alive through the sound of music and they are alive in Italy through the bells, through the churches which sound the bells, which sound the cry to come to worship, to come to the Lord. He is very present here in Italy and in the faithful. Their devotion to the Blessed Mother is so touching, as is their reverence for Mass, for priests and nuns, and for all the things of God.

Praying with My Mother

When I was not yet old enough to read, my mother read aloud to me, "The Prayer before the Crucifix." Encased in a small white plastic case, it had the prayer on one side and a crucifix on the other. I treasure this memento from my childhood, which I still have and keep with me. It represents the beginning of my own faith, a great gift which my mother passed on to me. Now, many years after her death, I am growing closer to her and learning to love her as I never did when she was alive. Holding this little white plastic case now connects me to my childhood, to my mother — and to God:

> *Look down upon me good and gentle Jesus, while before Thy face I humbly kneel, and with burning soul pray and beseech Thee to fix deep in my heart lively sentiments of faith, hope and charity, true contrition for my sins and a firm purpose of amendment; while I contemplate with great love and tender pity Thy five most precious wounds, pondering over them within me, while I call to mind what the prophet David put in Thy mouth concerning Thee, "O good Jesus: 'They have pierced my hands and my feet. They have numbered all my bones.'"*

Scripture Meditation

"Bless the Lord, my soul; all my being, bless his holy name! Bless the Lord, my soul; do not forget all the gifts of God, Who pardons all your

sins, heals all your ills, Delivers your life from the pit, Surrounds you with love and compassion, Fills your days with good things; Your youth is renewed like the eagle."

Psalm 103

Dear Lord Jesus,

To journey with You in faith is to be gifted every step of the way! You bless us through our memories, letting us walk back through our lives to receive Your grace and healing which we might have missed the first time around. You even bless us in our sleep, sending us dreams to heal our brokenness. No matter how far we stray from You, You stand by us patiently waiting for our response. Jesus, when will we wake up to the realization that You use everything to reach us, to call us, to awaken us to Your love? Even church bells! Open my ears and eyes, Jesus, to recognize You in Your gifts which surround me.

9

Buried Treasure

When I turned out the light before bed and opened the shutters to listen to the sounds of the night, I had no idea that I would open myself to all the mosquitoes in Montecatini! I didn't sleep a wink all night. One lone church on a distant mountain sounded it's bell every hour on the hour. Beginning with midnight, I heard every set of bells, and as soon as I'd begin to drift off to sleep, a mosquito would buzz my face, looking for a landing spot. I slapped myself about 100 times, each time a little harder, trying to kill the mosquito. It was like a nightmare, only a real one! I tried closing the shutters and nearly suffocated, it was so hot. My only defense was to fight the mosquitoes. I couldn't even go to the bathroom because it was two corridors away and I didn't know how in the world I'd ever find it without making a terrible noise and tripping in the dark. It was a dilemma which I wouldn't wish on my worst enemy.

I attempted to say the Chaplet of Divine Mercy, but the mosquitoes had me too enraged to pray. Around 6 A. M. I fell asleep for awhile, then decided to get up and move to another villa, if only to get some sleep and relief from the oppressive heat. The temperature here has to be well over 100 degrees.

Francis Turns Pain into Gift

I don't suffer these problems well, at least not like the saints, in particular not like St. Francis, who also spent a sleepless night when he camped out on a balcony at St. Clare's convent about a year before he died. But that's the extent of the comparison between St. Francis and myself! Francis was gravely ill and knew he would die unless he received some care, so his brothers brought him to San Damiano to be ministered to by Clare and her community. Francis was almost blind. He described the pain in his eyes as great splinters of glass, scratching against his pupils. He suffered from the stigmata, the wounds of Jesus in his sides, hands and his feet. His stomach was ulcerated from fasting and his spleen was almost destroyed. He slept on a little balcony at their convent. But he never slept. Apparently, all the animals of the night bit at his toes and crawled all over his open sores. When Clare went to see how he was feeling in the morning, she heard him singing a canticle to the animals and it was there on that little balcony where he sang that beautiful canticle of praise and thanksgiving to all God's creatures. Now there is the stuff of sainthood!

Francis Sings His Gratitude to God

Francis stayed at San Damiano for fifty days or more. There were so many mice that annoyed him not only at night, but during the day, that even prayer was difficult. When they sat at a table to eat, the mice climbed up on the table! Francis and his brothers were of the opinion that this was a diabolical intervention. One night, when Francis was feeling sorry for himself he prayed, *"Lord, help me in my infirmities so that I may have the strength to bear them patiently."* Then he heard a voice in his spirit which said: *"Tell me, Brother: if in compensation for your sufferings and tribulations you were given an immense and precious treasure, the whole mass of the earth changed into pure gold, pebbles into precious stones, and the water of the rivers into perfume, would you not regard the pebbles and the waters as nothing compared to such a treasure? Would you not rejoice?"* Blessed Francis answered: *"Lord, it would be a very great, very precious, and inestimable treasure beyond all that one can love and desire!"* "Well, Brother," the voice said, *"be glad and joyful in the midst of your infirmities and tribulations: as of now, live in peace as if you were already sharing my kingdom."*[1] Francis couldn't stop rejoicing at this great gift the Lord had given him, an assurance that he was sharing in His kingdom, that he composed the "Praises of the Lord," known as the "Canticle of Brother Sun" to be sung by all the Friars whom Francis called the 'jongleurs of God.'

A Healing Canticle

Not long after, Francis dispatched one of his brothers to go before the bishop and the podesta who were having a public feud, to sing this canticle to them. At the end of the canticle, the podesta cried out before the entire gathering: "*'In truth I say to you, not only do I forgive the lord bishop whom I ought to recognize as my master, but I would even pardon my brother's and my own son's murderer!'* He then threw himself at the feet of the lord bishop and said to him, *'For the love of our Lord Jesus Christ and of Blessed Francis, his servant, I am ready to make any atonement you wish.'* The bishop stood up and said to him, *'My office demands humility of me, but by nature I am quick to anger; you must forgive me!'* With much tenderness and affection, both locked arms and embraced each other."[2]

I Should Have Spread Bread Crumbs!

After breakfast I went in search of another villa. A billboard advertising a villa on "Montecatini Alto" had a picture of someone swimming. It looked so inviting. A 40 minute trek up the mountain, around some precarious turns finally brought me to this villa, which was closed. Now I was nowhere with no plan in sight. I should have spread bread crumbs along the way like Hansel and Gretel in order to find my way back down the mountain. I stopped a man driving a small garbage truck and asked for directions to town. He looked at me like I was crazy! How could he possibly direct me around so many twists and turns? He volunteered to lead me down the mountain as soon as he finished his garbage route. The view was breathtaking. But the smell from the garbage was repulsive and made me want to retch. What in the world was I doing following this garbage truck? How did I get into this mess? I felt sorry for people who earned their livelihood picking up garbage, especially the young boy who rode on the back of the truck who had to smell that all the time. What some people have to do to earn money and to make a living. Then I felt such compassion for these good people and for their work. If we didn't have garbage men our world would be a terrible place. They contribute so much to our quality of life, to making our world beautiful. What would we do without them?

Gifts in the Garbage?

All the way down I was wondering what lesson God was showing me through this experience. It all seemed like such a waste of time, and yet I knew better. I normally would have exploded with anger and frustration over this wild goose chase with a garbage truck. Instead I was thanking God for garbage collectors. Had St. Francis' balcony experience rubbed off on me? The way he turned his pain into gratitude and gift was heroic. Perhaps that is the lesson I'm to learn—to see the "garbage" in my life—pain, sickness, trials—as an opportunity to die to self so as to grow closer to God and His creatures. To see our "garbage" as gift is the stuff of sainthood!

My new hotel was adjacent to the famous mineral baths of Montecatini, where people come from all over the world to "take the cure," so they say, for what ails them. The water has a healing potential for intestinal problems, especially stomach and liver ailments. They bring cups to draw water from the fountains while opera singers perform on a huge outdoor stage accompanied by a full orchestra. I thought I'd "take the cure" but learned that you had to go early every morning on an empty stomach for at least five days for it to have any effect. I would only be here for another day, so it was out of the question.

My Insatiable Appetite to Know the Saints

After dinner I continued reading the life of St. Clare of Assisi. I want to be well acquainted with both St. Francis and St. Clare before I get to Assisi, my next stop. You can't read about her without reading about St. Francis because their lives were so spiritually entwined.

I really am enjoying reading about these saints. Their detachment and surrender to the Lord is so deep and complete. What a special call some of them have, like St. Clare, who lived a life of extreme poverty and generosity. They gave their wills totally to the Lord.

This challenges me to look at how God is calling me and my response. Is He calling me to such extremes? Why am I so attracted to their spirituality? Clare's life touches me so much, almost more than St. Catherine of Siena's, but I don't know why. All I know is that I have an insatiable appetite to learn about them, to sit at their feet and take nourishment from the ways they loved the Lord, and from the ways He loved them.

Clare's Mother Had a Vision

"Before the child's birth it was revealed to the mother that her offspring would be a brilliant light in the world. This light the mother detected in her daughter from her earliest years. Besides being favored with personal beauty, Clare possessed a charming personality and rare qualities of mind. She was a favorite in the family, and hardly had she attained to young womanhood, when several suitors sought her in marriage.

"But her virtues surpassed the gifts with which nature endowed her. She interested herself in the poor and frequently denied herself things so as to be able to give more to the poor members of Christ. She loved prayer, and it was her sweetest delight to surrender her heart to sentiments of ardent devotion before Jesus Christ in the Blessed Sacrament. Beneath her beautiful garments she wore a sharp penitential belt in order to honor the sufferings of Christ and to preserve herself a chaste virgin for His sake."[3]

She went to the Church of San Giorgio for a Lenten service one night when Francis was witnessing about living the gospel way of life. She saw the light and love in him and the joy he experienced in his life of poverty. She went to him after the service and said that she definitely knew she was being called to this life and asked for his help in entering the convent.

A Meeting of Hearts

Their meeting was a real union of minds and hearts. After sharing what was on her heart with Francis, and how she wanted to follow him, he said to her, *"You will have to know how to die."* *"What do you mean?"* she asked. Francis replied, *"On the cross with Christ."* His words burned into her soul and attracted her more deeply to the Lord, whom she saw in Francis.

They planned for her to enter the community the following week, on Palm Sunday. Clare attended Mass that Sunday in the Cathedral with all the young ladies of Assisi. The Bishop conducted the liturgy. After the homily everyone went forward to receive palms. The young unmarried girls of Assisi, of whom Clare was a part, were to be the last in the procession. They rose from their seats in all their new spring fashions and went up to the altar to receive the palms — everyone, that is, except Clare. She remained in her seat with her head down. Clare was fairly well-known because her home was next to San Rufino Cathedral, and the Bishop noticed her absence. So he went up to her and gave her a blessing and the palms.

Clare Professes Her Vows

That Palm Sunday evening Clare left home for the last time and completely broke away from her family. A friend of hers met her and they went to the Portiuncula, the tiny dilapidated chapel owned by the Benedictines which was given to Francis and his followers for the rental of a basket of fish per year. At that time it was almost a forest with the chapel in the middle. Francis had built little huts around this church where two of the friars were waiting for Clare and her friend. They led the girls through the brush, the thorns on the bushes ripping away at their Palm Sunday outfits. Finally, they arrived at the Portiuncula. Clare's friend removed all her jewelry. She replaced Clare's Sunday outfit with a coarse habit tied at the waist with a cord and then Clare was brought to Francis. The Bishop was aware of her being received into the order because a Father Sylvester stood in as the delegate for the Bishop.

Francis asked Clare, "*What do you want, my daughter?*" She replied, "I want only Jesus Christ and to live by the Gospel, owning nothing and in chastity."[4] She knelt before him while he sheared her magnificent blond hair from her head. He then placed a coarse piece of woolen cloth over her head. Clare was 18 years old and the founder of a new religious order known worldwide as the Poor Clares. Being very proper Francis brought her to stay with the Benedictine Sisters of St. Paul until he could set up a convent for her.

Clare Resists Being Kidnapped

The story continues that the uncle who had sworn to protect his brother's daughter got a group together to kidnap Clare. When Clare saw the army approaching she went into the church and stood at the altar, clutching the altar cloth. Her resistance was strong. At first the uncle spoke sweetly to her, but as she made it clear that she was not interested in coming home, they began pulling at her. At one point the cloth was pulled halfway off the altar. Clare prayed. It was as if legions of angels were called down from heaven with St. Michael in the lead. They couldn't pry Clare loose from the altar. Finally, she removed the woolen cloth from her head to reveal her shaved head. Too shocked for words, they decided they would henceforth treat Clare as if she were dead.

Agnes Barely Escapes Her Captors

Not too long after this, Clare's sister Agnes who had visited the convent everyday, and was overcome with the change she saw in Clare, decided that she, too, wanted to enter the cloister. She was 15. The uncle assembled another army to kidnap Agnes. This time they did capture her and dragged her through the streets of Assisi. Bloodied and hurt, she refused to get up. Her uncle was so overcome with anger he raised his arm to strike her. His arm became paralyzed in mid-air and he gave out a blood-curdling scream, the pain was so excruciating. The soldiers, fearing they had pushed God too far, scattered, and the uncle ran off, never to return. Clare came for her sister, who had been completely healed of all her wounds on the spot. Francis then found a place for the ladies at the Church of San Damiano, his very own special place, as it was where the Lord spoke to him from the crucifix.

Clare Wanted To *Be* Poverty

For her part, Clare stayed at the convent of San Damiano for the rest of her life. It remains very similar to what it looked like in Clare's day, which gives one a good idea of the extent to which Clare went to live her life of poverty. As much as Francis wanted to embrace poverty, Clare was determined to *be* poverty. She was a person who was used to the finest, never knowing anything but luxury. Here she was living with absolutely nothing, begging for everything, their food and, until San Damiano, their lodgings. Before long, Clare attracted women from all over Italy, in fact, from all over Europe. Many of them were from well-to-do families. This was so amazing. The more austere Clare's rule was, the more she attracted ladies from nobility. They wore no stockings or sandals at any time of the year. They lived in the worst possible conditions at San Damiano. They had no beds, they slept on twigs with patched hemp for blankets. There were cracks in the ceiling. Wind and rain seeped through the openings. They ate very little and no meat at all, and they begged for their food. Clare made sure that she fasted more than anyone else. When Clare's mother realized that neither Clare nor Agnes were going to return to their old way of life, their mother gave away all the beautiful things she had collected for her daughters' dowries. She took off her sandals, left their beautiful home near the church of San Rufino and joined her daughters in poverty at the convent of San Damiano. True to her name, Ortolana, which means "lady gardener," took care of the gardens at San Damiano.

God Wants Us To Unearth Our Gift

Clare inspires me so much! She heard God's call and she followed. I believe God calls every one of us to a vocation, to be open to the gifts He wants to give us. God's gift to each of us is faith. I believe that faith is the gateway to finding our true vocation, our work in life. Perhaps He is allowing me these experiences and inspirations to open my eyes to see where I am in relation to where He wants me to be, or rather to see who I am in relation to whom He wants me to be. God created each one of us as unique works of art to reflect His love and beauty in a very special way. He created us for a purpose, to play a role in life which no one else can do. Buried within us like the pearl of great price is a special gift or talent which sets us apart from the rest of creation. As our life runs its course, that special treasure is revealed to us. Some of us discover our gift early, some find it later. Some never find it. But He gifts us all and waits for us to dig it up and use it.

This trip is helping me dig up my gift! Through our gifts we uncover the presence of God more clearly and powerfully. Then we see that the gift is actually to be utilized for the benefit of others. I have a sense that the Lord is gifting me with a mission in relation to the saints and the Eucharist. Only God knows how a gift of this nature would fill me with joy. *I'd love nothing better than to share my love and faith in Jesus' Eucharistic presence.* It occurs to me that our gifts are not found without pain, without struggle, without suffering and disappointment, without the cross. We need to be purified of our "garbage," from the stuff that blocks us from utilizing our gift, so we can go out and bear fruit. In uncovering our gift, we discover the God within who empowers us to reach out to others with His love. The saints have responded so deeply to God's call. He has gifted them in order to gift others with His healing.

I'm so thankful for this opportunity to explore the lives of the saints in this holy land of Italy. I'm so blessed by their lives, by their teachings, by their sacrifice. The fallout of their love and faith is touching me deeply, stirring up a desire to give myself more completely to the Lord. How? Please show me, Lord.

Scripture Meditation

"The kingdom of heaven is like this. A man happens to find a treasure hidden in a field. He covers it up again, and is so happy that he goes and sells everything he has, and then goes back and buys that field." (Matt 13: 44)

Dear Lord Jesus,

How long does it take us to discover Your gift of faith, buried inside of us, just waiting to be tapped? Francis and Clare found it when they were young, and gave their all for it. You gift each of us with this treasure, Lord, which is the gateway to joy and fulfillment. You don't force it on us, You offer it and wait for us to discover it. How blessed are we to uncover it and appropriate it's contents. With Francis, we say, "Lord, it is a very great, very precious, and inestimable treasure beyond all that one can love and desire!" Thank you, Jesus.

10

Lesson of the Box

My primary task this morning was to mail home a box of unnecessary clothes. I realize how cumbersome all this luggage is and I really don't need half the clothes I brought. I already sent one suitcase home with Tommy. I've accumulated more stuff since then—some gifts and odds and ends, which I'd just as soon not be weighed down with for the rest of the trip.

Desperate To Mail My Box

The hotel concierge gave me some scissors, tape and a magic marker to prepare it for mailing. How I labored over my box! It weighed, I'd say, 8 or 10 lbs. Then he gave me a map with directions to the post office. It was so well marked I figured I wouldn't have any problem finding my way. It would have been too easy to go to the main post office in town; instead, he directed me to an out-of-the-way post office which only handled packages. I followed the map and went in a complete circle, ending up back where I started. I was already perspiring and the temperature was rising by the minute. Determined to get rid of this box, I set out again, following the map. It looked so easy, but somehow I turned off on wrong streets. I got lost. I asked somebody. He told me to turn around, cross the railroad tracks and turn left on the second street on the right and if I followed what he said, I'd find it. Again, I got lost. I was on this merry-go-round for an hour. I must have asked eight different people for directions. Each time, their directions were simple, clear, to the point and the one frustrating part was this: if I made one mistake, I had to pay dearly because the whole town is filled with one-way streets. So, if I did make a mistake, I'd have to go the opposite way for a long time until I could come back to where I needed to be. By then I was so lost I had no idea where I was. Twice I ended up back at my starting place. Once, I ended up on the outskirts of Montecatini.

I put 2,000 kilometers on this Fiat!

Driving Around in Circles

This wild goose chase felt vaguely familiar. This is like a rerun of the garbage truck episode. Now on the verge of tears, I ran my inner tape recorder: *Why is this happening to me? What in the world am I doing?* Here I was again, wasting a whole morning driving around in circles. What meaning could this possibly have?

It occurred to me that I spend a lot of my life running around, doing these kinds of things. I could have been sitting by the pool. I could have been listening to the beautiful concert next to our hotel this morning given by a female soprano; she was singing arias from Madame Butterfly and I briefly entertained the idea of staying there to soak in the beauty of the concert.

What drives me to do these things? What's in the box anyway that is so important that it's taking all my time? Perhaps that's the point. Perhaps I have too much. Perhaps I'm caught up too much in all these tasks and in having all these things which take me away from what I'm really about. Perhaps I'm so weighed down with the "boxes" of my life, I don't really have time for the essentials, like meditation and serving the needs of others. I don't know. I think there is a lesson in this. I decided to give up the idea of mailing the box.

Since I had already passed the store twice with the parchment of Gregorian Chant in the window, I decided it'd be easier for me to stop now and buy this gift for my pastor, than to find the post office. Finding these original 16th century pages was so satisfying, I bought two of them. He would be so surprised! Actually they were a centerfold and would have to be framed as such. It will make a beautiful gift and one man very happy.

My Box Couldn't Be Mailed!

Mustering what remnant of courage I had left, I asked the proprietor if there was any easy way to find the post office. *Easy, signora, it couldn't be easier to find from here!* Then he drew me a little map by which I actually found my way. I was so hot by the time I got there my blouse was wringing wet, but I was so relieved to be there I carried in my box and dropped it on the scale. People came out of nowhere telling me that they could never send this box, that it was improperly wrapped, that it wasn't taped right, that they couldn't read it and so on. I didn't know whether to laugh or cry. *What was the problem with this box?* I told them I'd fix it. I'd retape it. I'd write my name and address more legibly. Nothing seemed to satisfy them. If I cooperated with their specifications, they could possibly help me they said. I fixed the box and when it was ready they put it on the scale. Staring up at me from under her glasses the post office superintendent said in Italian, "$100.00." At that moment I made the quickest decision of my life. *Thank you very much, but I'm not going to mail this box,* I said, and took the box to the car. I dreaded the thought of carrying this box with me for the rest of the trip. *It's meant to remind me of my preoccupation with things that don't matter.* What am I doing to create these situations, these fruitless endeavors? I spend a lot of time spinning my wheels. There are other important things to be done. I'm tired of running around in circles. Maybe I just better keep the box with me for the rest of the trip and I'll let it serve as a reminder to simplify and prioritize my life. I'll focus on doing things that have meaning and that I feel the Lord is directing me to do. I'm becoming my own worst enemy.

Lord, Deliver Me from Myself

On the way back to the hotel, which I prayed now to be able to find, I asked God to deliver me from my myself. I probably could make a very good pilgrimage if I were stashed away in a convent for a week or two where I could obey all the rules, follow the routine, pray and feel very good about it all. Left to my own devices I can drive myself crazy running here and there and getting caught up in so many pursuits. *Lord, please deliver me from myself and heal that self that is so frantic and in need of busyness or activity.* It seems I have to create activities to keep me happy. I'm in Italy and I don't need to make work for myself, especially by driving in Italian cities looking for out-of-the-way post offices!

I stopped at a little deli and bought a huge bottle of water and a roll for lunch. Back at the hotel I took some time to cool off and then spent an hour at the pool swimming laps and frolicking like a seal. It was so refreshing.

Reliving the "Death" Of Witness Magazine

Rereading my journal renewed my gratitude for this trip. Looking back over last year's entries, I realized what pressures and trials we endured — trials involving several of our children, our own relationship, the death of my Dad, and the demise of the publishing ministry I started nine years prior, otherwise known as *Witness Magazine*. It seemed as if everything converged at once.

I had poured my heart and soul into *Witness*. It started with an inspiration I had while I was taking a shower one morning and ended nine years later as a professional-looking magazine, put together by a volunteer group, which had a worldwide circulation of eight hundred subscribers. It's not that it wasn't good; it was really good. We know from the response it generated that many people were touched by the personal stories of faith of which it was comprised. It was an enormous amount of effort for a handful of people. We were like a little fish swimming alongside much bigger fish in the publishing ministry. It seems we had to re-invent the wheel with each issue we produced and we were always in a hole financially. We struggled to expand, to get subscribers, to make connections, to gain recognition in the publishing world. Then there were the rejections, each one of which I took personally. I believe *Witness* was inspired by the Holy

Spirit, but I believe also that the signs of its demise were obvious. It never took on a life of its own, and that is what we hoped and prayed would happen. One of the most difficult decisions I ever had to make was the one to close down *Witness*. Our small group knew long before it happened that it was going to happen; they waited patiently for me to give up and surrender.

Praying by Letters

But I grieved for it. It was a deep loss in my life. At a retreat some time after that, we were asked to write a letter to Jesus sharing some hurt or anger with Him. And then we were to let Him respond to us. Here's what I wrote:

Dear Jesus,

I can't find an early memory that I'm angry about. Yet I carry so much anger in me. Most of it I've turned inward—swallowed—and it has propelled me for years into activity of all kinds. I've had to find outlets for the anger and some of the things have been good pursuits. Like Witness Magazine. *It was a way for me to prove myself and share my faith at the same time. It was an outlet for all my bottled up energy and creativity and faith. It was a good thing. For nine years I tried to raise that "child," investing myself in her growth. I pushed so to make her succeed, to get her recognized and affirmed and to be noticed and valued. I wanted her to have meaning and value, to be important, to matter.*

Our time was up and we were instructed to let Jesus answer us. Here is what He said to me:

Dear Joan,

I saw your need from afar! From before you were born, I saw your pain, your attempt to fix your world, your self, your family; your attempt to heal them. Your needs were deep. You did the best you could, trying to fill yourself. The nuns helped you find Me. I heard your cries, your loneliness, your suffering. I always was aware of where you were, child, and what you needed. I sent you Gertrude to mother you, the nuns to teach you and discipline you, some good friends to love and play with you. I walked with you and helped you uncover your pain. Joan, I saw that your needs were taken care of, but waited until you were ready to begin to fill your real needs for love. I gave you Tommy and your family who nurtured you, then Witness *was my launching pad for you to set out on your own journey.*

My Inner Child Needed *Witness*

These words made me cry. *Witness* had been like raising a child and letting her go. Jesus was telling me *Witness* was a gift for *my inner child.* My inner child needed *Witness* to grow up! It was a vehicle for me to express and fulfill myself, to grow, connect with people, nurture and be nurtured. I thought my efforts were on behalf of the magazine—to be valued, to make a difference, to matter, to be important, to count—but underneath they were the striving of my needy inner child to find love and meaning. The rejections hurt so deeply because they were really the rejections of my childhood. The Lord gave me *Witness* to heal me; I needed it to bring me to this point on the journey. He said it was a launching pad. *A launching pad for what?*

In one of my dreams this past year, Jesus took me by the hand and we walked down a new path, a new road together. I didn't know then that *Witness* would be ending and we hadn't yet planned this trip. But this certainly seems to be a part of that new road that I'm walking down. It's a healing walk, a gift from my great big *Abba,* Daddy God, who's given his child the freedom and the wherewithal to travel and pursue my interest in the saints and the Eucharistic miracles. He probably has had it all arranged for eternity, knowing that I'd need to come away like this from my routine at home in order to learn the lessons He wants to teach me. Here I'm free, with no responsibilities other than to absorb what He's showing me.

I Gotta Be Me!

What I'm feeling down deep in myself is inadequacy. I'm trying to be a St. Clare or a St. Catherine. I'm trying to be someone I'm not. Do I think God will love me more or that others will love me more if I become like them? I want to be close to the Lord with all my heart, but I'm sensing that He's made me who I am, and I can't be a Clare. I can't shave my head and leave my family and join a convent. I don't want to and I don't think I'm being called to that. *I'm sensing a need to start living out of who I am instead of who I'm not.* I want to feel comfortable with the fact that I am here on this trip staying at these nice hotels and loving the Lord in this way. God has given me this and for me to always doubt whether I should be doing this means that I'm not accepting His gift. I'm always apologizing for having money and beating myself up for not giving it all up for a more simple life. The fact is, I've always had every material advantage imaginable. I'd like to believe that I could do without material possessions. I like nice things, but I am not bound by them in the sense that I'm living for them. My priorities in life are spiritual. If staying in a nice hotel means that I'm not loving God, then there's something wrong with my thinking. I can love God in a nice hotel as well as in a convent. This issue has been bubbling just under the surface for a long time, and this trip is forcing it to the surface.

Dinner Atop the Mountain

Tonight the concierge suggested I take the funicular up the mountain to have dinner at a little restaurant overlooking Montecatini. I recoiled at first because I'm so afraid of heights, but he assured me that it was like riding a train. The trip up the mountain was quite an adventure! The lights in the city below twinkled at dusk, and it looked like a fairyland. Riding this contraption made me miss my family. I thought of how they would be behaving now, how they'd be shaking the compartment trying to scare me, what they'd be saying, how they'd be laughing and enjoying themselves. Then I thought of all the places I've gone in life with friends, especially before I got married, and the fun we had. I imagined what a wonderful time we'd have if they were here now. People stare at me because I'm alone, but I'm getting used to it. My smile usually disarms them.

My Family

Jesus Is Giving Me Hind's Feet

I'm so content to be here. Again I felt so full and grateful for the ability and the freedom to roam around God's world. How many people have the opportunity to do this? Sitting at dinner up on top of the mountain was pure joy. I thought of the story of Much-Afraid and how she escaped from her Fearing relatives and went with the Shepherd to the High Places where "perfect love casts out fear:" "God, my Lord is my strength; he makes my feet swift as those hinds and enables me to go upon the heights." (Hab 3: 19) Jesus is giving me hinds' feet to jump around Italy in search of Him. *Hinds' Feet on High Places* by Hanna Hurnard is an allegory of our inner journey and speaks deeply to those who long for Love:

"But the High Places of victory and union with Christ cannot be reached by any mental reckoning of self to be dead to sin, or by seeking to devise some way or discipline by which the will can be crucified. The only way is by learning to accept, day by day, the actual conditions and tests permitted by God, by a continually repeated laying down of our will and acceptance of his as it is presented to us in the form of the people with whom we have to live and work, and in the things which happen to us. Every acceptance of His will becomes an altar of sacrifice, and every surrender and abandonment of ourselves to his will is a means of furthering us on the way to the High Places to which he desires to bring every child of his while they are still living on earth. The lessons of accepting and triumphing over evil, of becoming acquainted with grief, and pain, and, ultimately, of finding them transformed into something incomparably precious; of learning through constant surrender to know the Lord of Love himself in a new way and to experience unbroken union with Him—these are the lessons of the allegory in this book. The High Places and the hinds' feet do not refer to heavenly places after death, but are meant to be the glorious experience of God's children here and now—if they will follow the path he chooses for them."[1]

Listening to the "Still Small Voice"

God is being very patient with me, waiting while I learn how to listen to Him. The Holy Spirit plants the hunger and thirst in us in order to lead us to His will for our lives. He is continually converting our hearts to His will, leading us to our happiness and holiness, which I believe go together. By following His leading in our heart, we'll be filled with joy and peace.

For many years I thought that following the Lord meant living by what others wanted and certain rules. I'm beginning to know that it's not "out there" where we find the peace, but it's only by listening to the truth within, to that "still, small voice" that we can find the light and the love of Jesus.

God wants to gift us continually. Say He wants to give us a sweater. It's one thing for Him to give us the sweater, but if we don't wear it, it's not a very good gift. It's our wearing of the gift that gives joy to the giver as well as to the receiver. Unless the sweater is worn, the giver and the receiver don't really get anything out of it. I think God is pleased when we accept His gifts and wear them and when we take advantage of His goodness and say "yes" to Him, trusting what He wants for us is that which is the deepest hunger of our heart.

I'm glad I decided to spend this extra day here. I thought it was for a rest and, as it turns out, I think it was to put on the "sweater" that God gave me. I see how I prevent myself from enjoying His gifts and how I set myself up to reject His gifts. I learned some valuable lessons today for which I thank and praise Him. The more open we are to Him the more He can pour His grace into us. Yet we fear openness because we think He will take something from us rather than gift us.

There's an excitement building in me for leaving tomorrow and going to Assisi. I called ahead tonight to a hotel that's been recommended. When I spoke to the concierge I told him that I was alone and I asked him for a room, if possible, with a beautiful view. He told me that, of course, he would give me a beautiful room, I'm travelling alone and he would take very good care of me. Just one more sign that God watches over us through His people and is blessing and healing me through these people and this trip.

Scripture Meditation

"You know the grace of Our Lord Jesus Christ; rich as he was, he made himself poor for your sake, in order to make you rich by means of his poverty. . .If you are eager to give, God will accept your gift on the basis of what you have to give, not on what you don't have. I am not trying to relieve others by putting a burden on you; but since you have plenty at this time, it is only fair that you should help those who are in need. Then, when you are in need and they have plenty, they will help you." (2 Cor 8: 12-15)

Dear Lord Jesus,

Although it is good for us to give up the things of the world in order to free ourselves for You, You have told Your saints that the poverty You desire is for us to let go of all the ways we try to fill ourselves and to rely on You to provide for our needs. Thank you for the ways You get our attention to remind us that You want our total trust. You want us to abandon ourselves to You like children, trusting in Your care of us. Jesus, please give me the faith to surrender my ideas, plans, goals, desires and needs to You. Convert them into Your perfect will—for myself and for the good of others.

11

Assisi

Heading south on the *autostrada* toward Assisi accompanied by my ever-present bottle of water, I felt like singing I was so happy. To the east was Florence, cradled in the arms of the Tuscan hills, a city I called home for two years of my life and a place where I could easily spend the rest of my life. I said several Chaplets of Divine Mercy, offering each decade for someone at home. It helped passed the time and it also connected me to the people I love.

Driving Is Hazardous to Your Health!

The drive was hot and uneventful save for two incidents which nearly gave me a heart attack. Driving in Italy is hazardous to your life due to the lack of speed limits. European drivers think nothing of going 100 miles an hour. In the States I consider myself a fast driver, but compared to these Italian drivers, I drive at a snail's pace. Approaching a tunnel, I veered into the left lane to pass a huge truck on my right. It was a very dark, long tunnel, so I had my lights on and was sort of creeping along in the left lane, when, suddenly a car behind me sounded its horn. I almost jumped out of my seat. He flashed his lights signaling me to move, then sped away at breakneck speed. That's when I realized that he had purposely crept up on me without his headlights on in order to frighten me.

Another time a car came at me when I was in the left lane and the driver held his hand on the horn until I moved over to the right lane. I felt like screaming, but there was nothing I could do. Except pray. I prayed to my angel companions to protect me from these rude and impatient road runners!

Assisi Is a Sight for Sore Eyes

Assisi was beautiful to behold. Perched on the side of Mt. Subasio, it had an air of warmth and hospitality which was so welcoming. As soon as I found my hotel and parked the car, I headed for a deli to find some water. It was the middle of the afternoon and so hot, I decided not to leave my camera and film in the car for fear they would melt. In one of those little bars with the hanging beads in the doorway, I found bottled water and a hard roll. The lady proprietor was glued to her TV set, watching an Italian version of a soap opera. "What are you watching?" I asked, and without taking her eyes off the screen, she replied, "St. Barbara." I should have guessed! A soap opera named after a saint could only happen in Italy.

My hotel was adjacent to the Basilica of St. Francis. After checking in, I headed over there to see what I could before dinner. Once inside, I found my way to the Blessed Sacrament Chapel where I sat for awhile in the Lord's presence, feeling so peaceful and at home. St. Francis' tomb and some of his relics were downstairs, where I was drawn to the glass-enclosed case which holds the tunic he wore; a grayish brown undyed wool robe, sewn together in squares like a patchwork quilt. Next to it were some small shoes, like slippers with leather bottoms.

Standing with my nose pressed to the glass, I was taken aback by the similarity of St. Francis tunic with that of the one Brother Bill Tomes wears in Chicago. He modeled his denim robe on Francis', which he sewed together from seventeen pairs of blue jeans. The Lord called Bill from of a very active, busy life to give up everything and follow Him into the violent crime-ridden world of the gangs. His mission is to love his brothers. Appointed by Cardinal Bernardin to minister to the gangs in the inner city, he founded *The Brothers and Sisters of Love*. Bill and his associate, Jim Fogarty, literally lay down their lives for their brothers whenever there is gunfire; they run into the line of fire, hoping their presence will stop the bullets and bring peace and love into a dark and hopeless world. Brother Bill and his mother, Helen, are close friends of ours. I didn't know if my tears were for Brother Bill or St. Francis, or for the love that I felt in the both of them, so total, so unconditional, so Christ-like.

St. Francis of Assisi

Brother Bill Tomes joking with Demetrius Ford from Henry Horner Homes

The actual rock in which St. Francis is buried is exposed behind a grate in a lower level of the basilica. There's an altar in front of it where Mass was just about to begin. I felt so fortunate to be there with a youth group from Assisi who were part of a European movement dedicated to converting people to live for Christ, be they religious or married. Their faith and zeal evidenced by their active participation at Mass was so inspiring. Some of them were consecrated into this organization during Mass.

Christ's Young Apostles

The young gal who did one of the readings was probably no more than 20, just a little younger than St. Clare when she became the superior of her community at 21. The love between these young people was tangible, as they smiled and hugged and genuinely showed such affection during the kiss of peace. The young man next to me, obviously a member of the community, was from Africa. There were some that might have been 15 years old and some much older. At the prayers of the faithful, practically the whole little church prayed. Although it was in Italian, I did understand some of the intentions. The man in front of me asked for better communication in his family and some asked for prayers for relatives who were sick. Some said prayers of thanksgiving for different healings they had received or that their family or friends had received. It could have been morning Mass at my parish church, the prayer requests were so similar. Italian or American or Egyptian, our hungers and needs are the same the world over. So many came over and hugged me, an obvious stranger, and made me feel so welcome. One woman kissed me on both cheeks. *You will know they are My followers by the way they love one another.* Our love for Christ makes us one the world over.

I Want To Be Mary, Not Martha

Today was St. Martha's feast. The priest spoke about the need to reflect on what it was that was holding St. Martha back from finding her fulfillment. She was so preoccupied with so many things. How his words spoke to me! I'd like to turn the Martha in me into a Mary. The priest spoke about St. Francis and about his call to littleness and to simplicity, to littleness that the Lord might be big, and to poverty and simplicity, in order to give Him our all. Christ changes us, he said; He makes us a new creature. We can't do it, but He can. I've heard the reading many times, but today it spoke to my heart. I need to change, but I need to let the Lord change me. All these crazy incidents that have been happening are showing me that I need to let go, to simplify, to be delivered from all the ego control and obsessions that have me running around in circles. I need to be delivered from myself, from the self that is trying to run the show. I think I've come to that dead end in myself, that bottom, which gives me the humility to know I can't do it. I can't make myself change but I am asking God to change me, to make me the new creature that He wants me to be.

"You should put away the old self of your former way of life, corrupted through deceitful desires, and be renewed in the spirit of your minds, and put on the new self, created in God's way in righteousness and holiness of truth." (Ephesians 4:22-24) In my 50 years, I've devoted myself to finding

my way on this spiritual journey according to my plan. In the years after 50, I want to try and live more by God's plan. I want to ask Him to let me know His will more than I have been doing. I need to know His will, to hear His voice, to feel His touch. *"Lord, deliver me from myself. Change me and make me into a new creature so that You can increase and I can decrease. Help me decrease the I, the ego, so that You can operate more fully."*

How Can I "Die" in the World?

I have to be willing, as Francis said to Clare, to die. But how do we die if we live in the world? I think that the dying is a spiritual death. It's a dying to self. It's a dying to our egos, to our compulsions and addictions. It's surrendering our wills and waiting on God. I think it's about putting God first. How can we live that out practically? How do I wait on God? For me it's learning to listen for Him and then following what I hear. If I really have an inspiration to do something, I must wait and check it out first with the Lord, *Is this from you, Lord? Do You really want me to do this?* Sometimes, if I want something and I'm not sure if the Lord wants me to have it, I'll give it up because I know if He wants me to have it, He'll give it to me. So, if it's truly of God, He will see to it that I have it. But, if it's not, then I don't need it. To listen for God's "go ahead" inside myself is to listen to the Holy Spirit who will lead us to all truth. To die to myself in the world is to listen deeply for God's will inside my own heart. Then I need to check it out to make sure the idea or the inspiration or even the dream or image is coming from Him.

Sitting in the little chapel of the tomb of St. Francis I felt so close to the Lord through the people and especially through the Eucharist. Jesus was so present. I wanted to set up a tent, like Peter, James and John on Mt. Tabor, to stay for awhile and savor His presence: *"How good it is for us to be here!"* they said. I felt that same enthusiasm. *Please, Lord, teach me how to surrender myself to You, to become little, to allow You to live in me and through me. Teach me simplicity in order to free me, and help me unclutter my heart so that there will be more room for You.*

St. Francis Was a Yuppie!

The french doors of my hotel room opened to a breathtaking view of the surrounding plains of Assisi. It's beautiful here, untouched by modern development and congestion. Cypress and olive trees continue to grow, adding an authentic resemblance to the Assisi which Francis knew. If anyone had become a new creation, he had. I had no idea he was such a rebel and had such a fierce battle within himself before he gave his life to the Lord. Sitting on my balcony with a small book of his life in hand, I read sitting at his feet, as it were, warmed and inspired by his struggle to find God. He came from a privileged background. Today we would call him a Yuppie; a wealthy and indulged young man who dressed in the finest clothes and aspired to be a prince. Described by G.K. Chesterton as "a courtier in a world of kings," he dreamt of a career of knightly chivalry. He had a zest for spending and a reputation of being a party-goer as well as a party-giver.

A Vision of Christ Crucified

Then God came into his life; or was it that Francis opened his life to God? He had a series of dreams which affected him deeply until he finally cried out, *"Lord, what do you want me to do?"* The Lord had plans to transform Francis' expansive personality and natural gifts into His own work of art. Francis spent days up in the mountains where, often accompanied by a friend, he cried anguished tears which he suffered because of fears and visions. One of those visions changed his life forever; it was a vision of Christ crucified. St. Bonaventure wrote that "St. Francis' whole soul seemed to melt away: and so deeply was the memory of Christ's passion impressed on his heart, that it pierced even to the marrow of his bone. From that hour whenever he thought of the Passion of Christ he could scarcely retain his tears and sighs.[1]

Then he made a pilgrimage to Rome to seek God's will for his life. Before he knew what he was doing, he exchanged his clothes with a beggar outside of St. Peter's, and stood there all day so he could learn what if felt like to beg. Francis was following the call he heard deep inside of him; he was cooperating with God's initiative to recreate him according to His purpose for him. It isn't as if Francis went about masterminding his life to become someone else. He simply gave in to the touches of God which he experienced in all different ways. In the process of surrendering, he was changed.

God Changed Francis

His story touched me so deeply. I learned from Francis. I saw his process of letting go, his deep listening to the Lord and the growth of his resolve to follow Him, no matter what the cost. Francis was merely a player in God's theater. He simply had to respond to God's direction. He really didn't have to *do* anything; he just had to be true to himself, and God would do the rest. God would change him into the person God wanted him to be, not into someone whom Francis thought God wanted. And to be changed, to be a new creation, was God's work, not Francis'.

At dinner on the terrace, a little white dove momentarily perched on the railing next to my table, as if to greet me and bid me welcome. It might seem silly, but it made me feel as if Someone were watching over me.

I phoned home tonight and told Tommy that this, by far, was the best yet and, hopefully, he and I will be able to return to experience this together. All is well at home, especially with the kids. It felt good to connect with him, however briefly. I wrote some postcards tonight, one of which was to Brother Bill Tomes. I found a postcard with a picture of St. Francis' robe on it, which I sent to him. I pictured his joy receiving this card and could just imagine the wisecracks he would make.

Scripture Meditation

"But because of Christ, I have come to consider all these advantages that I had as disadvantages. Not only that, but I believe nothing can happen that will outweigh the supreme advantage of knowing Christ Jesus my Lord. For him I have accepted the loss of everything, and I look on everything as so much rubbish if only I can have Christ and be given a place in him. I am no longer trying for perfection by my own efforts, the perfection that comes from the law, but I want only the perfection that comes through faith in Christ, and is from God and based on faith. All I want to know is Christ and the power of his resurrection and to share his sufferings by reproducing the pattern of his death." (Phil 3: 7-11)

Dear Lord Jesus,

What a model You've given us in Francis, whose love of You freed him from his "old self," from his compulsions and addictions so that he could follow You more completely. Jesus, You call me too and offer me the same love; when I open my heart to You, You fill me to overflowing with Your love and gifts. Help me Jesus to let go of my need to control; teach me to be a player on Your stage, waiting on Your directions. Give me the grace to say "Yes" to whatever You ask of me.

12

The Gift of Tears

Like Little Boys Singing to "Daddy God"

Today I feasted at a banquet table of spiritual delights. It began at the basilica at 7 A.M., where I sat enthralled while the friars chanted their office. Seated in choir stalls in a semi-circle behind the main altar, I don't know if it was the sight or the sound of them or a combination of both that affected me so deeply. Their singing was stirring, especially the refrain, "Il Papa Signore," which translated to me as "Daddy God," and which they sang repeatedly. I saw them as obedient sons of a loving Father, who have given over their lives and wills, deeply content in the knowledge they're cared for and safe in His love. How like little boys they were underneath those dark robes, so docile, so obedient, so surrendered—like Francis—to the Lord of their hearts. He must be pleased, I thought, with the large following of Franciscans who give up their all to devote themselves to spreading the Gospel. But then Francis knew this would happen, he had been privileged with a vision of the community which would exist in future generations, which he shared with his friars. Francis was going back and forth between having a great sense of the mission God gave him and his own sense of sinfulness and insufficiency. With tears and sighs he asked forgiveness for his sinfulness, confessing his fear that he would not be

equal to the work for which the Lord had chosen him. He and his brothers
were off in the mountains when he shared with them:

> My beloved, be comforted and rejoice in the Lord, and do not
> be sad because you seem to be so few. Neither let my or your
> simple ways frighten you; for the Lord has shown me that He
> will make us increase into a great multitude, and spread
> abroad to the ends of the earth. . .I have seen a multitude of
> men who come desiring to put on the habit of our holy
> vocation and to live under the rule of our blessed religion. . .I
> have seen the roads from all countries full of men coming
> here. . . .[1]

A part of that multitude was sitting in these choir stalls, and their full-
hearted song of praise and thanksgiving to our heavenly Father
reverberated in my spirit, making me cry tears of gratitude. I felt such
love for "Daddy God," for the friars, and for everyone—in this place of
incredible peace.

Their Singing Made Me Cry

I also understood the value of community in a new way; I was moved
by the depth of support and love they shared. My family is my first and
primary community, but outside of family, I really don't have a prayer
community. Each morning I went to listen to the monks sing their office,
and each time I cried. Why? Did they open a deeply felt need I have for
companionship, for support, for the caring presence of others who are
committed to their faith in the same way? They were touching a nerve in
me, perhaps opening some wounds left over from prayer groups in my
past. Whatever the tears signaled, I sensed the Holy Spirit urging me to
consider joining a prayer community.

Mass followed, after which I spent some time in the Eucharistic
chapel, where again I said the Chaplet of Divine Mercy for the intentions
for all the people I love.

Breakfast in Italy is such a treat. I don't know if it's the hard rolls and
jam, the freshly squeezed orange juice, the *caffe latte*, or a combination of
all of them that makes it so special. A gentle breeze was blowing on the
terrace this morning, where I sat overlooking Assisi, and where I was
about as close to heaven as I've ever felt. It took me almost an hour to scan
my guidebook in order to plan the day. I marked a good route for myself

on the map, portioning off sights for the morning and the afternoon, leaving out a big chunk of time during lunchtime when everything closes down for a few hours.

I Fell in Love with the Portiuncula!

I went first to the Basilica of St. Mary of the Angels, just down the hill from town, and a site to which my Florentine friend, Fratello Stephano, had directed me. He had written on a little piece of paper, "Don't miss the Portiuncula and the Feast of Pardons. . ." A big, beautiful structure, the Basilica houses the little church known as the Portiuncula. It was a precious, small hut-like church of stone which belonged to the Benedictines who gave it to Francis when he began his community. Francis loved the Portiuncula, which in his day was in the middle of a forest. The Portiuncula was the chapel around which Francis built 12 small huts, one for each of his friars. It was in this Portiuncula where Francis welcomed St. Clare on the night in 1212 when she fled down the hill in her Palm Sunday finery to make her profession of vows.

The Lord spoke to Francis in a vision in the Portiuncula, asking him what he wanted Him to do for the sanctification of souls. Francis asked the Lord to provide a way for people to be completely freed from the guilt and punishment of all the sins they have committed from the day of their baptism to the present. Eventually, Francis brought the matter before the Pope, who told him he was asking an awful lot and it wasn't the usual

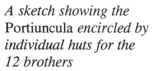

A sketch showing the Portiuncula *encircled by individual huts for the 12 brothers*

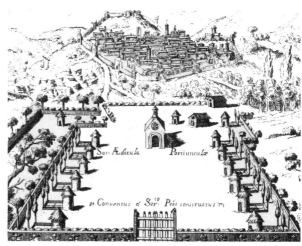

practice to grant such an indulgence, to which Francis replied, *"My Lord, it is not I who ask this, but rather He who sent me, the Lord Jesus Christ."* The Pope granted his request and established the Feast of Pardons, which continues to this day and is celebrated yearly in Franciscan and other

churches throughout the world. All those who go to confession and communion, pray for the Holy Father, and visit a church during a certain period, will receive forgiveness for their sins and be absolved of all the punishment due to them. It just so happened that I was in Assisi during the Feast of Pardons, which I recognized as a providential blessing.

The Chapel of Transitions in this basilica is a sacred spot, because it is where Francis died. Apparently, St. Francis knew he was dying, and asked to lie in the dirt to show that he lived his whole life, including his death, in poverty. He began to recite a psalm, which was interrupted only by his last breath, then he went to the Lord.

The Portiuncula *where Francis and his small community lived in the beginning of their ministry. Here, they received Clare, witnessed her vows and cut off her hair.*

The other interesting scene in this church is the rose garden in which grow today the unusual thornless rose bushes with reddish leaves. One night when St. Francis was suffering severe temptations, he threw himself onto the roses to castigate his body. The thorns and leaves were splashed with blood and colored red. Not only was he not hurt, but the roses all lost their thorns, and grow there to this day. As far as is known, they are the only thornless rose bushes in the world. Next to the rose garden is a chapel which St. Bonaventure built in order to commemorate this miracle.

Standing on Holy Ground

After lunch I bought an extra bottle of water and headed for the Church of San Damiano, which is where Francis heard the voice of Christ speak to him through the large Byzantine crucifix hanging overhead—and which is now in St. Clare's basilica in town. While kneeling in prayer, Francis heard a tender and compassionate voice which said: *"Francis, do you not see that my house is falling into ruin? Go, and repair it for me."* Trembling and filled with the consolation of knowing that it was Jesus Christ who spoke to him, Francis replied with all his heart, saying he would gladly help Him. That was Francis' formal commissioning, bestowed by the Lord Himself, to begin a life of extraordinary service to mankind.

A Dream Shows Me My Closed Heart

The church exists pretty much in the same condition as it did back in the 13th century. Not much has changed about it, which makes it all the more appealing. I immediately went in search of the chapel where Jesus spoke to Francis. It was dark and rather cool and I found myself just sitting and absorbing the atmosphere. I felt on the verge of tears, just thinking about how close Francis was to Jesus, how totally surrendered he was. I asked the Lord for the grace to surrender more of myself to Him. Then I remembered the dream I had last night. I dreamt about a young woman who came to me, having found me by some extraordinary means. She wanted fulfillment, she wanted to know what was missing in her life and how to get it. I felt inspired to ask her if she had faith. She just stared blankly and sort of shrugged her shoulders. I told her that it was already her gift. All she had to do was open her heart a crack and God would fill it to overflowing with His love and peace. Then I put my hand on her heart and prayed for her to open her heart to the Lord. That was the dream. *What part of me stares blankly ahead and shrugs its shoulders, not accepting the gift of faith?* I thought I had opened my heart to the Lord, but apparently I've not opened all of it. Through the dream the Lord was showing me that I've closed off part of my heart, and if I would open myself to Him in faith, He would give me the fulfillment that is missing from my life. Was that the part of me that I've been struggling with on this trip, the part involved in the box and garbage truck episodes? I've been asking the Lord to deliver me from myself. Now it seems He is showing me a part of myself that is "lost" and in need of healing.

Jesus Speaks to My Heart

This was awesome. *The Lord was speaking very directly to me through this dream, showing me what was keeping me from Him.* I was feeling so personally loved by Him when words began forming in my mind in Italian. Sentences were being written on the screen of my mind and I didn't know whether I was writing them or they were being written. Slowly I understood a message in the form of a loving, gentle admonition: *"If you want to surrender to Me, you need to be sorry for your many sins and ask Me for the grace of repentance. When you do, you will have opened your heart and surrendered to Me."*

These words made me cry; they spoke to my soul. I knew they were the truth and I knew they were from the Lord. Here, in the same chapel where St. Francis heard the voice of Jesus, was it possible that Jesus could be speaking to me? The words made sense; they melted into me. *It must be the Lord.* I prayed and asked Him please to give me the grace of repentance.

What Does Repentance Mean?

What is repentance? "Repent and believe in the Gospel" (Mark 1:15) cried John the Baptist. What does it mean? Translated from the Greek word *metanoia*, it means to "change your mind." A change of mind means a change of thinking, which should lead to a change of behavior. "Change your minds and believe in the Gospel" is what John the Baptist was saying. To follow Jesus is to accept the need to change. Jesus was asking me to have more faith and trust Him with my whole self; to surrender all the anger and fear and shame in me that was separating me from Him—and from others. He was answering my request of Him to "deliver me from myself." He was showing me that self who needs redemption, that self who is lost and needs to be found. It was the self involved in the incident of the box and the garbage truck, the self obsessed with pleasing others and with perfection. I was going down a wrong road in a wrong direction; I would never find the peace and joy of Jesus if I didn't *change.* I had asked the Lord to show me how to surrender more of my life. Through the dream and the words I heard in the chapel, Jesus was clearly showing me that I needed to open that closed-off part of my heart which was lost in the darkness of unforgiveness, and *let go* of my ego which was running the show. The Greek word for forgive is the word that means "let go." To follow Him I needed to release my control, and seek His forgiveness for my selfishness.

The closer we come to Jesus, the more need we have of repentance. I used to think those words of John the Baptist meant a one-time conversion, a willingness to turn our lives around and follow Jesus. But now I'm realizing that repentance is an ongoing process, a daily process in which we acknowledge the ways we have failed to give and receive love. St. Peter Julian Eymard, known as the "priest of the Eucharist," founded the Congregation of the Blessed Sacrament and the Sister Servants of the Blessed Sacrament. He has left us a spiritual legacy of inspired writing about the Holy Eucharist. In a small book of his I brought with me, his words spoke to me:

> "Self love is what makes life hard for us, what feeds our distaste for duty and the practice of virtue. Now the first effect of the love of God in a soul dominated by that love is to wage a relentless war on self-love, that is, on sensuality of life, on the ambition of the heart, on pride of the spirit, on the mind of the world, all of which are nothing but falsehood and egotism. The stronger divine love is in a heart, the more militant that heart is. It is not content with repelling evil, but it goes a step farther; it lays the foundation of its virtue on mortification and self-immolation, which bring perfect emancipation and complete freedom from oneself."[2]

A Eucharistic Miracle at San Damiano

I was eager to see the rest of the convent where Clare and her nuns spent all their time, but it was closed for renovations and I was so disappointed. There was one consolation and that was the chapel of St. Jerome where St. Clare and her community experienced a Eucharistic miracle. In 1241 the emperor Frederick II sent bands of mercenaries and Saracens to destroy castles and loot the cities. They came against Assisi, thirsting for Christian blood. They had already penetrated the outer wall of San Damiano and had entered the cloister. The nuns were frightened to death and ran to Clare, their mother, who was sick in bed. She asked for the Holy Eucharist, then gathered the community behind the cloister door. While kneeling and raising the Blessed Sacrament, Clare wept and, "pleaded fervently with the Lord of heaven in the words of the Psalmist:

'Deliver not up to beasts the souls that confess to thee, and shield thy servants whom thou hast redeemed with thy precious blood.' (Psalm 73, 19) A mysterious voice coming from the Host said: "*I shall always watch over you.*" Immediately panic seized the besiegers. A ray of brilliant light which emanated from the Blessed Sacrament had dazzled them. They fell down from the walls and fled from the place."[3] Clare continued: "*Lord, if it is Your will, please protect Assisi, which continues to live in your love.*" And Christ replied, "*It will suffer much, but I will come to its aid and protection.*" The Saracens ran for their lives. St. Clare said, "*My dearest daughters, as long as I am alive make certain that you tell no one of this voice.*"[4] This is considered a Eucharistic miracle and is recorded in several biographies of the saint.

The voice of a child came from the Host saying "I shall always watch over you."

The city officials commemorate this event annually on June 22 with a procession to San Damiano, where they offer candles in memory of the city's deliverance from the Saracens.

Standing in the small chapel of St. Jerome next to the cloister door where Clare and her nuns knelt, it was easy to visualize the scene. It was a powerful image, and a moving testimony to the Real Presence of Christ in the Holy Eucharist.

I Walked Down 500 Steps To Find Nothing

San Damiano was constructed like a huge fortress. Since I couldn't go exploring inside the walls, I decided to walk around it, hoping to find the balcony at the base of the convent wall where St. Francis spent his sleepless night when he was so sick and where he composed the Canticle of the Creatures. From the extended terrace at the back of San Damiano, there supposedly is a magnificent view of the Spoleto valley. I walked

*The Convent of San Damiano where the
Eucharistic miracle of 1240 occurred. St. Clare
held the Blessed Sacrament in the round window.*

down at least 500 steps to the rear of the convent, and found nothing except trees and brush. There was a view of Spoleto, but I had to imagine where Francis stayed, if, in fact, I was anywhere near the right spot. It was about 3:00 P. M. and so hot I was dripping with perspiration. Looking back up all those steps, I honestly didn't know how I'd ever make it. Thank goodness I brought the extra water today. I decided to take it slow, and to offer every step for the conversion and healing of friends and family. Every step sounds like such a small thing, yet I didn't know if I was going to make it back up because it was so steep and I had come much further down than I realized.

Then I thought of St. Clare, whom I never really knew very well before this trip, and now I couldn't take my mind off her. She was a voluntary prisoner at St. Damiano for most of her life. She lived behind those walls for Jesus, and yet she was free in her spirit. I thought of the way I am a prisoner of myself, of my selfishness, of my selfish desires; although I'm not a prisoner, I'm not free. I prayed to St. Clare, asking her to help me and the people I love become free for Jesus. Then I stopped; it was too hot. The perspiration was dripping down my face.

A Gift of Tears and Repentance

I felt vulnerable, an experience which was happening so frequently on this trip. First, I felt sorry for being on the outside, as it were, for wanting to see the convent so badly and not being able to enter. Then I began to feel sorry for my sins and for all the waste in my life. I thought back to Montecatini and to that box, which so clearly now represents all the fruitless, wasted efforts of my time and energy in pursuits which are really not of God. I felt sorry for my mediocrity, especially in relation to setting standards and an example for my children. I felt sorry for not being a better spiritual mother to them. I prayed for forgiveness, to be changed into a new creation, like the priest was talking about at Mass yesterday. I was helpless to change myself. I prayed to be healed of all that is keeping me a prisoner of myself. I thought of my drive around Montecatini. *"Lord, deliver me from myself."* This longing to be close to Jesus grew stronger. By now I was overcome with tears. Looking out over the Spoleto valley from behind this convent, while leaning up against the big old stones, I cried. I felt sad. I saw how all my preoccupations and projects lead me astray when they are not subject to the desires of Jesus. That Montecatini box is my living example of the extent of my fruitlessness. I just stood there for a long time and let the tears come. Somehow I wondered if St. Clare was giving me a special grace through this gift of tears and repentance. Perhaps this was the gift of repentance that I needed, that Jesus spoke about in the chapel only moments before.

My walk around San Damiano was very cleansing, and healing. I felt so much better, so much lighter, so much at peace. The walk back up the steps seemed to take forever, but I did make it eventually. I asked one of the Franciscan friars where the window was through which St. Francis threw the coins (which the priest had rejected) to repair the church, a gesture which shows how completely he had surrendered himself. That window was in another part of the convent which I would not be able to see. Then the priest offered me an unsolicited explanation about St. Clare and the miracle of the Eucharist. He was speaking in Italian, most of which I could understand. He said that when the Saracens were coming, Clare knelt behind the convent doors and cried her eyes out; it was then that the Lord performed the miracle. Only moments before I had been crying my eyes out. I just wondered why he told me that and was the Lord telling me, through him, that when we cry our eyes out before Him, He hears us and performs a miracle? Are our tears a grace that He gives us in order to show us that He's answering us?

The Saints Cried Buckets

The gift of tears is mentioned often in the lives of the saints. St. Ignatius of Loyola, the founder of the Jesuits, is recorded to have celebrated Mass in ecstasy and with the gift of tears. "After one of his Masses, a stranger who had attended, but who did not know of the saint's reputation for holiness, felt compassion for him. He approached Father Strada, who had served St. Ignatius' Mass, and said to him, 'He who has just said Mass must indeed consider himself to be a great sinner. Let us hope that God has forgiven him. He has wept enough.'"[5]

Many saints shed tears during Mass, and in front of the Blessed Sacrament. According to Celano, a contemporary of St. Clare, she often shed tears before the Blessed Sacrament:

> When Clare came to Holy Communion she wept hot tears of love, and was filled with the utmost awe and reverence towards the Lord of heaven and earth who thus abased Himself. She cried so much that it seemed as though her heart were being poured out. For her the thought of the consecrated Host was as awe-inspiring as that of God the Creator of all things. Even in illness she was always perfectly recollected in Christ, and always thanked Him for all her sufferings, and for this the blessed Christ often visited and comforted her, and gave her great joy in Himself.[6]

St. Catherine of Siena, who cried a great deal herself, asked God about her tears. He responded to her in "The Dialogue" explaining how all tears come from the heart, although there are stages of tears, from the imperfect to the perfect. We can experience all the stages of tears, and they can be life-giving if they are used virtuously. God told her that anyone who loves suffers and that suffering and sorrow increase in proportion to love. "When love grows, so does sorrow. So I say to you: 'Ask and it shall be given to you;' (Mk 11: 24) I will not say 'no' to anyone who asks in truth. . .The soul, therefore who chooses to love me must also choose to suffer for me anything at all that I give her. Patience is not proved except in suffering, and patience is one with charity, as has been said."[7]

God Explains Tears to St. Catherine

God continues His explanation of tears by using imagery:

> "The heart gathers them up from its burning desire and holds
> them out to the eyes. Just as green wood, when it is put into
> the fire, weeps tears of water in the heat because it is still
> green (for if it were dry it would not weep) so does the heart
> weep when it is made green again by the renewal of grace,
> after the desiccating dryness of selfishness has been drawn
> out of the soul. Thus are fire and tears made one in burning
> desire. And because desire has no end it cannot be satisfied in
> this life. Rather, the more it loves, the less it seems to itself
> to love. So love exerts a holy longing, and with that longing
> the eyes weep."[8]

God's timing is perfect. It was no accident that Fratello Stephano told
me about the Portiuncula and the Feast of Pardons. Then the words in the
chapel today about the need for repentance and my being here during the
Portiuncula Indulgence—it's providential. In the divine economy of things,
nothing is wasted, even our tears. On the contrary, they are like incense,
rising up to God's throne as an offering of our love and desire. Near the
end of "*The Dialogue*," the Father invites Catherine's tears saying: "Now I
invite you to weep, you and my other servants. And through your weeping
and constant humble prayer I want to be merciful to the world. Run along
this road of truth dead (to yourselves), so that you may never be
reproached for walking slowly. For I will demand more of you now than
before, since I have revealed my very self to you in my truth. Be careful
never to leave the cell of self-knowledge, but in this cell guard and spend
the treasure I have given you. This treasure is a teaching of truth founded
on the living rock, the gentle Christ Jesus, clothed in a light that can
discern darkness. Clothe yourself in this light, dearest daughter whom I so
love, in truth."[9]

Scripture Meditation

The Lord is merciful and loving,
Slow to become angry and full of constant love.
He does not keep on rebuking;
He is not angry for ever.
He does not punish as we deserve. . . .

As far as the east is from the west
So far does he remove our sins from us.
As a father is kind to his children,
So the Lord is kind to those who honor him.
He knows what we are made of;
He remembers that we are dust. (Ps 103: 8-10, 12-14)

Dear Lord Jesus,
Even your reproofs are signs of Your love. You bring us back into line so gently and with such tenderness. Your forgiveness is like oil which seeps into the rusted springs of our heart, enabling it to pump love again. You want us to stop running from ourselves and to extend the same unconditional forgiveness to ourselves that we must extend to others. Jesus, please release me from this prison of guilt and show me how to forgive myself. Free me to love.

13

Reconciliation

Today is the Feast of St. Ignatius, the founder of the Jesuits. I thought of all the Jesuit priests who have been in my life who have blessed me, our marriage and our children in so many different ways. I prayed for each of them at Mass, asking the Lord to send them special graces in return for all the gifts they've given us. The prayer of St. Ignatius seems particularly appropriate today:

> Take, Lord, and receive all my liberty,
> my memory, my understanding, and my entire will, all that I
> have and possess.
> You have given all to me.
> To you, O Lord, I return it.
> All is yours, dispose of it wholly according to your will.
> Give me your love and your grace,
> for this is sufficient for me.

While enroute to visit the Basilica of St. Clare I was enjoying the feel of the old cobblestone streets under my feet, when I noticed a sign on a small wooden doorway inviting pilgrims into a chapel. I entered an intimate chapel with a vaulted ceiling, adorned with brilliantly colored frescoes. Several nuns, kneeling on an oriental rug, were deep in contemplative prayer, adoring Jesus in the Blessed Sacrament. I joined them for awhile, saying my Chaplet of Divine Mercy, then just sat quietly in the presence of Jesus. How blessed the people of Assisi are to have Jesus so present. No wonder God blesses these people so much with many saints and visitations. They welcome Him. They're very hospitable to our Eucharistic Lord and He returns their favor.

Relics of St. Clare

Entering St. Clare's Basilica brought me another step closer to Clare. The little chapel on the right was part of the original church of San Giorgio, where St. Francis received his religious instruction as a child. Built in the 11th century, it was one of St. Francis' favorite churches. After Clare's death, the Poor Clare's gave up San Damiano and came to St. Giorgio's. Among the treasures in this basilica is the original crucifix, a painting of Christ on gesso, through which Jesus commissioned Francis at San Damiano to repair His church. In the rear of that chapel is a small room which has some relics of St. Clare, one of which is the dress she left behind when she fled to the Portiuncula that Palm Sunday afternoon to become a nun. It's a long, lace-type dress, with long sleeves and a high collar. There were some other robes there, a woolen one with a hood and some cloaks. Imagining St. Clare wearing these made her come alive. But what made her really come to life was her long blonde hair, preserved in a glass case! I had just finished reading about the first meeting between Francis and Clare. These relics brought them both to life.

Their first meeting had been arranged at the request of Clare, who longed to meet the man who inspired her with his words and lifestyle. When she told Francis that she wanted to leave the world and its riches to follow Christ, he told her that he didn't believe her. Then he said, "*Still, if you want me to have faith in your words, you will do what I am going to tell you: Change your clothes, put on an old sack, and go about the town begging your bread.*"[1]

Clare followed his advice, dressed herself in a sack, put a white veil on her head, and secretly left her house to beg on the streets of Assisi. That was the beginning of her surrender, soon to be followed by her leaving home forever.

Lord, Show Me How To Change

Wandering around the basilica I found the Chapel of the Blessed Sacrament as it is called, a very intimate place for prayer, lit only by the glow from the flickering votive candles. I sat in one of the choir stalls, resting my head against the side of it, so that I was partially hidden. My mind was cluttered with the cares of the world. I was Martha, coming in now trying to be Mary. I spent a long time trying to empty my mind of all the concerns I had about what gifts I was going to buy for friends and where I was going to find them. I was obsessed with canvassing the shops to find just the right holy water fonts for certain people.

Now in this sacred space I felt at home. I also felt connected to the many tourists of different nationalities who were walking around the basilica. I asked the Lord what must I do to receive the grace of repentance, to change my life. *"What do You want me to change? How do You want me to change? I know that I can't do anything on my own. I must allow You to recreate me. But I can cooperate. Please, Jesus, show me how."* No sooner did I pray this way than I pictured myself riding a bike around Assisi, going down the hills—out of control. I even felt myself physically trying to put on the brakes. I was going too fast and I needed to stop.

I Need To Stop Running!

I wondered what the Lord was saying to me. Am I going too fast? Am I out of control? What did this relate to? What do I need to put the brakes on? Then I thought of one thing in my life that needs changing—my relationships. There are some relationships that I have, including my relationship with my husband, that I must change, that I must mend. They're breaking. I have a responsibility not to allow them to break and not to allow any hurts to fester and go unnamed. In some ways, I'm running away from attending to those hurts and perhaps that's what the bike ride was signifying. I'm running and I must stop. I must stop and be accountable to people that I love by owning the part I played in creating the conflict. I must be open and brave and put the cards on the table in a loving way with people so that these separations don't continue. It's one thing if the other person says he or she doesn't want to continue a relationship. It's another thing to suffer by holding onto a relationship which is not mutual. Love is a choice and we're free to choose or not to choose. I must review the choices I'm making with my friends, treat them carefully and not let the dust of unconscious judgments and angry thoughts tarnish something that is really like a precious gem—and that is a friend. That goes for my relationship with my husband as well. I need to review how well I care for that precious gem of our relationship. Do I take good care of it or do I cover it with the dust of judgments and resentments so that after a while I can't even see the beauty of the gem?

Jesus Is Closer Than We Think!

I was glad for the privacy which the dim light in this chapel afforded me. Feeling vulnerable again, I thought back to my journals of the last year and recalled that I have been asking the Lord to hear His voice. Now He's reminding me of that in order to show me that I just heard Him. He's so close to us that we miss His voice because we think it's our voice. I'm pretty well convinced that Jesus is speaking to me through the imagery and the sensation I had of going downhill on the bike. It was His way of impressing His message on me. Jesus is closer than we think. We make Him so far away while He is within us; the hard part is to accept the fact that we can hear Him and that He does speak to us.

This is a gift for me today, to hear His voice and accept that I hear His voice. It's like putting on that sweater, the gift He's been giving me. But today I'm wearing it and receiving it and it feels good and I feel full. To add to the gratitude of that moment, there was a full-bodied chorus of male voices singing "Come, Holy Ghost, Creator Blessed," in English. I sang it with them in my heart, again rejoicing in the connection with strangers, yet people with whom I felt so intimate. We were one in the spirit.

Gratitude Releases Grace

A book which I've turned to often in my life is *The Healing Light* by Agnes Sanford. She has so much to say about how to open ourselves to God's healing presence. As we grow in accepting and appreciating the gift of His life within us, we will rejoice and give thanks for all the gifts that it is His will to give us, because He is love.

> We give thanks for them because we believe that we are receiving them. Therefore we do receive them. For our joyful thanksgiving testifies to our faith, and through the doorway of our faith He enters in. How many Christians down through

the ages have failed to receive the answers to their prayers by failing to take this last step—the step of giving thanks! God is standing before us with the answer in His hands. But unless we reach out our hands and take it by giving thanks for it, we are not apt to receive it. For while love is the wiring that connects our souls with His, faith is the switch that turns on the power. Our homes are full of things that run by electricity: lights, irons, sewing machines, toasters. . . Just believing that there is a power called electricity is not enough to make these things work for us. Every time that we want one of them to work, we must touch the button that releases the power in that one. Just believing a set of facts about God does not necessarily turn on the power in a single one of our prayer-objectives. In order to do that, we must believe that we are receiving the thing that we desire. If we really believe this, we will naturally rejoice and give thanks for it. And when our belief is weak, the act of rejoicing and giving thanks will awaken our faith.[2]

Agnes reminds us how full of praise the Bible is, and how continually the apostles and teachers of Christianity urged us to rejoice always, in *everything* to give thanks. They knew. Agnes Sanford concludes her thoughts on praise and thanks with the following:

Let us praise Him then, for His life in our spirits increasing in us the consciousness of being His children, light of His light, life of His life. And let us rejoice in His life in our minds, directing and arranging our thoughts, increasing our mental powers, giving us a better grasp of business and more wisdom in every line of work we undertake. Let us thank Him for His life in our hearts, ordering and controlling our emotions and filling us with His own love. And let us give thanks for His life in our bodies, recreating them after the image of His perfect health and strength. How easy this becomes when we know that our bodies are made of His own energy and full of His own light! How comforting to realize that when we expose our souls to Him in prayer, we absorb His life as simply and naturally as a leaf absorbs the sunlight. With infinite care He made the leaf so that every tiny cell therein can absorb the sun. With the same care He made us so that every cell within our frames can absorb Him. Therefore we need not hesitate to give thanks for each adjustment, however great or however small, that we would like His loving care to make in us.[3]

Her writing never ceases to inspire me. She really teaches me how to put into practice the deep things of God. Our gratitude releases God's grace and healing, especially when we thank Him through our tears.

Healed through Gratitude

I remember reading a story in Catholic Digest years ago which told about a priest who was diagnosed with inoperable cancer and who only had a short time to live. He decided to give himself a "farewell party" and so he invited all his friends and relatives in order to thank them for their friendship and say good-bye. In the process of planning the party, he was filled with joy and gratitude over the gifts of these people in his life. He found himself thanking God for his blessings. The party was a joy-filled experience for everyone, including the priest, who found out a short time later that his cancer was completely gone. What a convincing testimony of the power of the prayer of gratitude!

I Spoke to Clare like a Friend

I was never so glad to see anybody in all my life as I was to see the incorrupt body of St. Clare. She was buried in 1260 and when they remodeled the church in 1850 they exhumed her body—which they found in a perfect state of preservation. She is laid out in her habit for all the world to see and love. I approached the glass-enclosed saint and spoke to her like a friend, a sister, a mother, asking her to help me be a prisoner for Jesus. Just as she was a prisoner in San Damiano all her life, I asked her to guide me in my ability to keep out all that is not of the Lord in my life and to create space in myself for Him. St. Clare had heroic faith and I asked her to pass some of it on to me.

I also had a new understanding of why God allows these saints to remain perfectly preserved. They're intact bodies show us that they are human, just like us, but they have surrendered their humanity to God, serving Him with deep faith and love in this world. I think the Lord wants us to see how much He loves them and how He honors their faith, and He uses them to inspire us to love and serve Him as they did.

Today was hotter than yesterday so I took a slow walk back to the hotel, munching on a roll and a diet coke along the way. The stores were all closing and I was glad because I didn't want to look in them anymore. I wanted to go back and rest for a while in the air-conditioned room and just think about all these things.

My hotel was adjacent to St. Francis' Basilica. The church bells were my alarm clock

Confession, a Real *Kenosis*

After a brief rest I went over to St. Francis' Basilica, which is just across the courtyard from my hotel, and looked through the gift shop one more time. I was restless. It was too hot to go to the Hermitage and while wandering around the Basilica trying to decide what to do, I saw a sign for confession. I sought out a priest and had one of the most meaningful confessions I've ever experienced. A wonderful American priest listened to me, counseled and consoled me. It was a real *kenosis*, an unburdening, in which I emptied myself of all the hurts and sins of my life. I felt loved, renewed and forgiven. When we are loved in the worst part of ourselves we can begin to accept ourselves. By accepting the Lord's forgiveness, I was given the grace to accept and forgive myself, something I hadn't been able to do in a long time. I left feeling full of hope. At the very end he reminded me that this was the Feast of the Pardons and if I would go to Mass and pray for the Pope's intentions, I would have the benefit of the indulgence that St. Francis so dearly wanted for all the pilgrims who came to Assisi during this time.

Jesus instituted this Sacrament to give us a *ritual* of healing, a felt-experience of His healing love. *"If we say that we have no sin, we deceive ourselves, and there is no truth in us. But if we confess our sins to God, he will keep his promise and do what is right: he will forgive us our sins and purify us from all our wrongdoing."* (John 1: 8-9)

> "Sin is an offense against God, but it also inflicts a wound not only on the sinner, but on his or her neighbor, and indeed on the whole church. Parents sin by neglecting their children, but they also wound their children by this neglect. Children sin by abandoning their parents and not showing them gratitude and love, but they also wound their parents by such a lack of love. For the sin itself there is divine forgiveness; for the wound of sin there is divine healing. The wound of sin is an inner wound. The person is wounded in his or her self-esteem, self-image, relationships or memory. . .For the multiple wounds of sin there is a manifold gift of healing in the sacrament of reconciliation."[4]

Repentance And Healing Go Together

I'm taking this gift very seriously, believing that the Lord has invited me here especially to receive the grace of a repentant heart, something I didn't know I needed. Repentance, it seems to me, is a willingness to take down our walls of pride and rebellion, through which we've sealed others out, and ourselves in. Like the prodigal son, we've rebelled against God's providence and gone our own way. Our Father is always on the lookout hoping we'll return, and when He sees us, *He runs to us to welcome us home.* It is His grace which *calls* us home, and our willingness to surrender and confess our sin through the Sacrament of Reconciliation is to open the dam and allow God's graces to flood our soul, washing us clean like newborn babes. Like Mary Magdalene whose tears washed Jesus' feet, she was able to love much because she had been forgiven much. Repentance healed her and freed her to love.

Jesus tells us, *". . .when you stand praying, if you hold anything against anyone, forgive him, so that your Father in heaven may forgive you your sins."* (Mark 11: 25) The person we hold the most against is usually ourselves. Through the Sacrament of Reconciliation, the Lord provides a way for us to apologize for our sins, mend our brokenness, and "come home" to ourselves, to our loved ones, and to the whole body of

Christ—all at the same time. By seeking His forgiveness, He releases us from the bonds of guilt and shame which keep us locked in self-hate.

"I Am a Father Full of Compassion"

In one of Jesus' revelations to Sister Josefa Menendez, He spoke about His forgiveness:

> "I am Love! . . . I love souls so dearly that I have sacrificed My life for them. For love of souls, I instituted the Sacrament of Penance, that I might forgive them, not once or twice, but as often as they need to recover grace. There I wait for them, longing to wash away their sins, not in water, but in My Blood.
>
> I am God, but a God of love! I am a Father, but a Father full of compassion and never harsh. My Heart is infinitely holy but also infinitely wise, and knowing human frailty and infirmity stoops to poor sinners with infinite mercy.
>
> Never shall I weary of repentant sinners, nor cease from hoping for their return, and the greater their distress, the greater My welcome. Does not a father love a sick child with special affection? So is the tenderness and compassion of My Heart more abundant for sinners than for the just."[5]

How painfully I'm learning that for our conversion to deepen we have to be hollowed out to make room for Jesus, cleansed of our sins and our wounds. It seems that when we have the humility to face our darkness and sins and ask Him to forgive us, we allow Him to be our Lord and Savior. We allow Him to fill up those spaces in us which were filled with self—with pride and envy and sloth or whatever sins are on our hearts. We have to take ourselves off the throne in order to put Him on the throne.

Virtues Need Practice!

The priest cautioned me to slow down a bit, to put the brakes on. I didn't tell him about the bike ride; I didn't need to. He could figure that out on his own. I'm trying to be a new creature all at once, forgetting that conversion is a lifelong process. He spoke about developing virtues—habits—which come through practice. He helped me see that if I just take one virtue, for instance, that I want develop and practice it for a week, two weeks, a month and so forth, before long it will become a habit.

Then take another. The fruits of those labors will begin to flower in new strengths. But I have to remember that I'm not St. Clare and that I've got to go at my own pace. The Lord is leading me and I better be careful lest I go down that hill too fast.

I walked back to my room and fell on the bed, exhausted. The combination of the heat, the shopping and the spiritual soul-searching all converged at once, causing me to collapse. I closed my eyes and took a brief nap and was happily startled by the phone because I knew it must be Tommy. He didn't have any special news, but just was checking in and it was so good to talk to him. I needed to talk to him, to check up on him and the kids and to hear any tidbits of information about anyone or anything that was happening. He, in turn, was eager to have my news. I had been doing so much and seeing so much I didn't know what to share. I told him I had seen the crucifix through which Jesus spoke to St. Francis and that I had seen St. Clare's incorrupt body and what a veritable feast of spiritual delights is this trip. I would share in detail when I got home. I told him I missed him but that I still felt that I needed to be here for my own spiritual journey but also for the research on the miracles of the Eucharist. He was in agreement but I could tell that the time was dragging a bit at home all by himself. He and the children were planning to go to the lake for the weekend, which delighted me because I knew what fun that meant for everyone.

I Drank the Whole Bottle at Once!

Tonight there was no breeze on the terrace at dinner; it was hot and sticky. I ordered a quart bottle of mineral water with dinner, as I do every night, but tonight I gave the waiter a good laugh. He had no sooner brought it than he returned a few moments later with the salad — to find the water bottle empty. He was incredulous. I was so dehydrated from the heat of the day, I drank the whole thing down without stopping! I enjoyed the sunset, which was almost too beautiful for words, while writing postcards describing the crucifix I saw and the miracle of the Eucharist at San Damiano. These events took place seven centuries ago, and yet they might as well have happened yesterday, according to the fresh impact they had on me.

I could barely walk upstairs to my room. These days are long but never dull, and I'm always ready to fall into bed at night. I'm enjoying doing this tape recording; it's a lot easier than writing and I'm sort of excited about the fact that, when this is transcribed, I will have a detailed record of my experiences.

Tomorrow I'm planning to go to the Hermitage, or *Carceri*, a rocky cave on the mountain, a favorite place of escape for Francis and his brothers, where they would withdraw from the world to pray and contemplate.

Scripture Meditation

"So whoever is in Christ is a new creation: the old things have passed away; behold, new things have come. And all this is from God, who has reconciled us to himself through Christ and given us the ministry of reconciliation, namely, God was reconciling the world to himself in Christ, not counting their trespasses against them and entrusting to us the message of reconciliation. So we are ambassadors for Christ, as if God were appealing through us. We implore you on behalf of Christ, be reconciled to God. For our sake he made him to be sin who did not know sin, so that we might become the righteousness of God in him." (2 Cor 5: 16-21)

Dear Lord Jesus,

It is Your love that makes me a new creation. Like a sculptor who sees the beauty of the figure he wants to create inside a block of marble, You chisel away at our block of self—at our darkness and sins—which prevent the emergence of the person You created. Your love is hidden inside of us, covered over with the cold marble of unforgiveness. Our repentance releases us from the bondage of sin, and heals our heart, enabling us to love. Thank you for the grace of a repentant heart, Jesus, and please reveal to me daily every person and circumstance in which I am in need of forgiving. Especially myself.

14

Breaking Down Barriers

I awakened to another incredibly beautiful day, one of those typical summer mornings in which you can almost touch the stillness. At breakfast I was sitting on the terrace absorbing the beautiful view and listening to the sounds of the morning. The sounds of Assisi—the sounds of Italy—are unique. I finally asked Alberto, my waiter, what kind of an animal it was that squawked incessantly every morning. It was a parrot! He was loud and determined to perform for all of Assisi to hear. Then a rooster occasionally chimed in with his cock-a-doodle-doo. Add to that the sound of chirping birds, and a *caw caw* call of blackbirds in the surrounding trees. Bells from the nearby churches chime at irregular intervals, while motor scooters gun their motors racing around corners and ahead of cars and pedestrians. The sound of barking dogs is constant as is the grinding gears of tour buses winding up and down the hills of Assisi. Then at night the cicadas come out, blanketing the air with a steady hum. What a magnificent tape recording all these would make, a veritable concert of the sounds of Italy!

I got an early start, guidebook in hand, arriving at the Hermitage before the tour buses and before the sun was too high. The area around the Hermitage resembles a rain forest where the sun pours in through patches of openings in the trees and where you catch an occasional glimpse of the surrounding valleys below. It's no wonder why Francis loved to come here; the vistas are breathtaking. It's a hike to get here, even by car, because it's three or four thousand feet above sea level. I was relieved to learn that the friars rode mules up the mountain.

A Visit to "The Prison"

I went through the Hermitage once to see it, then again to savor the atmosphere. The old, original part was known as the "Carceri," which literally means "the prison"; it was known by Francis not as a jail, but as a place of seclusion. Francis was so drawn to prayer and contemplation that he used to come here often to find solitude. Francis slept in one room where you can see his bed carved out of the stone, and the other room is where he prayed and meditated. The chapel held a special interest because there was a fresco on the wall that probably dated from his time. This is where he and his little group celebrated Mass. I was moved by the sight of an elderly Italian lady leaning her head against the altar, in deep prayer.

Outside I walked along the ravine where I found a smooth rock to rest on while I soaked up this atmosphere with a book of stories about St. Francis. After the Order was established for a year or two, quite a few friars had joined him. He suffered with doubts over the direction his ministry should take; should he give himself only to prayer, a vocation which he called "the life of angels," or should he go out to preach? He wanted to know which of these the Lord wanted him to do. Fearful of self-will, he turned to others in order to know God's will.

Francis Seeks God's Will

He dispatched Brother Masseo to go to Clare and Brother Sylvester, two friends whose discernment he trusted, asking them to ask the Lord in prayer if Francis should devote his life to prayer or preaching.

Their answers were both the same. Francis asked Brother Masseo *'What does my Lord, Jesus Christ, order me to do?'* Brother Masseo replied that Christ had answered both Brother Sylvester and Sister Clare and revealed that, 'He wants you to go about the world preaching because God did not call you for yourself alone, but also for the salvation of others.' As soon as Francis heard this answer and he knew the will of Christ, he got to his feet and said to Brother Masseo with great fervor, *"So, let's go in the name of the Lord."*[1]

Francis Preached to the Birds

They set out immediately to go about the countryside preaching. Birds appeared to come from every direction, settling on the ground and in the trees, so that as Francis and the friars walked past them, the birds didn't move. Francis was filled with the Spirit and told his brothers that he was going to preach to the birds:

> "My sister birds! You owe God great gratitude, and ought always and everywhere to praise and exalt Him because you can fly so freely wherever you please, and for your double and triple clothing, and for your colored and most beautiful coat, and for the food you do not have to work for, and for the lovely voices your Creator has given you. . . God gives you rivers and springs to drink from, and hills and mountains, cliffs and rocks in which to hide, and high trees to build your nests in, and though you neither spin nor weave, He gives you and your young ones the necessary clothing. Therefore you must greatly love the Creator since He has given you such blessings."[2]

After Francis spoke to the birds, they opened their beaks and beat their wings, bowing their heads reverently to the earth. Francis made the sign of the cross over them, and they flew up and away, twittering happily. Apparently Francis' preaching to the birds was repeated in many places. He made friends with the animals wherever he went, including a wolf who was terrorizing the village of Gubbio. He went in search of the wolf and, when he found him, brought him back to town where he

St. Francis preaches to the birds by Giotto

became everyone's pet. Francis spent his life breaking down barriers, barriers in himself, with others and with nature, reaching out to all creation with love.

I followed the path along the ravine which led past the carved-out rocks where each friar had his own cubicle for meditation. A dove flew by! I looked up to see a little window which housed a whole roomful of doves. The Hermitage was a haven for doves; no doubt they've lived here since the day Francis blessed them, probably not far from this spot. One perched on a little bar as if to greet me as I walked past. They were very friendly and unafraid.

Gratitude Is My Constant Companion!

Francis craved contemplation. He craved a life of solitude to commune with his God. Here was the perfect place. But now the tour buses were arriving, which sent me off on a narrow path in search of privacy. I didn't have on the best shoes for climbing, but I held on to small trees and bushes to climb as high and out of sight as I could. I made my way up a rather steep hill to find a spot with a perfect view of the valleys.

Gratitude is my constant companion these days. I said my Chaplet of Divine Mercy, offering it, as usual, for friends and family at home. I was moved to pray for my brother who's having a hard time in his life right now. I prayed for a lot of people. Then I began to pray for my husband. I sensed his loneliness the other night. With me gone and the house empty, there are a lot of hours to fill; I felt a little sad about his lack of companionship due to my absence. I was asking the Lord to take care of him while I'm gone, to send angels to help fill his time. I started to get filled up with affection for him. I found myself thanking the Lord for him and for

#3 (Tom McHugh) excelled on the basketball court

his goodness. I thought back over our 25 years and I saw the *gift* he has been in my life, how he's been there through thick and thin. He's had to put up with a lot with me; I've been a thorn in his side, and I've caused a lot of heartache. We've had painful struggles for which I have to take much of the blame.

Tommy came from a wonderful family; he was the youngest of six. I saw him as the baby of his family, who had to struggle hard to keep up with the others, all of whom made names for themselves in sports and academics. Then came Tommy. I think he worked hard to have his star shine and he's been working hard all his life. He made a name for himself too, achieving much recognition in his own right. This trip has given me a chance to step back a little to gain some new perspectives, a special grace and something I've needed especially for our relationship. I know he's not perfect, but at least I feel a new strength to see the good in him instead of always focusing on the negatives.

I Put My Heart in Storage

The stories about St. Francis uniting himself so intimately with others and with nature set me thinking that I spent most of my life doing the opposite; I erected walls which kept me in and others out. I wasn't even aware that I was doing this as it was a behavior pattern that I adopted sometime during childhood. I built my wall brick by brick to hide behind as painful things happened. If I *pretended* that nothing bothered me, then I would be safe and happy. That was the delusion I set up deep inside myself. It was a way for me to help myself, to cope with a very painful reality, but it also cut my heart out of me and put it in storage!

I believe that we all suffer the fallout from being loved conditionally; that is, at some time or another, each child suffers from unmet needs of one sort or another. Depending on the problems or wounds of the parents, the children bear the consequences of *their* brokenness and inability to give and receive love. Some of us are more scarred than others. I covered up the pain in my mother and my father by absorbing it into myself.

I was completely unaware of my father's alcoholism as a child and adolescent; I adapted to his behavior by trying to take care of him and meet his emotional needs. And although I was aware of my mother's mental illness, I responded to that in a similar fashion: I *dealt* with her as if I was a social worker, clinically trying to assess the problem and find a solution. In both cases, I lived from my neck up, completely denying that I felt *anything*. Somewhere I learned that negative emotions were a sign of weakness and that they were to be ignored or squelched at all costs.

Feelings Trapped in My Unconscious

Growing up without emotional bonding left me starved for love and affection. I didn't know when I got married that I was carrying around a whole storehouse of negative feelings which I buried inside myself. There were years' worth of unacknowledged feelings in the basement of my soul; all the anger, fear, guilt and shame which I never admitted to, were trapped in my unconscious, causing an emotional malaise and depression which I didn't even know I had.

The problems in our marriage began when we were engaged. Tommy had just given me a beautiful diamond ring. In those days, it was safe to walk in Central Park in New York at night. We sat on a park bench near a lake in Central Park when he asked me to marry him and gave me the ring. I loved him so much and the ring was so beautiful I cried. I was as high as a kite—on love. My dad used to say to me, "Joanie, you're in love with love!" We were driving down Lexington Avenue and the ring sparkled under the street lights. In my euphoria I said to him, "I hear bells, don't you?" His flat, unemotional response triggered hurt in me that was out of proportion to the reality. I remember him dropping me off at my parent's apartment that night and crying myself to sleep, I felt so lonely and unloved. It didn't make sense, yet the feelings were so strong.

I could have saved the both of us so much heartache and struggle if I had known what was happening right there and then. Those emotions he triggered were in my storehouse, just waiting to be tapped. I thought he was causing me to feel so lonely and unloved; I thought his behavior was responsible and so I set a whole other behavior pattern in motion: I built up anger and resentment against him *without telling him*. "When partners don't tell each other what they want and constantly criticize each other for missing the boat, it's no wonder that the spirit of love and cooperation disappears. In its place come the grim determination of the power struggle, in which each partner tries to force the other to meet his or her needs. Even though their partners react to these maneuvers with renewed hostility, they persevere. Why? Because in the unconscious minds they fear that, if their needs are not met, they will die."[3]

Vulnerable in My Need to Belong

It is only by the grace of God that our marriage survived so many years of dysfunctional behavior. When I met Tommy, I saw him as someone who could give me all the love and intimacy I craved. My heart told me that he would take care of me in the way I really needed it; he would fill the emptiness left over from the emotional deprivation of my childhood. I was so vulnerable in my need to belong, I set him up as my knight in shining armor to take me to his kingdom where we would live happily ever after! What I wanted and needed most was his *presence*, emotional, intellectual, spiritual and physical. I entered marriage fully expecting Tommy to fill up what was lacking in me. The problems started when he failed to do that.

He also came into marriage dragging his own past and emotional storehouse with him. The fact of the matter is, we had a lot of breakdowns of communication and painful emotional struggles for many years; we had to learn slowly how to tell each other the truth, what we were really feeling and what we wanted and needed. The both of us had learned how to deny our feelings so well, that we played the blame game, the silent game, the punish game, the withdraw game, the denial game, the manipulation game; the list is quite long. We usually hurt others in the same way we were hurt. My main way of hurting him was through emotional abandonment. I learned so well how to isolate myself from him as a way of punishing him for not loving or responding or doing something the way I wanted. The other mechanism was to blame him for something, to project the problem or pain or whatever onto him, so that I wouldn't have to deal with it.

The Walls Went up in Our Marriage

So the walls went up all through our marriage; little walls, big walls, walls that most people couldn't see but we lived behind them. By the grace of God I became aware of the lie I was living, the duplicity. If our relationship was to grow, I would have to be honest with myself and then share that part of me with Tommy, otherwise our relationship would not be authentic. "The longest journey is the journey inward. *Bon Voyage!*" says Father John Powell. "Do I want to share my true gift with you, or do I want to play it safe and give you only my charade? My act is the price I pay for my safety and my strokes. It is the armor that protects me from getting hurt, but it is also a barrier within myself that stunts my growth. It is a wall between us that will prevent you from getting to know the real me. . . I will be taking a real risk, walking out from behind my wall. . . . I suspect that old Polonius knew this when he advised Laertes: 'To thine own self be true.' My courage will reap magnificent rewards: the statue will come to life; Sleeping Beauty will awaken. I will get to know who I really am. The real me will emerge from behind the mask, the sham, the pretense. I will begin to thrive in my relationships and grow into the best possible me. The ancient Greeks knew all this when they accepted as the summary of all wisdom: 'Know thyself.'"[4]

Jesus Has the Key to Free Us

I think I'm beginning to understand the healing that Jesus has been giving me, especially here in Assisi. He's been leading me to see the walls I've erected which have crippled me. At San Damiano, when I was crying and so deeply moved by the image of Clare living in a self-imposed prison for Christ, I believe Jesus was releasing me from my own inner prison, the walls I've lived behind all my life where I am trapped in the darkness of resentment, fear, guilt and shame. Those walls prevent me from loving and receiving love. Somehow those emotions fester and grow until they become rage. At the bottom of all the pain is self-blame, which emotionally paralyzes our heart. Jesus has the key to unlock us from this prison. And because our bodies never lose their memory and can never lie to us, they too bear the brunt of the violence we do to ourselves by hoarding these negative emotions inside of us. Thus, my tears have been an actual bodily release of these pains, some of which I'm sure are as old as I am.

After dinner I was sitting on my little balcony overlooking Assisi and rereading some of my prayer dialogues from the preceding year. I have prayed on paper for years, writing letters to Jesus and recording His responses. It has been a wonderful way for me to center and uncover repressed emotions. It also nurtures my relationship with Jesus. When issues rise to the surface, I can offer them to Jesus for His healing. I reread my "prison" dialogues which I had written several months ago; now they spoke powerfully to me.

Praying By Letter

Dear Jesus,

My freedom is gone. I am stuck without my shoes (a dream in which my shoes were missing) so limited, so vulnerable, so dependent. Also, the recent dream showing the concentration camp. Yes, I'm in that place of torture and pain, a place of hopelessness and despair, a dead end, no exit place within myself.

Who put me here? How did I get here? I've had so many benefits and privileges in life—material comforts, money, travel, friends, beautiful homes, a husband who gives me everything, four wonderful children, intelligence, faith, writing ability, enthusiasm, creativity, and *bam*—I'm locked in a prison and have no freedom.

How? By whom? When? Why am I not free? I take a lot of abuse, most of it self-inflicted. I "beat myself up" telling myself I shouldn't feel certain feelings, I should behave in certain ways, I oblige others in order to keep the *status quo*, I swallow rejections by friends and pretend they don't hurt, I hide a lot in order not to face people and situations. I do not know how to walk away from situations which are not good for me, or from people who hurt me. I seek them out. I give myself away in my totality to too many people. They have a hold on me and I then feel as if I owe them my vulnerability. I do things mostly out of a codependent need to belong, to be affirmed, to be supported, praised and loved.

What I do is violence to myself. I ignore my true self. I don't listen to my true self, I hide my true self, I squelch my true self, I behave contrary to my true self's needs. I attend to others out of a sense of obligation and fear that if I don't, I will be alone and cut off. My real self is crying and in pain because she has been abandoned by me—by her real self. She is behind lock and key, not thought about very much, not attended to, not comforted, not fed.

She is hungry for the warm milk of love. She thirsts for companionship, for friendship and intimacy. She has much to say if someone will listen and she has much to give if someone will receive. She has many gifts to offer to others if she is unlocked from her prison.

She wants to be free now. She has endured years of suffering, of being a victim, of crying herself to sleep, of loneliness. She is getting older now, fifty to be exact. How many years does she have left? Life is more than half way over. She wants to come out into the sunlight and feel the warmth on her face. She wants to feast her eyes on the colors of the earth, changing with each season. She wants to smell the salt air, home cooking, leaves burning in the fall, a pine forest, fresh brewed coffee in the morning. She wants to hear her own laughter, waves lapping against the seashore, the wind when it blows, raindrops on her roof, her children saying "Hi Mom" when they telephone. She wants to experience life, to let life happen to her, instead of always trying to make it happen. God, how do I get out of this prison?

Joan

My precious little one,

The door was never locked! You kept yourself in there with your own lock, your fear of being yourself. That fear forced you into a place of agony and aloneness and you have only yourself to blame. No one put you there.

When you were little — very little — you perceived that it was dangerous to be yourself because you would be considered weak and a cry baby. Your mom was so unhappy and you wanted to cry for her. Although you wanted love and hugs, you saw that you were unimportant compared to her suffering. You always tried to make her feel better. If she felt better then maybe she would take care of you.

So you built up a pattern of behaving as if others were more important than you were; their needs and problems were what mattered, not yours. You saw yourself as insufficient by comparison. You tried to blot yourself out, believing that you were in the way and you would interfere with the real business of life. You told yourself that you didn't really matter and instead you focused on people who did matter. You gave importance to everyone but yourself. You felt that you had no rights, even to your feelings and you automatically gave others power to love you or hurt you. You yourself had no power, you didn't think you deserved it. You felt you had to earn it.

So you strove to win your position with others by competing in things. If you did well, you would gain some measure of acceptance and recognition which would assure you that you were valued. Your own self-esteem fluctuated and depended on whether you performed well or got good marks or flunked exams or lost tennis matches. You identified yourself with your performance ability, believing that you were only as good as your achievements.

What pressure you lived under! What tension. What energy it took to keep up such efforts, especially when it went against your real feelings. Exhaustion set many times because there was a constant drain inside of you — the fallout from acting against your own feelings. Sometimes the fallout built up to such a degree that you overflowed with emotions. Those boiling points released you from the accumulated feelings which were clogging your system and causing the growth of bacteria in your blood.

Joan, you locked yourself inside your own heart and gave the key to very few people. I have provided you many opportunities over the years to share your truth and to be yourself with others. You have availed yourself of those opportunities and because of that your real self has breathed free a great deal. The pain intensifies because your real self has tasted and enjoyed freedom and love and acceptance. By contrast, life in a self-enclosed prison becomes darker, lonelier and more hurtful.

Joan you can have your freedom whenever you want it. I didn't put you in prison. A lot of people blame their imprisonment on Me, but they forget that I created the world and the sky and the sun and the moon and the stars, and people to share in the beauty and joy of life with Me.

It's people who have succumbed to fear and guilt who find themselves locked

I am the child of a King who lacks for nothing!

into an inability to be themselves. The door is open—you have only to take one step at a time and by doing that you will learn to enjoy your freedom.

'Let go and let God' is a saying which I like. Because anyone who walks away from the prison bars of fear and guilt and takes one step at a time in telling the truth, in being themselves, will find light and peace. My peace is given to those who walk in truth and the truth will set you free. Go, my child, take step by step in the present moment of being true to yourself. A circle of sunlight will follow you by day and a circle of moonlight by night. You will walk as a child of the light in a world of darkness. Your light will attract others who will find a refuge from their own darkness.

Jesus

I believe that is Jesus who is responding to me in the letter. I believe that whenever and however we reach out to Jesus for help, He answers us. He is more present to us than we are to ourselves; at any hour of the day or night He is beside us, so eager to be intimate with us. His response always leads us closer to the truth inside of us. Jesus is the one who removes the barriers that keep us from Him; He is the jail-keeper who unlocks our cells and leads us from our inner prisons into the warm sunlight of His love and healing.

Jesus Wants To Free Us For Love

He wants to unlock us from our self-blame and self-hate and free us to love ourselves. *"Love the Lord your God with all your heart, with all your soul and with all your mind. This is the first and greatest commandment. And the second is like it: Love your neighbor as yourself."* (Matt 22:37-39) What is love of self? "It is recognizing the presence of God within, that our bodies are living temples of the Holy Spirit, and living tabernacles of Christ Himself. *"Do you not know that you are God's temple and that God's Spirit dwells in you?"* (1 Cor 3: 16) We tend to belittle ourselves and condemn ourselves with thoughts, words and actions. We have difficulty in forgiving ourselves for our faults and inadequacies. Jesus wants us to love ourselves unconditionally as He loves us, as His Spirit loves us, and as our Heavenly Father loves us. We cannot truly love our neighbor if we are not loving ourselves. We cannot truly love God if we are not loving ourselves, for we are created in His image and likeness and placed here to love, honor and glorify Him. If we do not love ourselves we are not loving Him."[5]

My prayer for my marriage over the years has evolved from "Lord, change him," to "Lord, please fix the marriage," to "Lord, show me Your will for my marriage," to "Lord, show me how to love." It is this last prayer that I believe God is answering.

Scripture Meditation

"You shall be called by a new name pronounced by the mouth of the Lord. You shall be a glorious crown in the hand of the Lord, a royal diadem held by your God. No more shall men call you "Forsaken," or your land "Desolate," but you shall be called "My Delight," and your land "Espoused." For the Lord delights in you, and makes your land his spouse. As a young man marries a virgin, your Builder shall marry you; and as a bridegroom rejoices in his bride so shall your God rejoice in you." (Isaiah 62: 2-5)

Dear Lord Jesus,

It is your grace which makes me desire to be true to myself. You free us from the labels— "no good," "not worthwhile," "loser," "imperfect," which keep us locked inside ourselves. You give me a new name by which You free me to be myself, my true self; You call me "My Delight." Jesus, I want to spend the rest of my life giving glory to You by showing off the crown You gave me. I am a child of a King who lacks for nothing. Thank you, Jesus, for blessing me with Your gifts and favors.

15

Miracles in Cascia

The English-speaking Mass in the upper basilica this morning was attended by a handful of people. My confessor of the other day was the organist and it was wonderful to hear familiar music. It also felt good to understand everything for once, instead of having to strain over every word to catch the overall meaning of the prayers or homilies. Mass was concelebrated by six priests, one of whom was a Franciscan from Baltimore, who spoke to my soul. The theme was new life: *"For anyone who is in Christ is a new creation!"* St. Paul continues: *". . .you must lay aside your former way of life and the old self which deteriorates through illusion and desire, and acquire a fresh, spiritual way of thinking. You must put on that new man created in God's image, whose justice and holiness are born of truth."* (Ephesians 4: 22-24) I heard those words as if for the first time. To achieve that new life we must set our hearts on heavenly things, the Franciscan from Baltimore said, we have to die to whatever keeps us bound to earthly things. We have to allow God to remold us into His perfect image and to do that we need to let go of all the ego compulsions and desires born out of our false identity. It was the theme for the Mass but it was also the theme for my life.

Dying to Our "Old Self"

When Francis asked Clare if she'd be able to "die," this is what he meant; die to the sinful self, the ego self which wants to put itself on the throne of life. To follow Jesus is to nail that ego self to His cross with Him, to "lose" our life for His sake. Jesus told us that unless a grain of wheat falls to the ground and dies, it will not bear fruit. And if we lose our life for His sake, we will find it.

People like Francis and Clare have allowed their old selves to die and have truly become new creations whose justice and holiness are born of truth. God calls us all to be made new, but for many of us like myself, it takes a whole lifetime to "die." Death is painful; surrendering is painful, and yet when we do, we create a space in our hearts for God to fill with His life and joy. Jesus said to the woman at the well: "*If you only knew what God gives and who it is that is asking you for a drink, you would ask him and he would give you life giving water. . . The water that I will give him will become in him a spring which will provide him with life giving water and give him eternal life.*" (John 4: 10, 14) To have faith in Jesus is to have one's own flood-gates opened! The saints and mystics are people, it seems to me, who have done just that. They have known both the gift and the boundless munificence of the Giver.

Jesus patiently waits for us to say our "yes" to Him, to open ourselves to His grace so that we can have the same confidence as St. Paul in Him, "*who is powerful to do superabundantly above all we ask or think, according to the power that operates in us,*" which is to say, according to the life of grace energizing our whole being. If we really could surrender ourselves we, too, could be filled with the gifts and supernatural powers of Francis or Clare or Catherine or Rita. Jesus calls each of us. But He doesn't push. He offers His gifts and then He waits for our response.

Adieu, Assisi

What an inspiring *bon voyage* from Assisi. I waited to thank the priest for his uplifting homily, and together we walked down the steps of the Basilica while he jokingly complained about the steps and hills of Assisi, which he would never enjoy. "Ditto," I agreed, except they helped to burn the calories which, in Italy, was essential! This kindly and effervescent man had just celebrated his 54th anniversary as a priest. Thirty five of those years he spent living out of a suitcase, preaching retreats to young people all over the world. I found this very touching. He knew Maximilian Kolbe, he said, in fact he spent an afternoon picnicking and bike riding with him. What impressed the priest about Maximilian was that he was such an easy man to be with and he had a wonderful sense of humor. We had to take leave of each other, which I regretted, because I so enjoyed his company.

I felt a little sad winding my way down Mt. Subasio to leave Assisi; it was like leaving a good friend. It had been home to me for awhile, which in some ways seemed like a lifetime. I asked the desk clerk if the owner would allow me return sometime and stay here for a month or more to write a book. I can't think of anyplace more sublime!

Overcoming Obstacles Enroute to Cascia

Now all I had to do was face my fear of heights and drive over the mountains to Cascia. The memory of a trip over the French Alps with my parents when I was in 8th grade is still as vivid as if it happened yesterday. It was a very precarious journey and in those days the roads weren't as good as they are today. The roads were very narrow, with no guard rails on the side, and we had to climb 10,000 feet to cross the Gotthard Pass in Switzerland. With the road barely wide enough for two cars, we reached an impasse near the top and had to double back down. There was no other choice but to turn the car around. My father ordered my mother and me out of the car while he bravely took the wheel, inching his way around. It was frightening to watch those rear wheels hug the edge of the gravel, with nothing but a sheer drop down if they spun back another few inches.

I had visions of a journey like that this morning. Fortunately, the roads were good and wide and there were guard rails. The scenery is absolutely magnificent and the higher you climb the more you can see. The vegetation is lush; it's like being in God's garden. Just when I was beginning to enjoy myself, I had to contend with a group of motorcyclists who came speeding around corners. It must be a sport to drive motorcycles fast around the mountain because every now and then one would come whizzing past and frighten me to death. They were having some sort of a race. Just my luck! If I was nervous to begin with, these motorcycles put me over the edge. Other than that, the signs indicating straight climbs and "maximum caution" put the fear of God in me. I'd wait with my hand gripping the steering wheel for some steep straight climb which wouldn't be as bad as it indicated. The only other thing that destroyed my peace of mind was some big, black bug in the car which periodically jumped on me and frightened me. I guess you could say I was nervous, and the heat didn't help. But as I climbed higher, there was a breath of air and it felt wonderful. It seemed as if I'd never get to Cascia. A journey that should have taken an hour and a half took me three hours. The scenery grew more beautiful with every passing kilometer. Cascia in Umbria, known to everyone as the city of St. Rita, is also the place in which the relic of an extraordinary Eucharistic miracle that occurred in Siena in 1330 is preserved.

I found a hotel without any problem, choosing one adjacent to St. Rita's Basilica. I wanted to be near everything, seeing as I only had one night to spend in Cascia; there was no time to waste.

A Unique Miracle of the Eucharist

My purpose in coming here is to see the Eucharistic miracle, but I'm equally enthusiastic to be at the home of St. Rita, one of the great saints of the 14th century. I first went in search of the Eucharistic miracle, which was in the lower basilica in a special chapel. The sacred relic—a drop of Christ's blood on the page of a priest's breviary—is preserved in a marble tabernacle in a monstrance behind glass.

The story is that there was a priest, around the year 1330 in Siena, who was called to administer the sacraments to an ailing farmer. In haste, he irreverently put a consecrated Host between the pages of his breviary, closed it, tucked it under his arm and went on the sick call. He heard the man's

A special tabernacle holds the blood-stained breviary page. Many see the profile of Jesus in the blood stain

confession and when he opened his breviary to remove the consecrated Host, he was astonished to see how it had turned red with fresh blood, so as to have impressed both pages with blood. The priest, confused and penitent, went to the Augustinian monastery in Siena to share what had happened. As it turned out, he showed it to a very saintly man who was from Cascia, Father Simon Fidati, a renowned religious of the time. Father Fidati asked him for permission to keep the two blood-stained breviary pages. Some time after that, he took one of them to Perugia and the other to Cascia, his hometown, where the relic exists today.

This relic has been venerated over the centuries by the faithful from all over the world. Every year on the Feast of Corpus Christi the relic is borne in a solemn procession through the town. In 1930, on the occasion of the 6th centenary of the event, a Eucharistic Congress for the entire diocese of Norcia, the birthplace of St. Benedict, was held in Cascia. It was then that a special monstrance was made, a very artistic monstrance to display the relic, which exists now. One interesting thing about this relic is that many people have seen a suffering human face within the blood stains.

The Physical Proof of Jesus' Love

There was no one in the chapel when I went to see the relic. I knelt before the Lord in His presence in the blood on this page from the breviary. I wondered again why this happened. In the quiet of that chapel I began to hear a cry from the Lord. *I felt His cry through that blood.* I felt His passion, His sorrow, His suffering. It made it real somehow. I've known it intellectually, but to see it there so close to me, to almost be able to touch Him physically in a bloody presence, just brought Him so close. I saw Him carrying His cross and I imagined the physical anguish He experienced, not to mention the emotional and spiritual. His human cries pierced my heart with sorrow. *He is crying out to us through the blood on this breviary page.* He wants us to know the depth of His love for us, love that has no end, love that sacrificed itself to the death for us. And here is the physical proof of that Love.

The saints are reminding me of the central message of the Gospel—redemption. God, our Father, sent His Son to earth to redeem us from our sins, to save us, to lead us to the Kingdom. He won our redemption through His suffering and death. Until we can grasp the meaning for ourselves of Christ's suffering, we won't get the message. I recalled one of the first visions St. Francis had when he saw Jesus suffering

His Passion. That one vision was enough to give him a life energy which never stopped until he died, to give his all for the Lord.

How Do We Go "to the Death?"

Kneeling here, I asked the Lord to give me strength. Until now in my life I don't know that I've really been ready to accept a deeper conversion and all that goes with that. I don't know that I'm ready now. But I asked Him for the strength, for the faith to be able to follow Him and to die to myself to do that. I imagined the passion itself and what He went through. I saw myself there as a bystander. I actually felt present there, emotionally and physically. I know I would have wanted to help Him. I know I would have gone up to Him and in some way tried to relieve His suffering. The thing I don't know is how far I can go. I don't know if I could go to the death, which is what He's asking us to do. For that I need His grace and His strength.

How do we go "to the death?" What does that mean in everyday terms? It means to take whatever suffering we have, to take our pains, our problems, our hurts, our feelings of abandonment, rejection, sicknesses, failures, job losses, financial problems, loss of children or spouse, marriage problems, guilt, shame, compulsive habits and addictions, including chemical dependency and drug addiction, *everything* that pains our heart, for ourselves and for others, and lay it at the foot of the cross. St. Francis said it this way: "Above all grace and gifts of the Holy Spirit which Christ gives to His friends, is that of overcoming oneself and for the love of Christ gladly bearing pain, insults, disgrace and hardships. For we cannot glory in any of the other gifts of God, for they are not ours but God's . . . . wherefore the Apostle says: 'God forbid that I should glory save in the cross of Our Lord Jesus Christ to Whom be honor and glory, world without end, Amen.'"[1]

Francis Asks To Feel Christ's Pain

To bear the pain with Christ is to walk the way of the cross. Some of the saints *lived* the crucifixion in their bodies; they bore Christ's actual wounds. St. Francis asked the Lord for two things before he died. The first was to feel in his soul and body the sufferings Christ endured in His passion. The second was to feel in his own heart some of the love that moved Christ to suffer so much for us sinners. Christ granted him his first request one day through an apparition. While Francis was praying, he saw a seraph coming toward him from heaven. It had six luminous wings and as it got near he could see that it bore the image of a crucified man. Two of his wings were raised over its head, two were used for flying, and two covered his body. Francis was afraid when he saw this. He also was filled with indescribable joy because of the intimate look of love that Christ gave him, but then sorrow to see the Lord fastened to the cross. Francis was confused about the apparition because he knew a seraph was an angelic spirit who couldn't suffer bodily. Then Christ revealed to him that "God granted him this apparition that he should understand that not by bodily martyrdom but, by an inner flame, he was to be entirely transformed into the likeness of Christ crucified. After the wonderful apparition had finally departed, an excessive glow was left in Francis' heart with a living love of God and, in his body, the seraph left a wonderful image of Christ's sufferings. At once in his hands and feet marks like nails began to appear, so that they seemed perforated, and the upper side of the feet, and the points of the nails were in the backs of the hands and soles of the feet. . . . . and in his left side the image of a lance thrust appeared, red and bleeding and the blood often saturated Francis' habit. . . . . That night the glow on the mountain was so bright some muleteers got up and saddled their mules to start on their journey to Romagna for they thought the day had come." [2]

Rita's "Impossible" Life

I went upstairs to the main church where St. Rita's incorrupt body is on display behind a grill. I spent a few minutes looking at her and imagining her alive. She is known as the "Saint of the Impossible." Born to elderly parents who were insecure about her future, Rita was promised in marriage to a young man from Cascia. She married at twelve and bore two sons. Her husband was an alcoholic and abusive, and the sons were beginning to follow in their father's footsteps. The more Rita suffered, the more she turned to the Lord in prayer, begging Him to convert her husband and sons. They had been married for eighteen years when Paolo, her husband, had a miraculous conversion. He stopped his drinking and womanizing and abusing. He changed so dramatically that his friends became upset. Their drinking buddy was no longer a friend but a threat. His reform made them look bad, so they murdered him. Just when Rita's suffering had eased and her marriage was turning around, her husband was murdered. Her boys were so angry and filled with hate they set out to avenge their father's murder. Rita was so concerned for the souls of her boys that she prayed, *"Please, take my boys to heaven rather than let them lose their souls in killing my husband's murderer."* That winter both boys got very sick with the plague and died. Within the space of a year Rita lost her husband and her two boys.

Rita Received Her Sign

She went to pray up in the mountain near her home. Distraught because she didn't know if her husband and boys were with the Lord, she asked for a sign to show her if they were with Him. It was in the middle of winter and snow covered the ground. Rita asked for a rose to bloom in her garden as her sign. On January 24 she climbed up behind her house, as was her custom to do, where she prayed and where she cultivated a garden, and there, in the middle of her snow-covered garden, a bright red rose bloomed!

Rita was now free to enter the Augustinian convent in Cascia, a desire she had since childhood, where she spent the remaining 35 years of her life. Standing now in front of Rita's incorrupt body, I pictured her as a young wife and mother, troubled about many things. I could feel the pain she suffered, her anguish over her marriage and later over the deaths of her husband and sons. *She lost everything*. Her suffering was great. She used her suffering — she brought it to Jesus and He transformed it. He made miracles happen so that people like us, people like me, could be encouraged in our faith to trust Him more, to love Him more and to rely on Him more.

Rita's Obedience Bears *Fruit!*

I went on a tour of the monastery, which was adjacent to the church. It was so interesting to see where Rita spent so many years of her life, completely cloistered and solely dedicated to prayer. There was a little chapel where she spent five or six hours a day in prayer. The grapevines in the courtyard have been there since the 14th century. When Rita first entered the monastery, the mother superior told her to water a dead twig, planted near the steps of the courtyard. To practice obedience and to learn to submit to the Lord, she dutifully watered this dead twig everyday for months, patiently doing what she was told. One day, she noticed a tiny green shoot beginning to sprout. It blossomed into a grapevine, yielding a

St. Rita's miraculous grapevine still produces an annual crop. The dried and powdered leaves are sent all over the world to people who are suffering

rich harvest of delicious grapes which are still growing and which practically overrun the courtyard! God rewarded her obedience, the fruit of which is still nourishing others.

Christ Gave Her A Thorn From His Crown

Just off the courtyard was a small room containing the original fresco of Christ crucified, where St. Rita knelt one day praying, *"Jesus, how can I relieve your suffering?"* As soon as she said the words, Christ gave her one of the thorns from His crown which pierced her forehead and left a painful bloody wound which she bore until her death. It had a terrible smell which was so offensive that she had to isolate herself from the other nuns. It was all part of the Lord's plan to have her all to Himself. I was standing on holy ground. Not only did I love seeing these things up close, but I loved St. Rita. She was so human and yet so filled with faith. Another model, another friend! Her cell too was visible, where she spent so much time alone with Our Lord. She made of her cell a little Calvary; she actually built a small hill of rocks with the Cross on top.

These are but a few of the many stories about St. Rita's life passed down through her biographers. Visiting Rita's original home was another highlight. A very simple stone house with an arched doorway, it's now a chapel. I stayed there a long time praying to St. Rita for her intercession for the many people in my life who bear heavy crosses. That familiar vulnerability came over me again. Alcoholism affects so many families, as it did my family of origin. It's a physical and spiritual disease which is a destroyer of people, both the alcoholic and the people who live with them. She had firsthand experience with the disease of alcoholism. I tearfully asked for her help, to break all the

Painting in the Augustinian Monastery in Cascia of St. Rita receiving the stigmata in her forehead as she prayed asking how she could relieve the Lord's suffering

addictive patterns of drug abuse and chemical dependency that are being passed down through the generations of our families, both mine and Tommy's. I asked her to break the bondage of compulsive habits and to heal everyone in our family from this disease or from wounds related to the disease. Believing that her powers of intercession in heaven are great, attested to by the many miracles received by praying to St. Rita, I asked her to go before the Lord on behalf of our families to set us free.

Our Lord And Our Lady Visited Her

Climbing up the mountain behind St. Rita's house was a challenge as it was quite steep, and very hot. The views of the Umbrian mountains were worth the climb. The atmosphere here is very special; it's so pristine. St. Rita's rose garden still exists. Cuttings were taken from that rose bush and planted in the convent garden. Petals from those roses are sent to people who are suffering all over the world and many people of faith have been given cures. Three days before her death Our Lord and His Mother came to her telling her that she would soon be with them. Her cell was filled with light. She waited patiently and prayerfully, asking for the Eucharist. When she died, a sweet smell issued from her room and spread throughout the convent. She was seventy-six years old. The horrible scar on her forehead, still purulent, had turned red. Church bells rang constantly in Cascia, proclaiming her death to the world. Crowds flocked to pay their respect to the corpse, one of whom was a relative of Rita's who had a paralyzed arm. As soon as she entered the room, her arm was cured.

St. Rita's cures continue as people all over the world are healed through her intercession. The "saint of the impossible" has special access to the heart of God.

Back at the hotel tonight I sat out on my small terrace which commands a view of the Umbrian mountain ranges that is so gorgeous I can hardly describe it. We're quite high up, near the tree line. The amazing beauty is the silence; it surrounds you here. I sat on the balcony until dark—to listen to the silence. I feel more alone tonight than I have felt in a while, and yet I'm peaceful. There's an energy in me to study these saints and uncover these miracles. The more I read, the more I want to read. The closer I come to the miracles, the more they touch me or the Lord touches me through them. This is all gift. I keep thinking I'm doing this for others, so that I can bring all this information and these pictures home, which I will do. Perhaps I'll write about it, but I think it's really for me, for my own conversion, for my own growth, for my own healing. For the healing of my heart.

Scripture Meditation

"Yet ours were the sufferings He bore, ours the sorrows He carried. But we, we thought of Him as someone punished, struck by God, and brought low. Yet He was pierced through for our faults, crushed for our sins. On Him lies a punishment that brings us peace, and through His wounds we are healed." (Isaiah 53: 4-5)

Dear Lord Jesus,

Thank you for these Eucharistic miracles which are signs of Your very human suffering. Being so close to You in Your pain is a gift which You give to us to heal us. I want to ease Your suffering, Jesus, to help You like St. Rita, to be a consoling presence to You in the world. Teach me to embrace the cross, to unite all the pains and problems in my life and in the world to Your suffering, to redeem them.

16

The Oldest Miracle of the Eucharist

I took my pillow and blanket out on the balcony just as dawn was breaking this morning, and huddled low in the corner where the only person who could see me was God. If this view was pictured on the cover of *Life Magazine*, it would win a prize. But what moved me the most was the silence. While looking at one of the really tall peaks nearest the hotel, it occurred to me that the Christian call to sanctity is a call to climb the heights, as it were, to become perfect. The call to holiness is an invitation to climb the peak. *It is the way of the Cross*. Staring at this peak, I was thinking, *Well, how do we do that? What does it take? What if I was told that I had to climb that peak, beginning at ground zero, and I had a lifetime to get to the top?* It seemed to me that if I had to, I could do it. It might take forever, but I thought I could do it if I took my time and depended on others as well as ropes and ladders when the going got tough. It would take careful planning, ingenuity and intelligence. If I had to, I could cut down trees that were in my way; in other words, I could do many things to help myself on the journey. I'd need to be focused on what I was doing, because it's arduous and can be life threatening, all the more so if I'm not aware of the dangers.

Climbing the Mountain of Perfection

Climbing this mountain is like our journey to God. He's called us all to come to Him, to reach Him, and in the process we need to be perfected, which is to say, purified. The saints have made this climb rather heroically, utilizing all the gifts of the spiritual life. The sacraments are the ropes and ladders which strengthen and nourish us, giving us our fuel and energy for the journey. God came down to accompany and nourish us on our journey through His Son, Jesus, who is with us every step of the way, *especially* in the Holy Eucharist. Through the Sacrament of Reconciliation, the saints have freed themselves from the chains of anger and unforgiveness which bind them and keep them stuck along the way. They make their journey to God the most important thing in their life, and everything they do is in relation to whether it will bring them closer to God or keep them away from their goal. God gives them all the power tools they need to travel safely! If they do fall, they receive help from one another. And what joy they have in their companionship, of climbing with others who have the same goal. What strength and inspiration fellow pilgrims are!

I wondered where I was on the journey and how I was behaving. Was I struggling hard to go to God or was I more interested in camping out and enjoying myself along the way? In shopping? In buying nice clothes or dining out in great restaurants? It occurred to me that wherever we are is okay. We're all on this climb and we go about it in our own ways. The only sin, it seems to me, is not to go on the journey. It's not only an invitation that God gives us, it's a command. *"Be perfect as Your Heavenly Father is perfect,"* (Matt 5: 48) Jesus said. Become who God called you to be. Follow God's will in your life and be made whole. And holy.

It Looked Like the Jersey Shore!

I didn't want to leave Cascia. As I left, I pulled over at the outskirts of the city for a last, lingering goodbye and a parting prayer.

The ride to Lanciano was difficult because of the fast drivers and trucks. I always stay on the right, but somehow I'll be lost in thought when all of a sudden a car will whiz by me at 100 mph and frighten me to death. It was very, very hot. The Adriatic was on the left. Funny, I thought, this almost could pass for the Garden State Parkway on the Jersey Shore, it's so similar.

Somehow I thought Lanciano would be a small town like Cascia, but it was a big, bustling city, with a population of 35,000! *Here we go again!*

How to get from the *autostrada* to the center and then to find a hotel. Just as I was wondering where to exit the *autostrada* to go into the city, there was a highway sign with an arrow indicating 3 kilometers to the "Miracle of the Eucharist." How amazing to see this featured on a highway sign! That would never happen in America. A policeman directed me to a lovely hotel which was fairly new and had a pool. I've never cared about pools so much in my life, but you get so dehydrated driving and walking around in this heat, that it really does help to bring down the body temperature.

Lanciano is a very ancient city, reputed to be the home of St. Longinus, the centurion who thrust his lance into the side of Christ. Thus its name derives from the word "lance," and the Eucharistic miracle which took place in Lanciano in about the year 700 A. D. happened in the Church of St. Legontian, named after St. Longinus. The Church of St. Francis, which is where the Eucharistic miracle is now, was built over the ruins of the monastery of St. Legontian.

At 8 A.M. Tour Buses Lined the Square

The traffic in Lanciano was heavy at 8 A.M. when I left for the Church of St. Francis to see the Eucharistic miracle. Tour buses already lined the square, an indication that this miracle was, indeed, a very important one. I was really excited finally to be in Lanciano to see the oldest of the Eucharistic miracles, but I also had a lot on my mind this morning. Since yesterday, my tape recorder batteries died and my camera didn't work. I was also out of cash, and needed to find a small carry-on for the extra books and souvenirs I had collected. On top of that I desperately needed a haircut, and Lanciano was the perfect place to accomplish all these tasks.

I decided to go to church first; I would deal with all the rest later. The entrance to the Church of St. Francis is on a narrow street which was not terribly easy to locate. The arched entranceway has a magnificent bronze door with carved reliefs depicting various Eucharistic miracles. One relief showed the head and torso of a donkey, whom I read later was one of the main players in a Eucharistic miracle involving St. Anthony of Padua. It has become one of my favorite stories.

St. Anthony's Mule and the Eucharist

Much loved and revered as one of the greatest preachers in the Middle Ages, St. Anthony held crowds spellbound, especially when he spoke on the Eucharist. One day when he was preaching at Rimini, a seaport on the Adriatic, he attracted a large crowd, and among them some heretics, who jeered him. Rather than waste his time, he turned around and preached to the fish in the sea. The fish responded by raising their heads above the water to listen to him until he was finished! One of the heretics was so impressed with this, he told St. Anthony that if the saint could make his mule do the same thing, he would convert and believe in Christ and in the Holy Eucharist.

People marveled at how the fish raised their bodies out of the water as if to listen to St. Anthony

The mule bowed down on his front legs to adore Our Lord and Savior Jesus Christ in the Blessed Sacrament

They agreed to starve the mule for three days, at which time they would meet in the town square. St. Anthony would come with the Blessed Sacrament, and the heretic would bring the mule accompanied by a pail of his food. After three days, they all converged on the square, with almost the entire population of Rimini in attendance. St. Anthony went to one side with the Blessed Sacrament, and the heretic led the mule into the square. When the hungry animal was brought near his food, St. Anthony, holding the Blessed Sacrament, spoke: "In the name of my Creator, Whom I am not worthy to hold in my hands, I command you to draw near and prostrate yourself before your God, to give due honor to Him, that the heretics may learn from you how they ought to worship their God in the Blessed Sacrament."[1] As soon as St. Anthony spoke, the mule left his food, went before the Blessed Sacrament and bowed down on his front legs as if to adore the Savior. At the sight of this, the owner of the mule converted as did many that day. This is a true story and is memorialized in a statue which stands in Rimini today.

The Miracle Happens During Mass

The interior of the church of St. Francis was exquisitely beautiful. My eye was drawn to the altar immediately, the focus being on the two tabernacles, the lower one serving as the regular one and the upper one housing the reliquary which contains the sacred relics. Above the altar is a huge stained glass window featuring the Blessed Sacrament.

I sat down momentarily to appreciate the sheer beauty of this church and to savor the sacredness and mystery of those two tabernacles. There were quite a few people there, some kneeling, some moving about, and some climbing the stairs behind the altar to see the miracle. I made my way up the staircase which leads to the upper tabernacle. The tabernacle is made of glass on the back so that you can see clearly into it. The top part of the receptacle contains the circular Host-turned-flesh, and the bottom part holds an ancient crystal chalice with the globules of Jesus' blood visible through the glass. To the left is a podium with a booklet which describes this Eucharistic miracle in about ten different languages.

I tried to take in the enormity of what I was seeing and reading. First of all, this miracle is over 1250 years old, because it happened in about the year 700. It is recorded that a monk belonging to the Order of St. Basil was celebrating Mass. We are told that he suffered doubts about transubstantiation, the changing of the bread and wine into the body and blood of Christ. When he said the words of consecration during the Mass, the Host turned to live flesh and began dripping blood. There was much blood which eventually coagulated into five globules, each one differing in size and shape, yet each weighing the same.

The congregation came forward and witnessed the deep emotion of the priest, who wept and prayed with the people: "'O fortunate witnesses to whom the Blessed God, to confound my disbelief, has wished to reveal Himself in this Most Blessed Sacrament and to render Himself visible to our eyes. Come, brethren, and marvel at our God so close to us. Behold the Flesh and Blood of our most beloved Christ.' The people, having witnessed the miracle for themselves, began to wail, asking for forgiveness, crying for mercy. Others began beating their breasts, confessing their sins, declaring themselves unworthy to witness such a miracle. Still others went down on their knees in respect and thanksgiving

The Oldest Miracle of the Eucharist

This silver monstrance was made in 1713 and still holds the precious relics — which after 1250 years are still fresh without the use of any form of preservative

The Host-flesh is light brown and appears rose-colored when backlit

The Blood coagulated into five globules. Proteins in the Blood are fresh — a miracle in itself considering the Blood is over 1250 years old

for the gift the Lord had bestowed on them. All spread the story throughout the town and surrounding villages."[2] People have been coming to see it from all over the world ever since that day.

Throughout the centuries, the relics have remained unchanged; the host-flesh which has the same dimensions as the hosts used today in Latin churches, is beige colored and when lighted from the back appears rose-colored. It has not hardened but remains fresh and supple. The blood has an earthy color resembling the yellow of ocher.

Scientific Tests Are Performed

These sacred relics have been subjected to many tests throughout the centuries. The most recent of the scientific investigations were conducted by Prof. Odoardo Linoli of the University of Arezzo in 1970-71 and again in 1981. He and a team of scientists whose background is anatomy and pathological histology in chemistry and clinical microscopy reached the following conclusions: "The flesh is real flesh. The blood is real blood. The flesh and blood belong to the human species. The flesh consists of the muscular tissue of the heart. In the flesh we see present in sections: the myocardium, the endocardium, the vagus nerve and also the left ventricle of the heart for the large thickness of the myocardium. The flesh is a heart complete in its essential structure. The flesh and blood have the same blood type: AB. The blood is the same as that uncovered on the Holy Shroud of Turin. In the blood there were found proteins in the same normal proportions (percentage-wise) as are found in the sero-proteic make-up of fresh normal blood. In the blood there were also found these minerals: chlorides, phosphorus, magnesium, potassium, sodium and calcium. The preservation of the flesh and blood, which were left in their natural state for twelve centuries and exposed to the action of atmospheric and biological agents, remains an extraordinary phenomenon. In conclusion, it may be said that science, when called upon to testify, has given a certain and thorough response as regards the authenticity of the Eucharistic miracle of Lanciano."[3]

"Another unusual characteristic of the blood is that when liquified, it has retained the chemical properties of freshly shed blood. When we cut ourselves and stain our clothes, the chemical properties of the blood are gone within 20 minutes to half an hour. If blood is not refrigerated within an hour maximum, the composition rapidly breaks down. If blood were taken from a dead body, it would lose its qualities quickly through decay.

This blood is over 1250 years old and still contains all its properties, chemicals and protein of freshly shed blood. And yet in the testing, it was determined that *no preservatives of any kind* were found in the blood."[4]

Lord, Show Me Why

I stood there wanting so much to appreciate this miracle, to be with Jesus in His sacred presence in this form. It was difficult. Somehow this was harder to fathom, the flesh and the globules of blood. They were real enough, to be sure. Some other people were coming up the stairs and so I had to leave. My faith in this miracle and in all of Jesus' miracles is strong. *It's just that I wanted somehow to be able to feel this.*

I was struggling within myself. Here I was faced with the oldest recorded miracle of the Eucharist. Jesus is present in His actual flesh and blood right in front of my eyes. I'm standing next to Him, yet my mind is running all around Lanciano concerned with the errands I needed to run. Part of my frenzy was due, as usual, to the fact that everything would close down by noon. If I didn't find the things I needed, I'd have to wait till 4:00. In the heat of the day I just didn't feel like sitting somewhere this afternoon, because even the churches close.

I said the Rosary and the Chaplet of Divine Mercy. Then I decided I would go out for an hour and take care of some of my pressing concerns. I accomplished all my tasks easily and quickly, which freed me to go back to church.

Testimonies of Early Saints

I took some time the night before to read a book I had brought with me on the miracles of the Eucharist. It describes, from earliest times, the question that has always existed over the Eucharist as being Christ's actual body and blood. St. Ignatius of Antioch in 170, who was a disciple of the apostle John and one of the earliest defenders of the Eucharist, wrote the following concerning the heretics of those early times: "They have abstained from the Eucharist in prayer because they do not confess that the Eucharist is the flesh of our Savior, Jesus Christ."[5] St. Ignatius was a martyr, who was taken to Rome to be devoured by the lions. It is recorded that he wrote letters to St. Polycarp, another martyr, discussing the heresies regarding the Real Presence of Jesus in the Eucharist. *They died for their faith.* In 165, St. Justin wrote: ". . .We call this food "Eucharist," of which no one should partake who does not believe in the truth of our doctrine. . . . We know also that this food which in the natural order would become our flesh and blood, being consecrated in the prayer which contains His own divine words, is the flesh and blood of the same Jesus-made-man."[6] In 373 St. Ephrem said, "But if anyone despise it or reject it or treat it with ignominy, it may be taken as a certainty that he treats with ignominy the Son who called it and actually made it to be His body."[7] These testimonies are among hundreds—thousands—of people who have been willing to die for their belief in the Real Presence of Christ in the Eucharist.

Why, Lord, Did You Do This?

I stood again before the sacred relics trying to open my heart and mind to understand what this really meant. *Lord, help me accept You in this form, in this way. Why, Lord? Why have You done this?* No sooner had I asked the question than I perceived Jesus on Calvary, walking with His cross. I perceived Him in His suffering and I understood His intense sorrow over those who don't believe and who have closed their hearts. He gave His all for us. He loves us to the death, and yet people turn away in disbelief. He loves us so much to have given us the most intimate gift He possibly could give us, Himself in the form of bread and wine. What better way could there be to stay with us, to share His very life with us, than for Him to become part of our flesh and blood? There is no deeper intimacy.

I thought about the heresies that cropped up throughout the centuries. Christians were dying for their faith, but others were doing it great damage. I think I can understand the need for Jesus to give us a sign showing us what He meant, that He meant what He said. The Holy Eucharist is without question the greatest treasure in the Catholic Church, because it is Jesus Himself under the appearance of bread and wine. It must have been and continues to be incredibly painful for Him to witness the doubts, the indifference, the disbelief, the abuse of His gift of Himself in the Eucharist. I think that these are the reasons why Our Savior has deemed it necessary at times to show us His presence by performing Eucharistic miracles of different types. He wants desperately for us to know that He is really, truly with us, physically as well as spiritually.

I stayed there for a long time, marveling at the fact that this is the 20th century and that the Lord has been present in this manifestation since the year 700! I've always hungered to be close to Him, to be "one of His own" in the world. Now, this morning I was present with Him at Calvary.

My Wounds Are His Wounds

While praying I felt some pangs of pain from problems I've been carrying. I almost wished that I didn't feel them; I wished that I didn't have to deal with these certain things, that I could forget them. Then it occurred to me that maybe it was *because I'm here* that these were surfacing. Maybe this is what it's all about. Maybe these pains, these hurts, these problems, are what we can offer to the Lord and what we can sacrifice. Maybe the light of Jesus shines into our darkness to heal us. *Maybe our pain comes up because we are walking with Him.* It's His way of showing us that He's with us; that He suffers for us and we suffer for Him. Suffering has meaning; it redeems us through His dying — for us. But we must undertake the journey.

With only a few minutes left before the church closed, I didn't want to leave Lanciano carrying the weight of these heartaches with me. The more I felt like crying, the more I realized that Jesus was allowing me to walk with Him; that His wounds are our wounds, and our wounds are His wounds. It is in this wounded place where we are healed. I offered Him my heartaches and asked, in return, for the grace to bear pain in my soul.

The priest was eager to close up and I reluctantly left.

Heading South To See Padre Pio

It was going to be another long afternoon of driving. I was going further south, which meant it would be hotter. I fortified myself with some mineral water and left for San Giovanni Rotondo, the land of Padre Pio. The little town of San Giovanni Rotondo lies in a shell of the Gargano mountains about 1600 ft. above sea level at the foot of Mt. Castalano. It's not too far from the Adriatic, and the beauty and charm of its panorama makes it resemble a Swiss landscape. As I approached the city a lady was doing her laundry in a big washtub beside the road. It was obviously a poor place. How appropriate, I thought, for a man as holy as Padre Pio to be from here.

Someone had recommended the name of a hotel which I found very easily, and I was overjoyed to find it had a pool. My single room faces south and looks out on a huge crane used in the construction of a new building in the next lot. It's very hot here. This is the last lap of the journey. I'm starting to get those hunger pangs for home. I'm going to spend three days here because I want to let myself experience the world of

Padre Pio in a retreat fashion. From here I'll drive to Rome where I'll spend one day before I fly home.

Scripture Meditation

"The cross looks like sheer foolishness to those who are not on the way to salvation. But to those of us who are on the way, we see it as God's power to save." (1 Cor 1: 18)

Dear Lord Jesus,
Thank you for calling me to go on this journey of faith, to climb that mountain, to become perfect, which is to say, whole and holy. Jesus, I want to follow You. The journey is dangerous and painful, requiring us to surrender everything that keeps us separate from You. But it leads to Life. There is no other way. You are the Way, the Truth and the Life. Take my hand, Jesus, and keep me close to You on the path. Let me never be separated from You.

17

Padre Pio

If my room were an oven and my bed a cookie sheet, I was the cookie which baked all night! Even a small portable fan didn't help. I was restless and awake on and off most of the night. Not only that, but the crane operators came to work at 6:00 A.M. singing and shouting to each other outside my window, oblivious to the early morning hour. That, on top of everything, was just too much. I decided to ask for a better room on the western side of the hotel facing the beautiful mountains which encircle this little town, once referred to by an Italian cardinal as the "Bethlehem of Padre Pio."

I don't know what it is, but sometimes I seem to get the worst room in the hotel. A woman alone in Italy is very suspect; I don't think they know how to take me. I guess I shouldn't have been surprised when they gave me one of the hottest rooms in the back of the hotel. But something has changed since then because they've decided I'm not the loose woman they probably thought I was, and they're treating me with respect. When I asked to change my room they were most courteous and agreed to do it *subito*.

Our Lady of Grace Church and Friary

With that resolved I looked forward to seeing Padre Pio's Church and Friary which was just up the hill from my hotel, overlooking this small town and the Gargano countryside. Near the church is *The House For the Relief of Suffering*, a hospital which is one of the fruits of Padre Pio's ministry. It stands as a beacon of hope and healing to people of every nationality, who come seeking cures for their ills of body, mind and spirit.

People came by the thousands seeking Padre Pio's intercession when he was alive. He ministered to the whole world, and the people of the world came to say good-by to him when he died in 1968. With his last breath, he uttered the names of Jesus and Mary. His calvary was over after 58 years as a priest. I don't know how this small town accommodated the 100,000 people who attended his funeral. God used him mightily and powerfully. I'm just beginning to taste how deep and powerful was the love of God poured out for mankind through this man.

I headed for what I hoped would be a 9:00 A. M. Mass. Masses were ongoing all morning, every hour on the hour, and then again in the evening. Our Lady of Grace Church is large and artistically very appealing to the eye. It is also the home for the Capuchin Friary where Padre Pio came as a 19 year old priest and remained for the rest of his life. It is an oasis of holiness.

Struggling With My Self Image

Mass was so devotional, with bells and singing like days of old. That familiar feeling of vulnerability began to bubble up in me; I wondered if I felt the presence of Padre Pio. People say that miracles still abound and that his presence is very much here. I had never had any particular devotion to Padre Pio, and only through my Aunt Helen and her lifelong devotion to Padre Pio am I here now. I became increasingly uncomfortable during Mass. People looked at me like they usually did, (a foreigner) but this time they stared; some looked me up and down. It took me awhile but I realized that I was dressed for a summer picnic. I had on white bermuda shorts and a T-shirt. The congregation was dressed in working or Sunday clothes. I felt out of place, ridiculous. I wanted to leave. Here I was travelling in Europe, visiting these sacred places and why in the world didn't I dress accordingly? What was wrong with me? I'm a middle-aged woman and I dress like a teenager in shorts and tops. I squirmed in my seat.

I wondered if this was really about what I was wearing, or did it have more to do with a negative self-image? When Father Bob DeGrandis visited awhile back, he said he picked up a poor self-image in me. I never thought of myself as having a negative self-image. If anything, I thought I suffered from a superiority complex. Growing up I always felt I could accomplish anything. That was mostly due to the influence of my father, who insisted that "Joanie could do no wrong." I remember feeling shy and inferior as a child. I thought I overcame that because in school I behaved as if I had every confidence in the world. There was or is nothing that I won't attempt if I feel led to do it. I struggled during Mass, trying to hold back tears. This seems to be happening to me everywhere I go, but this morning it was very strong. I'm learning to bring lots of kleenex in my purse because I never know when I'll get these surprise crying jags. I decided that when I got back to the hotel, I'd change and not wear these shorts anymore in church. I'm too old to be dressing like this anyway; I'll start dressing as becomes a woman my age.

Touring the Friary

After Mass, I gave myself a tour of the church and friary. Signs indicated where you could find Padre Pio's room, the crucifix through which Jesus gave him the stigmata, his confessional, his tomb, an exhibit of his life and some of his possessions which are on display. There were very large pictures of his early life and his parents, of himself as a young priest, and then scenes related to different aspects of his ministry: his gifts of discernment in the confessional, his gift of healing, his celebration of the Mass. I stood for a long time in front of each picture, absorbing the spirit of love and faith inherent in each scene. Then we moved on to see his actual room, about a 10 x 12 foot very simple room with a bed and an iron headboard. At the foot of his bed was a painting of the Blessed Mother holding the Baby Jesus, which he obviously could see when lying on his pillow. Some of his many prayer books were on display under glass on his desk, as were his pens, and a small dictating machine. His correspondence was voluminous; he wrote and received thousands of letters during his lifetime. There were pictures of the Sacred Heart, the Blessed Mother, his parents, and there seemed to be one of a young-looking Bob Hope. The chair in which he died was there, well-worn from the thousands of hours he sat praying the Rosary. The physical austerity complemented the spiritual austerity of his life; he lived in a state of complete detachment and surrender, to be used by Jesus for the redemption of souls.

Padre Pio's Special Calling

"The source of Padre Pio's spirituality was his unconditional offering of himself to the Lord as a victim."[1] Francesco Forgione spoke of his desire to be a priest when he was five years old. When he was nine his mother found him sleeping on the floor with a stone for a pillow. He learned very early to discipline himself and do penance for the sake of others. At sixteen he entered the Capuchin novitiate to begin a life of extraordinary service to humanity. On the back of the holy card which Padre Pio gave out at his first Mass, he wrote: "A souvenir of my first Mass. 'Jesus, my life and my breath, today I timorously raise You in a mystery of love. With You may I be for the world, the way, the truth and the life and through You a holy priest—a perfect victim.'"[2] He knew very early that he had a special calling to suffer and to win souls for the Lord.

The Stigmata

Padre Pio was the first priest to receive the stigmata, very deep and painful wounds in his hands, feet and side, which he bore for 50 years. Many saints including St. Francis, St. Rita, and St. Catherine of Siena bore the stigmata wound; there are well over 300 documented cases in Church history. Padre Pio begged God to take away, not the pain, but the physical manifestations of it; he was mortified and embarrassed by it. "He knew even before he got the stigmata that his life was going to be a martyrdom. He knew that he was chosen by God as a collaborator in the redeeming work of Christ, and that this collaboration would not be realized without the cross....He was convinced that his entire life, like that of Christ, would be a continuous martyrdom."[3] He often spoke about the sadness in his heart and deep feelings of abandonment. Apparently Jesus spoke to him clearly, in word and in visions. He wrote, "Jesus made me hear His voice in my heart...My son, love is recognized in suffering; you will feel it acutely in your soul and even more acutely in your body...How many times would you have abandoned Me if I had not crucified you? Under the weight of

I rejoice now in the sufferings I bear for your sake; and what is lacking of the sufferings of Christ, I fill up in my flesh for His body which is the Church (Col 1, 24)

the cross one learns to love. I do not give it to everyone, but only to those souls who are most dear to Me."[4]

I could barely imagine his suffering and what it must have been like to lead such a consecrated life. More tears. I felt such love for this man who loved the Lord so much and whom the Lord loved so much. His life was totally dedicated to doing God's will, to immolating himself, to sacrificing himself for the needs of the Lord. The physical sufferings were of course the stigmata, but there were other sufferings that are recorded. For instance, he was given the crown of thorns to wear and received spiritually the scourging at least once a week for several years. He suffered incredible interior trials, especially with temptations against faith, hope and chastity. He also was faced with the physical and mental oppressions of the spirit of evil, fear, thrashings and persecutions. He certainly did walk the way of the dark night. He wrote early in his life, "The fury of the Most High has been confirmed and all the tempestuous billows surge upon me. Everyone detests me. Night and day I struggle and cry alone."[5] His dark night was one of abandonment. His whole life he experienced sorrow and suffering due to feeling so rejected, misunderstood and despised.

Padre Pio's Love for the Cross

I went to the choir stall to see the crucifix through which Jesus gave him the stigmata. It is a fairly large crucifix of a very anguished, dying Christ. Christ was so human! I've never seen one which exuded such a depth of emotion. I knelt there for a while with others who came to kneel and pray in front this sacred crucifix. The whole meaning of Calvary was right there; there is meaning to suffering; pain and love are interchangeable. That the proof of love is pain recurs persistently in the letters of Padre Pio. He wrote to his spiritual director, "I know well that the cross is the pledge of love. The cross is the down payment for pardon. Love that is not nurtured, not sustained by the cross, is not true love and it soon turns to ashes."[6] Padre Pio was possessed by this love. His love for the cross was extraordinary. Elsewhere he wrote: "It is then that man finds out in suffering the inner peace and even a spiritual joy: he overcomes that 'sense of uselessness' of suffering, by discovering the saving sense of it in the unity with Christ; 'he transforms that depressing sensation' into the exalting participation in the suffering of Christ; he keeps within himself the inner certitude that the man who suffers 'completes what is lacking in

Christ's sorrows'; he experiences the joy of being able, in the spiritual dimension of the work of redemption, to serve, just as Christ does, to the salvation of his brothers and sisters."[7] Padre Pio's entire life could be summed up by St. Paul's words to the Colossians, *"I rejoice now in the sufferings I bear for your sake and what is lacking of the sufferings of Christ, I fill up in my flesh for His Body, which is the church."* (Col. 1:24)

Still Grieving for My Dad

On my way out I decided to have some Masses offered for special people, including my dad. In the last months of daddy's life he suffered so, and I saw the same look in Padre Pio's eyes on a postcard this morning. I thought of my dad so much, especially during Mass. I think my tears were really for my dad. I thought my grieving was over, but it's like a fresh wound. I offered my communion for him. I still miss him a great deal and I pray that he is filled and happy somewhere with the Lord. Perhaps Padre Pio is interceding for him, bringing him into his full redemption. Or is it that my dad is showering me with love now, through Padre Pio?

There was a resemblance between Padre Pio and my Dad. Here's Dad enjoying one of his own stories – and a La Corona

Padre Pio was said to have "The eyes of a saint"

Inspired Prayers For My Children

I decided to fast today. I started the trip limiting myself to one roll for breakfast with no butter and a little marmalade. Somehow I graduated to two rolls and two butters with lots of marmalade. I've lost my discipline completely and my clothes are getting tight. I want to see if I can stop, plus the fact I would like to incorporate fasting into my life. It adds power to prayer. I bought a bottle of water and went home to my hotel for a siesta. I don't know how I went from the ridiculous to the sublime, but now I have a huge room with a little balcony facing the mountains. Today there's a beautiful breeze and this is like my little corner of heaven. I was tired after my restless night, so I laid on the bed for a while and on the wall facing me is a picture of Padre Pio at prayer. I must have been praying about my children because all of a sudden the thought came to me, *"Consecrate them to the Immaculate Heart of Mary."* It was a different thought; it seemed to almost have come from Padre Pio. I thought about it while I walked back to church. *What a beautiful idea.* I wanted to say the Rosary while kneeling beside Padre Pio's tomb. His presence, like St. Francis', is so tangible. But there were too many tourists, so I left. Instead I went up to the main church and was fortunate to be there in time for Adoration of the Blessed Sacrament. The ushers passed out a leaflet with Our Lady of Medjugorje on the cover and inside a Consecration to the Immaculate Heart of Mary which Our Lady dictated to Jelena Vasilj, one of the seers in Medjugorje, Yugoslavia. Not only had I been inspired to pray to her, but now I had been given the prayer itself and a whole community of people with which to pray it. Praying it in front of the Blessed Sacrament meant so much to me. My children mean the world to me and I carry them with me every moment of the day. Their welfare and protection is always uppermost in my mind, as well as each one's particular needs and problems. I've been praying for God's will to be realized in each of their lives, asking Him to lead them to the next step of truth and love on their journey. Now I put each of my children into the loving arms of the Blessed Mother, *consecrating* them to her care. I prayed for them:

O Immaculate Heart of Mary, ardent with goodness,
show your love towards us.
May the flame of Your Heart, O Mary,
descend on all mankind.
We love you so.
Impress true love in our hearts
so that we have a continuous desire
for you.
O Mary, humble and meek of heart,
remember us when we are in sin.
You know that all men sin.
Give us, by means of your Immaculate Heart,
spiritual health.
Let us always see
the goodness of your maternal Heart
and may we be converted by means of the flame
of your heart. Amen.

A Growing Desire For His Real Presence

I sought out the intimacy of a small chapel where Padre Pio heard confessions. He had the gift of reading hearts, and it is said that he spent as many as 16 hours a day hearing people's confessions. He knew what people were going to say before they said it. He knew the state of their soul. It was a gift and a burden. It is said that he heard millions of confessions in his lifetime. A person was limited to three minutes when they went in with him and they had to speak Italian or Latin. But they really didn't even have to speak because he knew what was in their heart and he gave them advice and counsel as if it came from the Lord.

I knelt in a pew right next to his confessional and again the feeling of his presence was so strong. I was quiet and very peaceful and, as always, so grateful to have this time. Prayer comes so easily here. Whether or not we feel anything when we pray is of no consequence because every prayer is heard and cherished. I just seem to have an abundance of feeling on this trip and an abundance of vulnerability. I think I'm becoming more interested in spending more time in prayer. I can feel the desire growing in me to sit for longer periods in front of the Blessed Sacrament, just to be a Mary, just to listen. Perhaps I've been influenced by Padre Pio and Rita and Clare and Francis. Devotion to the Real Presence of Jesus in the Blessed Sacrament was at the center of their lives. One day a friend approached Francis and asked him: "Father, what do you do during those long hours before the Blessed Sacrament?" Francis replied, "My son, in return I ask you what does the poor man do at the rich man's door, the sick man in the presence of his physician, the thirsty man at the limpid stream? What they do, I do before the Eucharistic God. I pray. I adore. I love."[8]

What A Gift to Be Here!

It was a beautiful night. A gentle breeze was blowing, providing blessed relief from the heat of the day. Standing in the piazza in front of Padre Pio's church, seeing the little town spread out below the hospital, I had the feeling that God's in His kingdom and all's right with the world, a world which Padre Pio helped restore and which he continues to help restore. So many people are healed bodily and spiritually through his intercession.

I'm glad to have a few more days here. I'm drinking from these wells of spirituality. I have much to learn, but my thirst is being quenched by reading and absorbing the fruits of Padre Pio's relationship with the Lord. I have been struggling so over the question of pain in our lives. I think Padre Pio is helping me understand it.

I sat on my balcony after dinner. I think of home a lot, of what everyone's doing and I miss my family terribly. But, there's a peace in me here, a peace that comes from knowing I'm where I'm supposed to be. With less than a week left, I want to experience every day to the fullest, especially here in San Giovanni. I've been thinking tonight that when you open your heart to the Lord, even a crack, He'll take whatever you give Him, to make it benefit you. Just like Mary Pyle, a wealthy woman from New York who came to San Giovanni Rotondo and never left; she opened her heart little by little until finally she just gave her all. I know we're asked to give our all. I know we're not all meant to come to San Giovanni to become Third Order Franciscans, but we are meant to find our path, which is to say our gift, wherein we can give and receive God's love to the fullest. When we find God's will for us we'll know it, because in His will is the peace and joy which the world cannot give.

Scripture Meditation

"Behold, I stand at the door and knock. If anyone hears my voice and opens the door, I will enter his house and dine with him, and he with me." (Rev 3: 20)

Dear Lord Jesus,

You come gently knocking at the door of our hearts, patiently waiting for us to open the door. When we are attentive and prayerful we hear You, like Padre Pio, who opened himself to You as a young child. I want to listen to Your "knocks," Your nudges and inspirations, Your dreams and images, Your pain and sorrow. Teach me, Lord, how to welcome You in my heart where You reside as My Divine Guest. Then we can dine together, in intimacy.

18

A Continuous Martyrdom

I never thought I'd last this long on my own in Italy. I worried before I left home that this would be too long a span of time to spend by myself. I'm usually ready to go home after three days on a business trip. Strangely, I haven't had that anxiety. Perhaps just a fleeting glimpse of it, but I'm very peaceful and dedicated to what I'm doing. My homespun retreat is so spiritually nourishing and satisfying. I'm absorbing the faith, teachings, and example of some of the great saints of the Church. These guides are expert at helping me find my way up that mountain! They've "been there," they've walked the walk, emptying themselves of their own defects and weaknesses to give Christ full possession of their souls. Into their emptiness God has poured Himself, Whom we see reflected in them and in the fruits of their lives. Padre Pio is one of these. To see him is to see Jesus.

This morning I decided to wear a more suitable outfit to church, so I picked a matching skirt and blouse, which I hadn't yet worn on the trip. I felt good wearing it. I've thought about my "Bermuda shorts episode" again, and decided that the Lord probably "couldn't care less" what I'm wearing. If I went to visit Him in Nazareth or Bethlehem, I think He'd accept me no matter what clothes I wore. The issue is not what I'm wearing, but what doesn't "look good" on the inside. Some part of myself feels that it doesn't measure up; that old inferiority complex is still with me.

House for the Relief of Suffering

After Mass this morning I took myself on a tour of the House For the Relief of Suffering. It was enormous, clean and had a very gracious feel to it. Their list of departments was long and impressive. They had everything from nuclear medicine to maternity. Adoration of the Blessed Sacrament was taking place in one of the chapels I found, so I decided to sit for a few minutes while I said my Rosary. It was an intimate chapel with beautiful stained glass windows behind the altar depicting the Eucharist. Many of the people making a visit were dressed in white jackets, which meant they were doctors. How wonderful, I thought, that they come to draw strength and nourishment from Jesus Himself in the Holy Eucharist in order to be Eucharist for their patients. Mother Teresa and her nuns begin their day with Mass and Holy Communion and they end it with one full hour of Adoration of the Blessed Sacrament. She says that unless they believe and can see Jesus in the appearance of bread on the altar, they will not be able to see Him in the distressing disguise of the poor. In May, 1988, at her co-workers chapter meeting in Paris she said: " If you are looking for vocations as a community have adoration every day. Once the Missionaries of Charity started daily adoration their vocations doubled."

Graced Moments at Bellevue Hospital

This hospital chapel transported me back to my freshman year of high school in New York City when a group of us went to Bellevue Hospital on Sunday mornings to teach catechism to the children. Mass was at 8:00 A.M. in the hospital chapel on the sixth floor. I'll never forget the smell of urine that greeted one when the elevator doors opened. It was the same in the chapel. There were so many sick people who came to Mass in their robes, on stretchers, in wheelchairs and so forth. Afterwards, we'd go into the children's ward to teach them Bible stories. I remember one little boy about 5 years old who had no arms and legs. He waited for me on Sunday mornings and as soon as I walked into the ward, his face lit up like a Christmas tree. I loved Paul and asked my father if we could adopt him. I went there for two years and I know I got more out of it than I gave. God was beginning to teach me some valuable lessons about His kingdom; that it's like finding a buried treasure in a field. You'll give up everything to have it. As I look back, I know it was God's presence in those people, especially in the children, which was so filling, so *satisfying*. I can almost cry when I think of the goodness and love in that little child with no arms and legs. He was five and had a lifetime ahead of him of learning to live with his handicap. I remember that he didn't seem to act as if he were handicapped.

Those were graced experiences. I remember wanting to follow the Lord then, to be one of the workers in His vineyard. He calls us from the time we're little and, when we respond and give ourselves to Him, those are the graced moments of our lives. I've always wanted to respond, but have not always succeeded. In fact, most of the time I haven't responded.

Lord, How Can I Serve You Now?

Now, so many years later, in another hospital chapel, I thought of how God calls us and asks us to be with Him in so many ways, for so many needs. How often do we say, "Yes"? I have so many desires! I'd like to be His scribe, like Maria Valtorta. But I'd like to know *His* desire for my life, for the work He wants me to do. Is it to spread the message about these miracles of the Eucharist? Is it to write this book? To give slide presentations on His miracles and His saints—all in relation to the Eucharist? When I visit these sacred places and see the manifestations of Jesus' Presence in the Eucharistic miracles, I want to go home and shout this from the rooftops. Americans need to know about this! I went to Catholic school all my life and never once heard about any of these miracles, including the Corpus Christi miracle. *How can these awesome happenings be going on all over the world without us knowing about them?* If our God has seen fit to allow the Eucharistic miracles to happen, then our Church should see fit to spread this news. It's not that I'm so caught up in the miracles; it's my love and faith in the Real Presence of Jesus in the Holy Eucharist that drives me.

Praying with the Body

It was high noon when I left the hospital; the sun never felt hotter, it was boiling. I decided to fast again. Fasting is the prayer of the body, I read somewhere. Our Lady of Medjugorje has been asking for us to fast at least twice a week—on Wednesdays and Fridays. Jesus began His public life by fasting; it is just as important for us in order to make up for our sins and the sins of others. It was harder today because I was hungrier, but, nevertheless, I decided that I was going to learn to discipline myself to grow strong spiritual muscles, to add "weight" to my prayers and also to learn to sacrifice. I'm so inspired by Padre Pio's suffering. This seems like a good way for me to begin a more disciplined prayer life.

A "Smile-In" at the Pool!

Finding my way back to the hotel in this town is so easy. Basically, I just go in a circle from the hotel to the church and back again. No more walled cities or rush hour congestion with which to contend. By comparison this is a piece of cake. At the hotel I took a break and went for a swim in the pool. It's a lovely Olympic-sized pool, against a backdrop of the Gargano mountains, and it made for an hour of total refreshment. While I was in the pool a little boy about 5 years old came running out. Upon his discovery of the pool, he couldn't hold back his delight. He looked at me enjoying myself in the water and he broke out in a grin that went from ear to ear. For about a minute we had a "smile-in," he and I just smiling at each other! He was vicariously enjoying my fun. His ten year old brother came running out looking for him and began scolding him. Shaking cupped fingers at him, he yelled in Italian, *"Don't you know we're eating? What are you doing here? What are you staring at, dummy? Come in for lunch."* The five year old couldn't stop staring and smiling. Then the older brother looked at me in the pool. If looks could kill, I would have been dead in the water. His eyes told me I was responsible for his brother not being at lunch. Now I couldn't stop smiling! It was such a funny scene it still makes me laugh when I think about it.

Mass Was Calvary for Padre Pio

I went back to church for Adoration of the Blessed Sacrament in the late afternoon. It's no wonder there is adoration everyday as well as so many Masses and confessions and Holy Hours. Mass and the Holy Eucharist was the center of Padre Pio's life. He said often that, "It would be easier for the earth to exist without the sun than without Holy Mass." "Holy Mass was Calvary for Padre Pio, but it was also his Paradise. He saw the heavens open, the splendor of God, and the glory of the angels and saints."[1] "The Mass of Padre Pio visibly reproduced the Passion of Christ, not only in mystical form, but also physically, in his body."[2] He spent two hours preparing for each Mass, which was the peak of his day. There was such a rush to come to his Masses that people took up lodgings nearby and queued up for the church doors to open at 4:30 A.M.

"Calvary is a definite place, and the crucifixion of Christ took place at a definite time; but by his mighty words, 'Do this in commemoration of me' — Christ instituted the Sacrifice of the Mass as the real renewal of that death, in an unbloody manner, 'from the rising of the sun to the going down thereof,' as the prophet Malachias had foretold. After that, every moment became a mystical Calvary, for at every moment of the day and night, somewhere in the world, Christ is brought on the altar by the words of a consecrated man whose priesthood gives him the power to command Divinity, and is immolated anew in a bloodless manner.'"[3]

The Sacred Heart Nuns Taught Sound Theology

The Sacred Heart nuns gave me a deep understanding of and appreciation for the Sacraments and most especially for the Holy Sacrifice of the Mass and the Eucharist. I remember Mother Brennan in senior year of high school spending weeks — months — on the Mass and its meaning for our lives. Jesus Christ voluntarily mounts the Cross — the altar of sacrifice — offering Himself as a perfect victim to the Father on our behalf. Jesus, the God-man, offered Himself as an *infinite gift* of love for our redemption. At the Last Supper, Jesus presents Himself as the new Passover victim to be fed on at the supper. We perpetuate this memorial of His sacrifice in an unbloody manner through the Mass, in which the priest who represents Christ, consecrates the bread and wine which becomes the body and blood of Jesus Christ. We are co-offerers with the priest who share in the redeeming power of Christ's sacrifice.

A Priest Remembers Padre Pio's Masses

A priest who had the privilege of serving many of Padre Pio's Masses writes: " The Holy Mass. . . was his life, his calvary, his crucifixion, his paradise. It lasted about three hours. I would follow him with great attention and emotion in the various phases of the celebration. At the Memento for the Living, his meditation was deep, lengthy, interminable and interrupted only by some painful sighs. He proceeded slowly in the painful ascent of his mystical calvary and he arrived exhausted to his crucifixion. The moment of consecration was the climax of his passion; it was the crucifixion with Jesus. As he pronounced the words of consecration, one noted on his pale and exhausted face signs of

"This is my only comfort, that of being associated with Jesus in the Divine Sacrifice and in the redemption of souls" Padre Pio

indescribable internal suffering, the horrible martyrdom of the tortured one on the cross. He looked like Jesus crucified. After the consecration, with tears in his eyes and some sobbing, he slowly continued. . . ."[4]

Padre Pio Suffers the Crucifixion

Padre Pio described his own experience: "During the celebration of Holy Mass, I am hanging on the cross together with Jesus and I suffer all that Jesus suffered on Calvary, as much as is possible for a human nature."[5] Padre Pio bears powerful witness to the Holy Sacrifice of the Mass being a *sacrifice*, a reenactment of Christ's death on the cross. In the Mass, as at the Last Supper, the sacrifice of Calvary is repeated. At the Last Supper, on Calvary and in the Mass, Christ is the victim offering Himself to the Father on our behalf. At the Last Supper He gives Himself under the appearances of bread and wine; on the cross, he offers Himself as a broken, bleeding victim, and in the Mass, He gives Himself to us in the form of bread and wine. To be at Mass is to be at the foot of the cross, a witness of Jesus' sacrifice in which He sheds His blood and dies—for us.

Padre Pio and Christ were intimately united on the altar. "When he pronounced the words: "This is my body," "This is my blood. . ." he, the new Christ, was entrusted to continue and complete the passion of his Teacher. Looking at the face of Padre Pio, wet with tears, one immediately thought of the sins that he took upon himself in the unending hours spent in the confessional every day. Humiliated under the weight of the sins of others, he climbed the altar of His God to offer himself as a victim, together with Christ, and to represent in his own person the suffering Jesus."[6]

Prayer and the Holy Eucharist

Prayer for Padre Pio was a continuous dialogue with Christ, with Our Lady, with his Guardian Angel, and with St. Francis of Assisi, who would appear to him under visible forms. Whenever he prayed for a sick person, he would ask that the sufferings of the sick person become his. The Lord would hear him. Padre Pio would become ill and suffer. The sick person would become well. This is the key to the miracles; he prayed and he suffered.

The center of Padre Pio's life was the Eucharistic Jesus. His devotion polarized around the tabernacle. Jesus, the Word incarnate, was not distant in time and space to Padre Pio, but very close to him, living with him under the same roof, hidden under the Eucharistic Species. Hour by hour, day and night, he would linger in conversation with the Divine Inhabitant of the tabernacle. When asked where he could be found if he was not in his cell or in the confessional, he answered, "Come and look for me in the choir, in the presence of Jesus in the Blessed Sacrament."[7] In a letter to a friend he wrote: "What hurts me most, dear Father, is the thought of Jesus in the

The moment of Consecration was the climax of his passion—it was the crucifixion with Jesus

Blessed Sacrament. My heart feels drawn by a higher force each morning I am united with Him in the Blessed Sacrament. I have such a hunger and thirst before I receive Him that I almost die. . . .and instead of being appeased after I have received Him sacramentally, this hunger and thirst steadily increase."[8]

Coming Closer to Jesus Through Padre Pio

After Benediction and Adoration, I decided to return to the choir loft to pray before the crucifix which was so special to Padre Pio and from which Jesus gave him the stigmata. I was half-kneeling, half- sitting just looking at the crucifix. The corpus of Jesus was so sad and suffering. I saw myself as an infinitesimal drop in an ocean of people and I felt small and insignificant. *Lord, what do You want? What can I do? How can I help? You have people like Padre Pio. What in the world can someone like me do for You?* If anything, one of the gifts I've been given since I've been here is the new gift of humility to see myself for who I really am, at least more clearly than I have before. Perhaps Padre Pio is giving me discernment to see what work I need to do on myself, or rather what God needs to do in me in order to serve Him. I see so much of my own imperfection, so much of my self-will, so much of my self-serving. I see myself as going through the motions a lot in my spiritual life.

Coming here has opened me to the need to concentrate on who I'm following; I'm not following a doctrine; I'm following a Person. *What do You want, Lord? How can I help You? What can I do? God, will You speak to me? I know I'm unworthy, but we're all unworthy. No one could be worthy of You, but as a grace would You just clearly, audibly speak to me?*

No one happened to be there at the moment and when I looked to the left, I noticed a plant on one of the choir stall chairs. It was just across the aisle from me, about three feet away and one aisle behind. There was a sign on the chair, saying, "This is the chair Padre Pio sat in praying before the crucifix when he received the stigmata." When I read that it moved me so much. I felt so close to Jesus in His presence in Padre Pio. It made me want that same intimacy. Then I understood, almost as if words were spoken to me, *"I have been present. You've been hearing me in your heart."* Yes, I realized that I have been hearing the Lord in my heart. He's been speaking quite clearly, giving me direction, images, tears, sensations, dreams and so forth. Those are His graces. He's especially there when I feel lost or in pain. I have to remind myself that He wants contact and intimacy with us more than we do, so that He's already there waiting for us to open our hearts.

What I'm Learning From Padre Pio

I knelt in that sacred place for a long time. I didn't want to run off to read or feed the hungry or write a book. I just wanted to be with Him. I asked Him again, "What do You want?" And that's what He seemed to want. I think He just wants us to love Him, to kneel there, to befriend Him, to accompany Him. Yes, to serve Him. But if we serve Him without being with Him, we're really not serving Him. We're serving ourselves. If we're with Him, He'll send us out to serve. That is to say, He will serve through us. This is what I'm learning from Padre Pio, the need to be for Jesus, the need simply to be, to be open and willing to be present, to love, to receive Him in the Eucharist, to create space in my own heart where He can find refuge. How do we do this? How do we create this space? How did Padre Pio create it? He created it by spending time in prayer, by just being there before the Lord. That's the commitment. It's not to go out and do all these great things. That happens perhaps if the Lord uses us that way, but it's to be a follower who's willing to spend time and a follower who's willing to live by God's agenda, not our own.

At dinner the waiters now give me a very friendly smile and greeting. After I sat down, an elderly lady walking through the dining room waved at me and smiled. I waved back. I don't know why, but this little gesture of acceptance made me feel so good.

Scripture Meditation

"Remain united to Me and I will remain united to you. A branch cannot bear fruit by itself; it can do so only if it remains in the vine. In the same way you cannot bear fruit unless you remain in Me. I am the Vine and you are the branches; whoever remains in Me, and I in him, will bear much fruit." (John 15: 4-5)

Dear Lord Jesus,

There is no deeper intimacy than to be united to You at the altar of Your crucifixion, the Holy Sacrifice of the Mass. Your Body and Blood is poured out for us like sap which gives life to our branches. Jesus, I want my branches to be filled with the fruit of Your love! Jesus, thank you for Your Real Presence on our altars and in our tabernacles. Please give me a hunger for You.

19

Spiritual Warfare

I made another new friend today, St. Michael the Archangel. He's a good friend to have, considering what a great "defenseman" he is. For years we invoked his protection at the end of every Mass:

> *St. Michael, the Archangel, defend us in the day of battle; be our safeguard against the wickedness and snares of the devil. May God rebuke him we humbly pray; and do thou, O Prince of the heavenly host, by the power of God, thrust into hell Satan and all other evil forces who wander through the world seeking the ruin of souls.*

What a pity we dropped that prayer, especially now when we need his protection more than ever in a world growing deaf, dumb and blind through the darkness of evil. The Lord referred to Satan as "the Shining Darkness" in private revelations to Zdenko "Jim" Singer in Ontario, Canada, a man originally from Zagreb, Croatia, who now lives in Ontario, Canada and who has experienced many apparitions of the Father, Son, Holy Spirit and the Blessed Mother. In the last ten years especially, people from all over the world have been receiving apparitions and locutions from Christ and the Blessed Virgin, who plead with us to open our eyes to the evil around us and to lead souls back to God. Satan is poisoning the souls of men, undermining our dignity as human beings, and stealing all the beautiful gifts God gives his children. The lie which does the most damage is the one which says Satan doesn't exist, because it leaves us vulnerable to his deception.[1]

Biblical References to Satan

We have only to look in the Bible to reaffirm the sinister reality of the evil one and his cohorts. When the bad angels fell away from their allegiance to God, St. Michael joined forces with the good angels in heaven to drive out Satan and his legions and plunge them into the depths of hell. In the New Testament, when Christ commissioned his disciples, *"He called the twelve together and gave them power and authority of over all devils and to cure disease, and he sent them out to proclaim the kingdom of God and to heal."* (Luke 9: 11) Of the many miracles Jesus performed, eight of them involved cures of demonic possession. Jesus Himself was tempted by Satan: *"Then Jesus was led by the Spirit out into the wilderness to be tempted by the devil. . . ,"* and He replied, *"Be off Satan! For Scripture says: 'You must worship the Lord your God, and serve him alone.' Then the devil left him, and the angels appeared and looked after him."* (Matt 4: 1, 10-11) St. Paul warns us that *"our struggle is against the Sovereignties and the Powers who originate the darkness in this world, the spiritual army of the evil in the heavens."* (Eph 6: 12-13)

St. Michael and His Appearances

The great prince of the heavenly court, St. Michael, who led the chosen people through the desert and who will, at the end of the world, destroy the Anti-Christ just as he did Satan, has appeared to people throughout history to protect and defend them from danger. We learn that he often accompanied St. Joan of Arc in battle and, "the Emperor Constantine, grateful for the victories gained over his enemies, which he attributed to the protection of St. Michael, built a magnificent church near Constantinople in honor of the Archangel which he called Michaelion. It became a place of pilgrimage, and many sick and infirm were cured in it by the intercession of the Archangel. Constantine's successors erected no less than fifteen churches in Constantinople itself to St. Michael."[2]

I drove a short distance to Mt. Gargano this morning, one of the most celebrated apparition sites of St. Michael, to see the sacred grotto and church dedicated to him. The drive reminded me of a scene out of an old John Wayne movie. It was an arid, mountainous area, with scant vegetation or animal life. It was a good road and a beautiful drive but I wondered what I would do if I got a flat tire because there was no one else on the road. I enjoyed the feeling of space and openness, and asked St. Michael, St. Raphael and my Guardian Angel to watch out for me.

This shrine of St. Michael the Archangel on Mt. Gargano "has been a sacred place since the days of Pope Gelasius (492-496). At that time St. Michael appeared in visible form in a cave in the mountainside and revealed to the local bishop that the mountain was under his special protection for the honor of God and of the Holy Angels. It was indeed providential that this shrine, which is practically the only notable one dedicated to the Holy Angels, is

Padre Pio had a great devotion to St. Michael whose grotto is situated only fourteen miles from San Giovanni Rotondo

situated but a short distance from Our Lady of Grace Friary in San Giovanni Rotondo. When Padre Pio came to live in this friary situated on the slopes of Mount Gargano he seemed to have an arrangement with the glorious Prince of the heavenly hosts. St. Michael would assist him in defeating Satan and his followers in the battleground for human souls, while Padre Pio would direct and encourage people to go to St. Michael for help in warding off the attacks of the evil one."[3]

His Sacred Grotto

The grotto is a carved-out area deep underground, the focal point of which is a raised altar, behind which stands St. Michael the Archangel, carved in white Carrara marble. He wields a golden sword with which he has slain a grotesque monster underfoot. There were some side chapels around the grotto, one of which contained a silver crucifix bearing a relic of the true cross donated by Frederick II. Another chapel was dedicated to St. Francis who made the trip to Monte San Angelo and, when he arrived, he felt unworthy to go into the grotto; he first carved a cross on a rock outside before entering.

Mass was about to begin. They sang my favorite, "Rest With Us, Don't Leave Us Lord." It was so familiar to me now, much the same as "Here I am, Lord" in America, and I welcomed it. I stayed afterwards to say the Rosary. I felt as if I had been personally introduced to St. Michael. I recommended my friends and family to his care and protection, asking him to bind and destroy the power of darkness and evil for each person and situation.

Meeting a Shepherd on the Road

On the drive back to San Giovanni Rotondo, I encountered a shepherd pasturing his sheep. Driving toward them I pulled over to take a picture. They were walking pretty fast, so I grabbed my camera, and zoomed in on them as they approached. A sheep dog started barking and came running toward me. He showed his teeth. I took one picture and ran back to the car, frightened to death. I even closed the windows because I was afraid he would jump through them! By then the shepherd caught up to me, obviously aware of what just happened. *"It looks like you were afraid. What were you afraid of?"* he said with such warmth and concern, I relaxed. "The dog," I said, "He showed his teeth." He assured me that he

The sheep dog is headed straight for me! *"Do not live in fear, little flock. It has pleased your Father to give you the kingdom."*
(Luke 13:32)

wouldn't hurt and that I had nothing to worry about. Just then a car approached, separating the shepherd from a lamb on the other side of the road. He made eye contact with the lamb, who was tentative and unsure of where to go and what to do, and he kept his eyes on him until the danger passed. *He reassured the lamb with his eyes, and held his gaze with such sensitivity.* It was a fleeting incident which spoke volumes to me; I saw Jesus in the action of the shepherd. If this shepherd is so focused in his care of animals, how much more attentive must Jesus be to the needs of His flock, the souls of men? This shepherd probably knew each one of his sheep intimately. Sheep are really quite dumb; they follow each other into danger. Our Good Shepherd, Jesus, knows exactly where we are on the journey and He's particularly sensitive to us during our times of trial, danger, sorrow, sickness, or desolation. He will not take His eyes off us. If one of us should become lost, He will go in search of us, leaving all the rest of the sheep in the desert until He finds us. Despite our guilt or fear or our running away, our Shepherd continues to seek us out. A shepherd is one with his animals. Jesus is one with His flock.

Jesus, Our Good Shepherd

I thought about this all the way back to San Giovanni Rotondo. I was so grateful for this experience, particularly for the insight into Christ's love and care for us. Jesus, our Good Shepherd, came to life in a new way, as did the Scripture verse: *"I myself will pasture my sheep; I myself will give them rest, says the Lord God. The lost I will seek out, the strayed I will bring back, the injured I will bind up, the sick I will heal. . . shepherding them rightly."* (Ez 34: 15-16) Just as a shepherd takes his flock out to pasture, so does Christ refresh the faithful with spiritual food, his own Body and Blood. *"The Good Shepherd gives his life for his sheep."* (John 10:11) That is why Jesus said that he would lay down His life for His sheep. His flock matters more to Him than His own life and when they are in danger, the Shepherd even will give His physical life to save them.

The Rosary, a Powerful Prayer

I remembered that today was the day I had a Mass offered in Florence for my children. It was just about time for that Mass to take place, so I went to church to say the Rosary and ask the Blessed Mother's intercession with her Son on their behalf. I once heard an Irish priest in Medjugorje give an inspired talk on the Rosary, saying it was the highest form of contemplative prayer. Praying it enables us to "lose" ourselves in Jesus' birth, death and resurrection, through the eyes and experience of His mother. What better way can we approach Jesus than through the heart of His mother? Our Lady has been recommending the Rosary to saints for centuries: to St. Catherine of Siena, St. Bernadette of Lourdes and to the three children of Fatima, promising salvation and graces to all who pray it. Recalling her first apparition of Our Lady of Lourdes, St. Bernadette recounted how Our Lady held the Rosary over her right arm and followed along the beads with her, joining in at the Gloria between decades. At Fatima, after the children had just completed saying a Rosary, they saw a "Lady dressed all in white, more brilliant than the sun." Her parting words were, *"My children, go on always saying the Rosary."*

On nearly every occasion that the Blessed Mother has appeared on earth, she has stressed devotion to the Rosary. She has increased her appeal for the Rosary to be said in the last fifteen years especially, through her appearances at Medjugorje and in so many other countries around the world. In one of her many messages to the visionaries in Medjugorje, she said: "My *children, I urge you to ask everyone to pray the Rosary. With the Rosary you will overcome all the troubles which Satan is trying to inflict on the world. Give time to the Rosary."* (June 25, 1985) The Blessed Mother has given so many specific messages about the need to fight Satan. In a message given to the visionaries on July 25th, 1993 she said:

> *Dear Children, I thank you for your prayers and for the love you show toward me. I invite you to decide to pray for my intentions. Dear children, offer novenas, making sacrifices wherein you feel the most bound. I want your life to be bound to me. I am your mother, little children, and I do not want Satan to deceive you, for he wants to lead you the wrong way. But he cannot if you don't permit him. Therefore, little children, renew prayer in your hearts and then you will understand my call and my live desire to help you. Thank you for having responded to my call.*[4]

Healing through the Rosary

I only began saying the Rosary several years ago; it helps me appreciate the mysteries of Christ's life. It is so powerful to pray this way. It takes my mind off myself long enough to focus on Jesus and His life. *Focusing on*

Him is healing. Jesus tells us, *"Unless you become as a little child you cannot enter the kingdom of heaven."* (Matthew 18: 3) The Rosary allows us to become that child; by praying the mysteries we let go of ourselves and become intimate with Jesus and Mary, our real parents. Our intimacy with them opens us to grace, which empowers us to change and grow in virtue. I enjoy the thought that, when a child needs something, he or she will often go to its mother first, because every child knows that the quickest way to get what it wants from the father is through the mother! I take that one step further: the quickest way to God's heart is through the heart of His mother.

Padre Pio clutched his beads morning, noon and night, saying many Rosaries daily and urging everyone to pray it in order to "empty Purgatory." Jesus and Our Lady often appeared to Padre Pio and on one occasion he describes her physical presence as she accompanied him to the altar for Mass: *"With what care she accompanied me to the altar this morning! It seemed to me as though she had nothing to think about other than filling my heart completely with saintly affections. . . . !"* [5]

A Fellow Friar Remembers Padre Pio

I was getting to know my way around Our Lady of Grace church very well. After Benediction I went to the sacristy in search of Father Joseph Pio, a namesake of Padre Pio's whom a friend suggested I contact. From Brooklyn, New York, he came to Italy on a business trip as a young man and was introduced to Padre Pio. He returned to have another meeting with Padre Pio, who asked him to stay, saying he would become a priest. That was in 1964. He knew Padre Pio when he was mostly withdrawing from the world, when he was beginning his process of separation and death, when his suffering was probably the most difficult.

He spoke of him with such genuine affection, I had the feeling he had been like a father to him. He said Padre Pio was a mystery; he lost a cup of blood per day from his stigmata, had only about three hours of sleep per night, and doctors said that Padre Pio didn't eat enough to keep a four year old child alive. Yet he wasn't anemic nor did he lose weight. Father Joseph Pio said he saw his wounds on his hands and chest and he saw the suffering, the pain the man lived with, especially during Mass when he suffered the crucifixion. It's a wonder he could function after undergoing what he did. But Fr. Pio said he had a wonderful sense of humor and he was such a warm, happy and joyful person. He had the true peace and joy of the Lord. Whatever Padre Pio did, he did in the light of his priestly ministry; so that if he took a nap, it was only in order to prepare himself for his Confessions. Everything he did was for the purpose of serving the Lord and saving souls.

His Mission Was to Save Souls

"Are we all meant to suffer like this, or was Padre Pio especially called?" I asked. Yes, he was especially called, he thought. Father Pio referred to the inner locution and vision which Pope Leo XIII had in 1884 in which Satan and Christ spoke and Christ gave Satan unbridled power over the 20th century.[6] We are living in those times now, an age of apostasy, of great unbelief, in which Satan is working overtime to spread his lies and destruction. It seems God has always raised up great saints during the darkest periods of human history in order to combat the adversary. Padre Pio helped win millions of souls for Christ during his lifetime.

A week before he entered the novitiate, Padre Pio celebrated his 15th birthday. When he was meditating one day wondering how he could bring himself to say good-by to the world and dedicate himself to God in a friary, he had a vision in which he found himself in a meadow standing between some very beautiful people and some dark and dangerous people. Among the latter there was a monstrous, evil giant whom Padre Pio knew he would have to fight. He was so afraid he wanted to run away, when a guide stepped forward from among the beautiful people. The guide gently confirmed that he would have to fight the monster but the guide promised to stay at his side and help him. With that, the monster attacked Padre Pio. They fought. With the help of the guide, he overcame the monster who fled amidst shouting, cursing and deafening cries.

Padre Pio Battles Satan

Some days later Padre Pio understood the vision to mean that by entering religious life and dedicating himself entirely to God, he was exposing himself to a continuous conflict with Satan and his cohorts. But he had nothing to fear for the good angels would ever be present to help him in his battles. The person who acted as his guide was Jesus Himself. As time went on, the struggle would become more and more intense, the temptations more subtle and stronger. God would even allow the devil to physically manhandle him. But in his role as victim for the salvation of souls, the more he suffered the more effective he was in snatching souls away from the domination of Satan and opening them up to the saving power of Christ. The dream was prophetic; Padre Pio battled with Satan his entire life.

"In many of his letters to his spiritual director, he would mention apparitions, persecutions, trials, provocations and fierce assaults from the devil and his satellites, who gave him neither respite nor rest. He wrote that he was tormented day and night with angry aggressions, deathly beatings and iron weapons."[7] Satan tried to trick Padre Pio by appearing at his door dressed as his spiritual director. One night he came and told Padre Pio to stop saying the Rosary and doing so much penance; he needed a rest. Padre Pio was suspicious and said to his "spiritual director," "*Say praise be the name of Jesus Christ!*" At the mention of *Jesus Christ*, the apparition vanished and left a terrible stench of sulphur in the room. In one of the many recorded instances of his bouts with Satan, Padre Pio was hurt so badly, he couldn't say Mass for a week.

> "Sunday, July 5, 1964, 10 P.M. 'Help me! Help me!' This was the cry that was followed by a heavy thump that shook the floor. The Padre was found by his confreres face down on the floor, bleeding from the forehead and the nose, with a serious wound on the right eyebrow, that required two stitches. Unexplainable fall! That day the Padre had passed in front of a possessed woman, from the town of Bergamo. The following day, the devil, through the mouth of this possessed woman, admitted that at 10 P.M. the preceding day "he had been to visit someone. . . he had sought vengeance. . .this way he will learn for another time. . ." The Padre's swollen face showed the signs of the violent struggle with the devil, which, in fact, was almost uninterrupted during his entire earthly existence."[8]

We Must Fight Satan Daily

The battle we are fighting and that Padre Pio fought is for the salvation of souls. The battle has already been fought by Christ who has won over the power of darkness and evil. "Spiritual warfare is the effort we exercise to walk in the Light of Christ. . . It is a constant battle between eternal reality (which is God, in His holy and triune form) and temporal reality (which is the world in which we live and the lures of Satan). It is a battle which takes place in every moment of every day with every breath we take. We must realize that we cannot escape this battle. It wages within every human heart and soul. . . The battle between rampant self-indulgence and self-sacrifice. "*. . . if you are guided by the Spirit you will be in no danger of yielding to* *self-indulgence, since self-indulgence is the opposite of the Spirit, the Spirit is totally against such a thing, and it is precisely because the two are opposed that you do not always carry out your good intentions."* (Galatians 5: 16-17) To be victorious. . .we must learn how to keep our every thought, deed, action, and word centered in Christ Jesus. . .Unless we are people of intense prayer we cannot survive the onslaught of attacks (temptations in thought, action, word, and/or trials) that we undergo in any given day."[9]

Blessed by Father Joseph Pio

Before leaving I asked Father Joseph Pio about all my tears. He nodded with understanding and said he thought it was probably grace acting in my soul through the intercession of Padre Pio. When I mentioned about Padre Pio looking like my dad, he said Padre Pio probably was healing my grief over the loss of my dad. Then he told me that Bob and Penny Lord were arriving in San Giovanni tomorrow afternoon. How unfortunate that I had to leave for Rome tomorrow. I would love to be able to stay and meet them because their book, *"This Is My Body, This Is My Blood, Miracles of the Eucharist,"* has been one of my guides to the Eucharistic miracles. The Lord is using them powerfully in opening peoples hearts to experience God's love for us in the Holy Eucharist and in the lives of Saints. Father Pio took one of Padre Pio's fingerless gloves which he wore to cover his stigmata wound and blessed me with it. As he did so, the power of the Spirit was so strong I nearly fell backward in a faint. *Thank you Padre Pio, and thank you Jesus, for the gift of Your presence, so loving and healing!*

Can I Follow Christ the Way He Wants?

Tonight was especially beautiful. Leaving St. Mary of Grace Church there was more of a breeze than usual; it was wonderful. I looked forward to dinner because by now my stomach was running on "empty." My encounter with Father Joseph Pio left me feeling unsettled. I think it has something to do with seeing your shadow when you're standing in someone's light. I feel unworthy, full of ego and imperfection in contrast to Padre Pio who was so purified and full of light. I'm such a beginner on that climb up the mountain of perfection, just barely asking the question: *Am I willing to die to myself? Am I really willing to love Christ the way He wants to be loved? Am I really willing to offer Him total submission? And if I am, how do I do that?* Padre Pio counsels:

> *"The field of battle between God and Satan is the human soul. It is in the soul that the battle rages every moment of life. The souls must give free access to the Lord so that it be fortified by Him in every respect and with all kinds of weapons; that his light may enlighten it to combat the darkness of error; that it be clothed with Jesus Christ, with his justice, truth, the shield of faith, the world of God, in order to conquer such powerful enemies. To be clothed with Jesus Christ it is necessary to die to oneself."[10]*

I feel surrounded by mystery and I can't really see my way very clearly. While lying on the bed reading, something Padre Pio wrote in one of his letters consoled me: "The darkness that sometimes surrounds the heaven of your soul is light. Because of this you think you are in the dark and you have the impression of being in the center of a burning bush. In fact, when the bush burns, the air around it is filled with smoke and clouds, and the bewildered soul is afraid of not seeing, of no longer understanding anything. But it is then that God speaks and is present to the soul who hears, understands, loves and trembles. Therefore, do not wait for Tabor to see God when you already contemplate Him on Sinai."[11]

Scripture Meditation

"Put God's armor on so as to be able to resist the devil's tactics. For it is not against human enemies that we have to struggle, but against the Sovereignties and the Powers who originate the darkness in this world, the spiritual army of the evil in the heavens." (Ephesians 6: 11-13)

Dear Lord Jesus,

You have told us to be meek as doves and wise as serpents. The enemy prowls about like a roaring lion, seeking to hurt us in any way he can. The more we are aware of him and his tactics, the more power we have to defeat him by naming him and sending him to the foot of Your cross. Jesus, help me to be constantly alert to his lies, manipulation and deceit, especially his negative spirits which lodge themselves in my conscious and unconscious mind like a fungus, seeking to enslave me. Please cover me in Your Precious Blood Jesus, and with St. Michael and his allies surround us, our families, our friends, our Church, our country, and our world, with Your protection.

20

Rome

I couldn't decide how I wanted to spend my one and only day in the Eternal City. My heart was already on its way home and I was running on reserve tanks of energy. It was 110 degrees in Rome and I didn't feel like sightseeing. In a section marked "Additional Suggestions" in my Michelin Guide, a Basilica named "Saint Sabina" caught my eye. I didn't have the faintest idea who St. Sabina was, but as soon as I saw it, I knew I wanted to investigate; Sabina was my mother's name.

The Basilica was not easy to find; it was in an old section of town clear across the city. On my way there I became excited. I wondered if my mother had been named after this saint. I wondered why I cared so much all of a sudden. I hadn't thought of my mother a great deal. Although I hadn't been close to her, since her death I've cried a lot of tears over the breach between us, the deprivation we both experienced due to our lack of communication and closeness.

Painful Memories of My Mother

I was married and had four children when I saw "One Flew Over the Cuckoo's Nest" for the first time. The pain was so wrenching I couldn't stop crying. The scenes in which they showed shock treatments opened up memories of my mother pleading with me not to let them give her shock treatments when she went to the hospital. I was in high school and trying to cope with my mother's problems in a very clinical, detached way. I thought shock treatments were great because they always brought her back to reality, so I tried to silence her "hysterical" cries rather than really listen to her and help her. The movie gave me my first realization of the horror of those shock treatments and what suffering she endured. I cried years' worth of tears for my mother's pain, which I buried while she was alive, and for my own selfishness and coldness as a daughter. When I had my own children I was able to taste the pain of rejection she must have experienced from me; I couldn't bear to think of how difficult it would be if one of my children behaved toward me as I did to my mother.

Bathed in Love and Forgiveness

Some years ago on a charismatic retreat given by Barbara Shlemon Ryan, I went back to my seat after I was anointed with oil and began to sob from some deep place of pain inside of me. An elderly woman sitting next to me put her arm around me. *I welcomed her love as if she were my mother.* I folded myself into her warm embrace and rested my head on the nape of her neck. My lips were just about touching her face. While I was crying, the affection I never received from my mother came to me through this woman. She was a complete stranger but, at that moment, Jesus used her to fill my empty heart with my own mother's love. I felt like an infant cradled in the arms of its mother, something I never remember experiencing in real life. Jesus' healing was like a cleansing; I felt bathed in love. He healed me of the terrible hate and bitterness I felt toward my mother which I had allowed to build up for so many years. I was able to forgive my mother for her inability to mother me in the ways that I wanted and needed. In time, the Lord showed me that I had to forgive myself for the ways I reacted to the pain and problems at home. I asked Jesus to help me forgive the both of us, and His healing still continues to this day, many years later. In place of all the negative emotions there came new love for her, new warmth, new appreciation for her gifts, new understanding of her problems and empathy for her pain. God was mercifully replacing my old stony heart with a new one that was stronger in the ways of love. *"I will sprinkle clean water upon you to cleanse you from all your impurities, and from all your idols I will cleanse you. I will give you a new heart and place a new spirit within you, taking from your bodies your stony hearts and giving you natural hearts."* (Ez 36: 25-26)

Standing on Early Christian Turf

As we approached Saint Sabina's Basilica, I couldn't help but notice the street names: Via Santa Sabina, Via Priscilla, Via Aquila, names dating back to the first and second centuries. Aquila and his wife Priscilla were early converts who earned their living by making tents. They probably lived in this old section of the city along with St. Peter and a growing Christian community. Scripture tells us that they met up with St. Paul in Greece, where they went about preaching the Gospel with him.

"Aquinas Hides out at St. Sabina's!"

The basilica was constructed during the period of barbarian invasions and the destruction of ancient Rome, around the year 422. It stands today mostly unchanged from its original construction. Its existence was due to the vision and labors, as well as of the wealth, of one Peter of Illyria. He was a priest belonging to the diocese of Rome who decorated and consecrated this church as he did that of St. Mary Major, built about the same time. As Sts. Jerome and Peter were both Illyrians, this would no doubt help to explain the choice of the site for this church.

I was fascinated to learn that, in the thirteenth century, St. Thomas Aquinas hid out in St. Sabina's from his angry mother who was pursuing him to persuade him to return home. She wanted him to join the Benedictines, probably hoping that he'd become the abbot of Monte Cassino. Instead, he joined the Dominicans, a mendicant order of preachers. When she arrived at St. Sabina Basilica, she was bitterly disappointed to find out he and some friars had already left. What lengths some mothers go to in order to control the lives of their children! Even St. Thomas Aquinas struggled in his relationship with his mother.

I was amused at the thought of St. Thomas Aquinas sneaking around the massive pillars inside this enormous basilica trying to hide from his mother! This had to be the largest church I've ever been in; the sheer volume alone was awesome. It was classic in its proportions and simplicity and all around the perimeter on the ceiling were large arched windows which let in great amounts of light. One of the artistic treasures are the original doors of the basilica. It is considered somewhat of a miracle that they have been preserved to this day. They're hand-carved dark cypress wood depicting scenes from the life of Christ. I felt so at home when I came upon an altar to St. Catherine of Siena and to St. Francis — my new friends whom I love so much.

St. Sabina's Bones under the Altar

Then I found an unexpected treasure. Under the main altar lie the bones of Sts. Sabina and Seraphia, who were martyred about the year 125 under the emperor Hadrian. Seraphia was a Christian from Antioch, a close friend and quite possibly a servant friend of Sabina, a widow of noble family. It was from Seraphia that Sabina received her introduction to the Christian faith. Both were accused of being Christians, but the local prefect, while condemning Seraphia to be beaten to death, hesitated at first to proceed against a lady of noble lineage. Sabina accompanied her friend to her execution and afterwards buried the body of the martyr in the tomb she had prepared for herself. Eventually Sabina was also condemned to death. She was beheaded on August 29 and was buried with her friend.

I approached the main altar and knelt in front of their tomb. I automatically loved St. Sabina. That familiar vulnerability surfaced. I was mysteriously being drawn into the life of this saint, and through her, to my mother. I knelt there for a long time. God must have brought me here. I never intended to look up St. Sabina and now I felt so graced, so blessed in knowing about her.

Remembering My Mother's Suffering

I pictured her as a young convert. She obviously had a lot of courage to be executed for her faith. I found myself thanking her for giving so totally of herself—for being a martyr. Then I thought of my mother, another kind of martyr. She really suffered so much in her life; physically, mentally and emotionally and especially in her unhappy marriage. She was trapped inside a broken heart, unable to find an outlet. Except her piano. Her music was an outlet of sorts. She played the piano with her soul, releasing her pain through Chopin, Mozart, Beethoven, Liszt and Rachmaninoff. She never realized her dream of becoming a concert pianist. Before she died, she was so physically sick and she'd say, "I don't know, but God must have a reason for this suffering." I know now that her suffering was not in vain.

My mother lived her purgatory on earth. I sensed the reward she was experiencing, the "concert" she was giving in heaven. A concert filled with peace and joy and love, which was falling down on me now in this church bearing her name. In rare memories of happy times, I do remember how deeply she smiled and how gracious and hospitable she was to others.

Feeling My Mother's Presence through St. Sabina

I took a picture of the tomb and sat in one of the choir stalls to await Mass. The priest walked over and presented me with a little holy card of St. Sabina. I thanked him and cried. I can't explain it; I felt my mother's presence and perhaps the presence of St. Sabina. I don't know, but I felt so loved by my mother, with a love that I had never really enjoyed, love that I had never allowed.

The gifts on this pilgrimage keep coming, even on the last day. This is the icing on the cake. During Mass a man played a flute giving a heavenly, ethereal sound. I closed my eyes and savored being in the Basilica of St. Sabina almost more than I appreciated being anywhere. What a gift this was to connect with my mother and now with another new friend, St. Sabina. I prayed to both of them and asked them to watch over my brother. On this very day he was entering the hospital for tests in New Jersey. I gave them charge over him; how fitting that they look after him. My mother loved my brother so much. He was her firstborn son and I knew the warmth in her heart for Howie. She is loving him from heaven and will watch over and care for him as only a mother can. I offered my intentions at Mass for my brother's family and mine. If anyone would intercede before the throne of God for us it would be our mother! I had to keep my face cupped in my hands during Mass because I couldn't stop crying.

Grateful Prayers in St. Peter's

The taxi dropped me off at St. Peter's and I must say it felt good to be there again. Like coming home. I found my way to the chapel reserved for Perpetual Adoration of the Blessed Sacrament, which Pope John Paul II opened for the laity in 1981. Known for his deep devotion to the Holy Eucharist, he has been reported to spend entire nights in his private chapel sometimes prostrate before the Blessed Sacrament in prayer. I said the Chaplet of Divine Mercy, placing the needs and intentions of all the people I carried in my heart in the Heart of Jesus.

I reread the sixth chapter of John's gospel in which Jesus gives His Bread of Life discourse. His words meant even more to me now that I had witnessed His flesh and blood Presence through so many Eucharistic miracles. *"I am the bread of life,"* Jesus told them. *"He who comes to me will never be hungry; he who believes in me will never be thirsty. . . . I am telling you the truth: if you do not eat the flesh of the Son of Man and drink his blood, you will not have life in yourselves. Whoever eats my flesh and drinks my blood has eternal life and I will raise him to life on the last day. For my flesh is real food: my blood is real drink. Whoever eats my flesh and drinks my blood lives in me and I live in him."* (John 6: 35, 53-57) When the crowds started walking away because the teaching was too hard, He turned to his twelve saying, *"And you, would you also like to leave?"* (John 6: 67)

Lord, I Want To Witness to You!

"No, Lord, I would not like to leave," I prayed. "I want to hang in there and help spread the word that You are really present in the Holy Eucharist, Your Body, Blood, Soul and Divinity, and that You hunger for our faith in You. Nothing pleases You more than our faith, period." I felt such joy bubble up in me when I thought of sharing all I had seen with others. *Nothing will give me greater joy than to witness to the Real Presence of Jesus in the Holy Eucharist!* On my way out of the Vatican I did a double take as I walked past the statue of St. Longinus, another old friend! *I had just been in his hometown, Lanciano, the site of the oldest miracle of the Eucharist.* Suddenly I felt connected to the entire world.

Alone in the Flesh But Not in Spirit

Tonight while packing my suitcase for the last time, I was reflecting on how alone I've been for almost three weeks. It hasn't really bothered me, but for one moment tonight I felt really alone. On this trip I've been alone in the flesh, so to speak, but in the spirit I've walked in the company of saints. I feel a new connection to my mother and my father. This morning's visit to St. Sabina put me in touch with my mother in such an intimate way. It's almost as if I had a brief meeting with her. The walls continue to come down, enabling love and healing to flow between us.

Memories of My Dad's Welcome

For some reason memories of my father were surfacing now, specific memories of the many times Daddy welcomed me home when I came to New York to nurse him back to health after his radiation treatments for throat cancer. When I opened the apartment door, Daddy would rise from his chair, smile, and raise his voice in a high-pitched greeting, *"Joanie!"* He said my name with such delight and anticipation of being with me that it used to make me giggle. I was always surprised by it because I couldn't imagine why he'd be so glad to see me. Even if I'd call him on the phone from Chicago unexpectedly, there'd be that same high-pitched welcoming response to my 'hello': *"Joanie!"* I was thinking now about how much that meant to me. I never thought it meant anything when it was happening, but now in this hotel room in Rome I can hear him greeting me with such gladness in his voice, delighting in my presence. I've thought of him a great deal over here, especially through Padre Pio. It's like I've also had a visit with my dad. He's become so real, so alive. My spirit attests to my parents' presence; I sense them trying to reassure me of their love and their continuing care for me, especially tonight when I'm feeling so alone.

Our Heavenly Parents

If I can feel the love of my earthly parents so much, how much more is the love of my heavenly parents for me, for us. I think that when we come before the Lord in prayer, He says our name with gladness in His voice. He delights in our presence! Our Lord and our Blessed Mother yearn to give us all the things our human parents can't. They are our real spiritual family, ordained by God to watch over and care for our deepest needs. Not only do they know what we need, they can give us whatever it is that will bring us more fully into God's will for our lives — whether it be a job or a mate or a new house or food on our table; they are there for us 24 hours a day. They can heal us of all our hurts, and re-parent us in the ways our earthly parents couldn't. When we approach them I can imagine how they welcome us and delight in our presence. *"You are precious in my eyes, and glorious, and I love you. . ."* (Isaiah 43: 4), says the Lord. Our earthly parents are but a faint reflection of the unconditional love of our heavenly parents, Our Lord and our Blessed Mother.

How Well You Treat Us, Daddy God

How loved and cared for are we, as God's children and members of His Mystical Body.

> *"For you did not receive a spirit of slavery to fall back into fear, but you received a spirit of adoption, through which we cry, Abba, 'Father!' The Spirit itself bears witness with our spirit that we are children of God, and if children, then heirs, heirs of God and joint heirs with Christ, if only we suffer with*

him so that we may also be glorified with him." (Rom 8:15−17)

We are watched over, guided, sustained and nurtured. As people of faith, we live in this world, but are not of it. We belong to the spirit world of the saints and of Our Lord and Our Lady and ultimately, to God, our Father, who the friars in Assisi address as "Daddy God." Though Jesus called God "Abba," meaning "Daddy," and urges us to do so as well, I think God embodies both male and female attributes. Many times in both the Old and New Testament, feminine images are used to describe God. We are His precious children and He treats us with the strong, faithful, masculine love of a father and with the sensitive and compassionate love of a mother. In addition to this, Jesus gave us His own mother, to mediate God's love to us as only a mother can.

El Greco's The Dead Christ in the arms of God the Father

Scripture Meditation

"While he was still a long way off, his father caught sight of him, and was filled with compassion. He ran to His son, embraced him and kissed him." *(Luke 16: 20)*

Dear Lord Jesus,
Even though I've wandered away from You and sinned against You, when I come home, You come running to meet me! As soon as You see me, You call my name and raise Your voice in welcome, throwing open Your arms to embrace me. I love you Father! I come to You like a child, needing the comfort and security of Your love. Please hold my hand and keep me by Your side, never letting me stray from You.

21

Going Home

Somewhere over the Atlantic I realized I was flying home on the feast of St. Clare of Assisi. I couldn't have been happier if someone told me I just won the lottery! She might as well have been sitting next to me on the plane, I felt so warmed by her friendship.

I was excited to be going home but the trip was painfully long and would have tried the patience of Job. It was like an endurance contest lasting 24 hours, door to door. Due to bad weather on the East Coast, we were rerouted to Bangor, Maine, where we landed around 6 P.M. — which was 1 A.M. Italian time. We filled the waiting room where we sat like refugees in a holding camp, until the middle of the night. Nothing could shake my peace though, including the long line at the cafeteria. It was worth waiting for a cheeseburger and fries and a wonderful cup of American coffee.

Flying Home On Inner Joy

I flew home on an inner cloud of joy, so grateful for my new relationships with the saints, for a deeper appreciation of Jesus in His Eucharistic Presence, for the healing, the tears, the dreams, the insights, and the direction I received on this pilgrimage. Too excited to sleep, I stared out the window enjoying every bit of the starlit night. A magnificent full moon illuminated the earth below, giving a clear view of sleeping New England towns. It was so good to be *home*, to be back in America. I felt new appreciation for my country, for our beautiful land, for our natural resources, and for the creativity, intelligence, ingenuity and efficiency of American people. I realized how I take for granted all the benefits and comforts that we enjoy.

Dreams – The X-Rays of My Soul!

I had plenty of time to review the entries in my journal to reflect on what my dreams had told me. The 911 dream was the most powerful, showing me the poisonous residue of negative emotions stored in the basement of my subconscious. These dreams had shown me my shadow, that part of myself which I hated and hid from view, which was now clamoring for acceptance. In one, a woman who wandered off from her community was sick and in need of a doctor. In another, a depressed and angry woman took sick all of a sudden and just disappeared from the scene. These reflected the sinful, separated part of me who needed to seek forgiveness and repent of my "disappearance" and forgive—myself and others. By failing to acknowledge this other part of me who swallowed so much fear and shame, I actually fueled her negative feelings. One "trigger" was usually enough to ignite the rage, just waiting to explode. No wonder my dreams were telling me I was sick and angry. I was literally a house divided against itself.

In Italy God was pouring His grace into those hard, dried crevices of my unconscious, watering my soul with tears. Being in the presence of Jesus in the Blessed Sacrament so much was to absorb His healing love—just by sitting there. Much like sitting in the sun and getting a tan, you can't escape the rays of the Son's love when You are in His presence. Through the "Bermuda shorts" episode, I believe God wanted to heal the shame I was feeling down deep, the feeling of not being good enough or not measuring up to others' standards. Unless and until that "old self" is dealt with, I will continue to be in pain and I will continue to suffer from bondage which keep me from giving and receiving love.

Sin and Spiritual Sickness

There were several dreams involving priests, both of whom represent parts of myself that I don't like. These wounded masculine sides of myself were hard things to face, but my dreams weren't lying. They were helping me see where I was broken and hurting. They were leading me to see that cold, arrogant and unforgiving part of myself which keeps others at a distance. By separating myself from others, I was also separating myself from God. Sin is really sickness in our soul which separates us from our own truth and therefore from God who is Truth; it prevents us from loving ourselves and others. One of the great gifts Jesus gave me was to show me my need for repentance. He made me realize that repentance is a daily process, a daily emptying of the ways I have failed to love and obey the Lord. I saw the connection between sin and sickness and how we block God's love in us by living with unrepented sin. When we are willing to acknowledge our sin and seek His forgiveness, God just pours His healing into those damaged roots, restoring our spiritual health. One of our great evangelists, Father John Bertolucci, tells us that repentance is like good medicine—it heals us. Unrepented sin can lie at the root of our physical sickness and can create an obstacle to receiving God's love.

Nurses and Doctors of the Soul

In the beginning of the pilgrimage, I prayed asking the Lord to "deliver me from myself." He answered my prayer—first, by delivering me into the hands of people who have been like nurses and doctors of the soul. I've had an apprenticeship in their schools; they've taught me new attitudes and have inspired me to develop new spiritual muscles. The saints have worked out in their spiritual gyms, training for the long race to which St. Paul refers. The equipment they used was sacrifice, truthfulness, humility, prayer and fasting, generosity, suffering, trust, endurance, faith. I've also had the opportunity to sit at the feet of the Master Himself, especially in His Eucharistic Presence. To be bathed in so much love and light causes us to be cleansed of our darkness. In Italy God was showing me that part of myself which was lost and broken and in need of His healing love. *"Whoever finds his life will lose it and whoever loses his life for my sake will find it."* (Matt. 10: 39) Jesus can gift us with new life when we're ready to surrender control and let Him lead us.

New Love for My Husband

There were a few dreams about marriage and marriages that don't work out right. In a dream about divorce, a woman said to me, "You aren't expecting your husband to change, are you? If you are, you better forget it, because he'll never come to accept this like you want." I slapped her across the face! At a deep level I didn't want to hear that. I wanted my husband to change, I wanted him to be the problem in our marriage, not me.

In Italy I was given new eyes to see the depth of my husband's goodness and my own inability to be truthful and up front with my needs and feelings. I felt new hope and strength in coming out of hiding with my feelings, and a desire to stop protecting him from my negative feelings. The Lord was removing my spiritual blindness by showing me that while I was trying to remove the

Tom and Joan happily reunited

splinter in my husband's eye, I had to first remove the wooden beam in my own eye: *"How can you say to your brother, 'Let me remove that splinter from your eye,' while the wooden beam is in your eye? You hypocrite, remove the wooden beam from your eye first; then you will see clearly to remove the splinter from your brother's eye."* (Matt. 7: 4-6)

Pain and the Cross

I'm grateful for my new understanding of pain and the cross. The cross is everything because it brings us to Jesus. Without it, we don't find Him. Suffering is a mystery. We think "Why should God treat me like this? What have I done wrong to deserve this?" No matter how deeply we believe in God, we ask those questions in moments of anguish and suffering. Even in the secular world, the cross is used to honor war heroes. We award soldiers for their gallantry by "decorating" them with crosses, which in different countries are named the Service Cross, the Victoria Cross, the War Cross and so forth. And in the spiritual world God also gifts His heroes and heroines with a cross. We usually don't think of it as a gift—our crosses come in forms we would not choose ourselves—marriage problems, relationship struggles, illness, financial difficulties—yet by embracing those trials we will find God. St. Thomas Aquinas said he learned more from the crucifix than from all the books of theology he read. It was usually a cross through which Jesus spoke to the saints or gave them the stigmata, and it's through that same cross that Jesus presents Himself to us. I met some of God's heroes and heroines in Italy who inspired me by the way they carried their crosses and embraced pain. They renewed my courage to do the same. We want to live a resurrected life without dying—and it's not possible.

> Oscar Wilde said, 'Each man kills the thing he loves.' Those who stop short of evil in themselves will never know what love is about. They will never receive the crucified. . . Man's self-hatred is not only the obstacle to his acceptance of God's love. It is the medium in which God's love is revealed to him as it transforms it. I meet God's love not by turning away from the hatred of myself to another motif, but as a climax of my self-hatred, its crisis and resolution. God does not just give me a reason not to hate myself. He transforms my self-hatred into love. That is the meaning of the cross.[1]

When St. Francis had the vision of Jesus' Passion and Crucifixion, it filled him up so totally with love and compassion for Jesus, there was no room left in him for self, let alone self-hatred. The cross and Jesus are inseparable. They are Love.

My appreciation for the Mass and the Eucharist has grown by leaps and bounds. The awesome gift of Christ's Presence is made available to us on every altar and in every tabernacle in the world. By uniting with Him in the sacrifice of the Mass, *He gives us a way to crucify ourselves with Him,* to redeem our lives by offering them to the Father through Jesus. *A prayer of infinite merit!* To attend Mass is to surrender, to empty ourselves, to die to ourselves, so that we can have the life Jesus promised His followers.

Reunion with Katie

My daughter, Katie, came to stay for a few days, and while we were sitting on my bed I showed her all the souvenirs I had collected. While I talked non-stop about one experience after another, Katie asked if I had met any people on the trip. *"Met any people! Did I ever meet people, Katie!" "Who, Mom?" "Oh, I met tons of people. . .they're the most wonderful people you can imagine. . .they're dead now, but they're really still alive: St. Clare, St. Francis, St. Rita, St. Catherine of Siena, Padre Pio. . . .!" "Ohhhhhhh, Mom,"* she giggled and fell back on the bed in amused disbelief. My children have a low tolerance for my religious zeal and resist all my efforts at evangelization. I try to respect their need to find their own path and when I don't they let me know it! I love them more than life itself and thought of them constantly in Italy. Now I could hardly wait for a reunion with my sons who were in Canada with their dad, fishing, and would be home in two days.

Witness Ministries is Born

Imagine that I went to Italy to receive an enormous gift from God which I opened during my pilgrimage. *The trip was only the top layer of the gift!* The pilgrimage laid the groundwork for a new apostolate which took shape day by day. I used the *Witness* logo from the magazine I once published and named my new work: *Witness Ministries—An Apostolate to Foster Devotion to the Real Presence of Jesus Christ in the Holy Eucharist.* Through the medium of slide presentations, videos, books and pamphlets, my wish is to bring people into a deeper awareness of this great Sacrament of Love. *"You will be My witnesses. . .to the ends of the earth!"* (Acts 1: 8) Jesus said. I feel as if He has personally commissioned me to spread the Good News about what I have seen and heard. I want to go around like the saints and show everyone how REAL Christ is, how present He is in our world, especially through the Mass and the Eucharist. He relies on our generosity and our energy to wake up the world to His reality. This desire to witness to His Real Presence impels me daily—to write, create, and speak about the love Jesus has for us in the Holy Eucharist. I spent the better part of a summer writing *Feast of Faith*, which seemed like it was writing itself because of the enthusiasm I had to work on it.

I have been giving slide presentations for small and large prayer groups, for people in nursing homes, for entire parishes, for Ministers of Care. Father Joe Whalen, a cherished friend, invited me to St. James parish in Danielson, Connecticut to present the program to his parishioners. From there we went to Father Ed McDonough's *Healing and*

Restoration Ministry in Watertown, Mass., where a Healing Mass followed the presentation. Hundreds of people were set on fire with new love for Our Eucharistic Lord. Each night the Holy Spirit filled us with His presence, gifting everyone with a sense of His love and peace. On another night we went to St. Ambrose parish in Dorchester where Father Vincent Von Euw held Adoration of the Blessed Sacrament. He allowed us to kiss the container which held the Sacred Host. What a special outpouring of love and healing there was that night, as people came with such open hearts to be anointed during a healing service. It has been an extraordinary gift for me to witness the deep love people have for our Eucharistic Lord—*and His love for them.* People are so hungry for Jesus, and they want to touch the hem of His garment. I watch in awe and with tears to see and feel His presence so deeply.

Marriage Problems

Contrary to my expectations, and despite all the graces and gifts we received in Italy, in the ensuing months after my return home, I was not free from emotional pain, especially in my marriage. In fact, the pain seemed to intensify. At times, something would happen between us which would cause me to sink into a black hole where I would anguish for hours, sometimes days. All the prayers, tears, dreams and insights in Italy were a preparation for the spiritual surgery God was planning for me.

One weekend our youngest child flew to California to visit Santa Clara University. With less than a year before he would leave home for good, I grieved as if he had already left and dreaded the prospect of being an empty nester. Like the woman in my dreams in Italy, I felt lonely and abandoned, a tinder box of emotions just waiting to ignite. "I seem to realize that this pain in the relationship has been there since before we were married," I wrote in my journal. I recalled a time near our wedding when I felt this pain and spent a sleepless night struggling with fear and a desire to end the relationship. Tommy had reneged on a commitment to meet at our new apartment, without explaining why. I felt dismissed and abandoned. Over the years I have felt that anguish so much. In the last two to three years it has gotten stronger. Using the example of St. Catherine of Siena's four petitions in "The Dialogue," I relied on every ounce of faith I had and asked God the following questions: 1) should I separate from Tommy and if so, how? 2) Is the pain due to the dysfunctional relationship or is it due to my own wounds which needs healing? 3) How can I put out the fires of repulsion, dread, fear, disgust, disappointment and anger which rage inside of me and are often triggered by my husband's behavior? 4) What is the way to your peace? *Jesus, God, I beg You to answer me. Please.*

Coming Out of Denial

At a retreat in Pecos, New Mexico, given by Dennis and Sheila Linn, Fr. Matt Linn S.J., and Fr. Jack McGinnis, more light was shed on this dark painful area. Entitled "Belonging: Bonds of Healing and Recovery," the retreat focused on recovering our true selves by exploring how our sense of belonging may have been damaged and how it can be restored. During one of the talks I began to realize how sexually abused I was as a child, both through the experience I had with uncle Jim when I was twelve and through emotional incest. Sheila's talk loosened the hard scab of denial which had covered the wounds. I saw my own desperate attempts to adapt to my father's needs and desires as a result of my own need to be loved and nurtured. Fearful of being abandoned, I became emotionally responsible for him and stood in the gap, so to speak, trying to fill the vacuum in his relationship with my mother, all the while negating myself and my needs. Lest I appear weak or unable to cope, I repressed any negative emotions. But the anger and shame which I stifled as an adolescent ended up stifling me, or at least that young part of me that I silenced out of fear and embarrassment. By squelching her I squelched my real self.

What cripples us is the way we turn on ourselves and blame ourselves because we automatically assume the guilt for what's happened. As Christians we're taught to forgive, but in reality, we often use Jesus to escape from our feelings. We don't have a right to forgive until we've listened to our own feelings, to the voice of the real self which says, "I didn't deserve to be abused." Then, our forgiveness can be authentic. I grew up thinking I could pray away my negative feelings. I learned to "offer" them to the Lord in prayer, incorrectly assuming two things: 1) that He would take these problems from me forever so that I would not have to deal with them, and 2) that I was earning spiritual "Brownie" points by being a sort of martyr. I thought I was dealing cleverly—and spiritually—with hurtful situations, while in reality I was behaving codependently by burying the problems and feelings deep inside myself and setting up a process of denial, the mind's way of protecting itself from experiencing pain. It was a process which protected me as a child but which suffocated me as an adult. The beginning of religious addiction is to deny what we really feel. I had no idea that I was actually doing violence to myself by cutting off a part of myself. Was she the part of me that often fell in the dark hole and felt such pain? Was she the woman in my dreams who had disappeared from her community and was lost and wandering around on her own? Was she sick and in need of a doctor? I believe she was the abused child in me who split off and went into hiding. At the retreat we were asked to reflect on an area in our hearts that keep us in bondage and then urged to invite the Lord into that area at the Eucharist. *Thank you Jesus for opening my eyes to the bondage of sexual abuse. I give you this closed-up, guilt-ridden and fearful part of myself, this abused child who split off, went into hiding and never grew up. Please lead her out of the desert of separation and make her well. Just say the word, Lord, and she will be healed.*

Facing the Pain

Some months later I read an article on "Spiritual Bonding" by Serafina Anfuso, Ph.D., in which separation from God, others and the self was presented as the wound to be healed. She presented her own story of generational non-bonding, her search for bonding and explained inner healing, rebirthing, and reparenting as the spiritual process of restoration. After reading the article, I knew this was the path I needed to follow, but since she was from Roseville, California, I didn't know how I'd be able to connect with her. Not long after this I learned that she was coming to Chicago to give a workshop on "Healing the Mother/Father Wound." I signed up for the workshop and private counseling. Serafina was the spiritual surgeon God sent to operate on my soul and expose the pain of my experience with Uncle Jim, pain which I had so quickly repressed as a child. In one session she put the evil part of him in the chair next to me and asked me to dialogue with him. At first it was awkward and I felt shy and silly. I went through the motions of talking to him, mostly to please her. She asked me to tell him what I was feeling, then helped me dig down underneath layers of denial and get to the core of the hidden emotions. There was a storehouse of feelings—of anger, shame, rage, fear, repulsion, dread and guilt, coupled with feeling trapped and paralyzed. The nerve was exposed and no amount of pounding pillows or sticking imaginary knives into this man would satisfy me. Then I impulsively reached for his imaginary hands and broke his wrists—and spent my rage.

For all the years I tried to snuff her out, my twelve year old remained alive by blaming others for her pain and making them responsible for her feelings. Over the years my husband took a lot of the flack that belonged to Uncle Jim. By hiding her inside of me, I hid so much of myself, of my femininity and sexuality, my trust in men, spontaneity and affection. It's as if part of me froze and couldn't grow up until I called her out of the darkness and let her breathe free and be herself. Freedom comes when we welcome our feelings and our true self without judgment. I cried bitter tears over the way I had abandoned her and left her for dead. She was not dead after all, only asleep like Jairus' daughter. When the therapy session ended and the therapist asked me to look out the window and tell her how the world looked, I responded, "Clean." I felt cleansed of those dark emotions which robbed me of so much light and life.

My perceptions were changing. I began to see the problems that my own denial of myself had caused, and now I felt empowered to be open with Tommy and share my need for intimacy and my desire that we take steps to heal our relationship. I wanted to build bridges in our relationship, bridges of understanding, openness, listening, truth and affection. In place of those negative emotions, there was new space in my heart for joy and spontaneity and affection. I wanted our love to be life-giving.

Scripture Meditation

"For this reason, I remind you to stir into flame the gift of God that you have through the imposition of my hands. For God did not give us a spirit of cowardice but rather of power and love and self-control. So do not be ashamed of your testimony to our Lord, nor of me, a prisoner for his sake; but bear your share of hardship for the gospel with the strength that comes from God." (2 Tim. 6-9)

Dear Lord Jesus,

Thank you for the courage You give us to undergo the spiritual and emotional surgery so necessary to heal our wounded, sinful selves. You yearn for us to be made whole—and holy—and wait ever so patiently for us to allow You to operate so You can free us from the disease which causes such pain and division within ourselves. No matter what we've done or what's been done to us, we need not be ashamed to reveal it because our healing gives glory to You, our Divine Physician.

22

My Sacrifice of Thanksgiving

The contents of this final chapter are so personal as to leave me completely vulnerable to my readers. Although this healing happened after I returned home from Italy, it is integral to the inner journey of repentance and renewal to which the Lord was inviting me, and thus I am including it. It is a healing gift from the heart of Jesus which I believe He wants me to share. I pray it will encourage you to put all your trust in our Eucharistic Lord and rely on your faith to guide you and heal you. *"Lord I am your servant. . . you have loosed my bonds. I will offer a sacrifice of thanksgiving and call on the name of the Lord. I will pay my vows to the Lord in the presence of all his people. . . ."* (Psalm 116: 16-19)

More Surgery Needed

In a follow-up therapy session it soon became apparent more surgery was needed. When the therapist asked me if I'd ever had any miscarriages or abortions, I admitted the truth to her and told her I had suffered both. These are difficult things to share, especially the abortion, which I had before I was married while I was living in Italy. The miscarriage happened before our last child was born, and resulted from the use of an IUD, a form of birth control which is now considered an abortifacient because it prevents implantation. I have lost two children, one of which my husband knew about (miscarriage), the other of which he didn't.

I have asked myself so many times how I could have done it. In the first case I was 23 and fearful that a baby would force me to spend the rest of my life in Italy married to a man I wasn't sure I loved. Knowing full well that life begins at the moment of conception, I deceived myself by telling myself that, because I was barely pregnant, the baby wasn't developed yet; it was only a blob of protoplasm. At four to six weeks old that "blob" already has a beating heart, the foundations of the brain, the spinal cord and nervous system are established, and arms, legs, eyes and ears have begun to show. Yet in one moment of decision, all my faith and years of Catholic education went down the drain. The guilt I felt in betraying my values and conscience sent me in search of a priest to whom I poured out my heart and confessed my sin. Then I so completely blocked the abortion from my memory that it seemed as if happened to someone else—until I'd see photographs or a video graphically demonstrating how life begins when the sperm joins the ovum to form a cell. *That cell contains the genetic blueprint for every detail of the child's development.* I'd feel the pain of having to wonder forever who and where my child was. The Church has always maintained a strong position on the sanctity of human life from the moment of conception. *"Before I formed you in the womb I knew you"* (Jeremiah 1:5), said the Lord. Our legal system has turned abortion into a "choice." The one who paid the price for my "choice" was my unborn baby.

Secrecy Divides and Deceives

The abortion is at the root of the emotional pain for which I've sought relief most of my life. Tied to it like barnacles on a rock is the shame and guilt, the sense of abandonment and emptiness, the depression and anger, the denial and deception and the pressure and conflict of living with this deep dark secret. Attempting to conceal my pain for so many years, I bottled up my emotions. Repressing emotions only makes them come out sideways, and unfortunately the person closest to me received the brunt of my feelings, my husband. The aching sense of loss inside of me created a deep wound, a void inside myself which I wanted him to fill. Nothing he did could fill the gap. The intimacy that I so craved was impossible as long as this secret existed between us. It was divisive. It caused deception and division in our relationship that prevented real intimacy. Keeping such a secret from my husband prevented truth from flowing between us. It's as if we were each standing on the precipice of a mountain with a deep crevice separating us. As long as the deception and the secret existed, we could never bond in true intimacy. Intimacy presupposes connection. We were disconnected at our core. The unfinished business of the abortion created a division between me and myself, first, because my heart was not really connected to the wound of the missing child. A second division existed between me and the father of the child. Inasmuch as I acted independently in regard to our child and made the decision without his knowledge, I needed to bring this to prayer and ask the Lord to forgive me and release him of the hurt and separation that this wound caused him. And thirdly, there is a division between myself and my husband because of the secret.

Sharing My Secret with My Husband

Healing is a process, the first step of which I took by sharing all this with the therapist. The next step was to share it with my husband. I didn't know how I could bring myself to share this with him—twenty eight years after the fact. I never shared it before we were married because I wasn't sure how it would affect him. Would he really want me to be his wife and the mother of his children? I told myself he'd never forgive me and buried my secret rather than lose him. He has taken so much flack from me over the years for his unwillingness to open up and share his feelings with me. I often made him responsible for my emptiness, wanting him to change in order to meet my needs. Now I had to allow him to nail me to the cross of my own hypocrisy, to the ways I had blamed him for not sharing himself with me while I hid so deeply from him. But I knew that the health of our marriage rested on the establishment of truth between us and I trusted the promise of Jesus that the truth would set us free.

My own lack of trust had prevented me from fully sharing myself with Tommy, whose understanding and compassion had attracted me to him in the first place. When I finally found the right time to tell him, I shared everything, explaining how this whole thing had blocked my ability to love and had damaged and divided our relationship. I felt sorry for the hurt and pain this would cause him, but there was no way around it. Our marriage was at stake and I wanted to build a bridge of intimacy by opening the dam and allowing the blocked up love and truth to flow.

He listened with understanding and made it easy for me, yet the pain came the next day during a marathon marriage counseling session in which we left no stone unturned in uncovering every last hurt and grievance that existed between us. When a wound is cleansed, the pus coming out is actually a sign of healing and makes the pain tolerable. In the same way, we were willing to take the pain and drain the pus rather than continue to live with the infection that was slowly killing us.

Embracing My Lost Children

In a previous private session, the therapist helped me release some of my unresolved grief by setting up an imaginary encounter between myself and my two lost children. I knew they were both boys and I even knew their names because they had come to me quite spontaneously during a Mass of generational healing I attended several years prior. At that time the priest invited us to name our aborted or miscarried children and commit them to God through the holy sacrifice of the Mass, thus allowing the love of Jesus to wash over them and all deceased members of our family tree. The child I conceived in Italy I named "Giovanni" or John, and our miscarried son I named "David." Having offered their souls to God, I thought I could put them to rest, until the therapist opened the door for me to personally bond with them and grieve their loss in my life.

My inner resistance to a guided imagery exercise was strong. Unable to conjure up an imaginary meeting with them and at the point of giving up, I pictured a tent in our backyard and a family reunion in progress. Then in walked my two boys whom I had never met. They were grown up (30 and 20), handsome, full of life and excited to be there. They knew each other, but no one else, yet they acted as if they were completely at home. *They were at home.* I ran to greet them. When they saw me coming they opened their arms and the three of us enfolded each other in an embrace. I was sobbing. It was a moment of profound joy and forgiveness. Their love released me from all the guilt and self-hatred I had lived with for so many years. I kept looking at them and touching them, wanting this union to last forever. It was the happiest moment of my life. "*I will turn your mourning into dancing,*" said the Lord. When abortions and miscarriages are not dealt with, they represent hidden grief. As soon as they're grieved, they become our intercessors, our joy, which I was now experiencing.

During our marathon counseling session, the therapist asked Tommy what he would do if he saw John and David standing nearby at a family party. He thought for awhile then with deep feeling said he would embrace and welcome them home. At that moment I felt his love so deeply, his loyalty, his commitment—to life, to love, to me, to us. He sealed his love by spiritually fathering my children that day and brought us to a new level of intimacy in our relationship.

Sharing with My Children

Finding just the right moment and with my husband beside me, I shared the whole story with my children. This was difficult and painful because I would make myself so vulnerable. They would see a side of their mother that would shock them. They have known some of the problems we've suffered in our marriage, and I felt they deserved to know the entire truth. Inasmuch as our relationship was hurt by this, so was the family. They also needed to know that they had two brothers in heaven. It is one thing to keep secret that which is sacred and not cast our pearls before swine, but we should not keep secret that which is evil. I prayed that the truth would set them free also, and that my sharing would strengthen their faith and love. *"For nothing is hidden that will not be disclosed, nor is anything secret that will not become known and come to light."* (Luke 8:17) God was pouring His grace into our marriage and healing our relationship, and I wanted the blessings to flow into their lives. They received my long, tearful sharing with tenderness, sensitivity, honesty and gratitude. It elicited much frank dialogue, a gift of love for all of us. Three hours flew by in a flash. In conclusion, I told them that when I die I want to leave them something other than furniture and silver. Those things could all go up in smoke tomorrow anyway, and then they wouldn't have anything. I want to leave a legacy of love, and that legacy is the truth of my life. This is the best gift I can give them, and I give it with all my love. Each child hugged and thanked me for this love.

Connecting with My Lost Siblings

My mother had left me her own legacy by making herself completely vulnerable to me in her suffering. I always appreciated her telling me that I was the first child to live after four miscarriages. That helped explain the eleven year age difference between my brother and me, he being the oldest. Some of the babies were pretty well along before she miscarried them, and at least one she described as a hemorrhaged mass in which she could discern the little body of a boy. My mother told me this when I was in my twenties and still living at home, but it had little or no impact on me until much later in my life when I became interested in healing the family tree. At that same Mass I described earlier, when the priest asked us to name our aborted or miscarried children, I also thought of my mother's four lost children *who were my brothers and sisters*. I gave each of them a name, or did they give me their names? At any rate, their names came to mind quite easily: Maria, William, Michael and Agnes.

Just as the life of Jesus comes into the bread and wine when the priest says the words of Consecration during Mass, so does it come into the people who are being offered to the Father, both the living and the dead, in this prayer for their complete healing and salvation. I offered my Communion for Maria, William, Michael, Agnes, John and David. Dr. Kenneth McAll in *Healing the Family Tree* writes that a dead child who has not been lovingly accepted by its family and committed to God will cry out to a living family member for love. Extensive research and interviews with people who have been healed by praying for deceased relatives support this belief, as well as testimony from Elizabeth of Hungary, Teresa of Avila, Thomas Aquinas and St. Malachy about the healing power for the living of the Eucharist offered for the dead. That praying for the dead is acceptable comes from the prophet Daniel, who asked for God's forgiveness for present sin and for the sin of his forebears.

So pleased with Daniel's prayer was the Lord that He sent Gabriel with an answer of forgiveness for the present and past sins that had been confessed. Also Baruch prays and asks Yahweh to forgive and 'remember not the misdeeds of our fathers' (Baruch 3: 1-8) "The apparent injustice of 'the sins of the fathers' being punished until the third and fourth generation is reconciled when it is understood that God is, in fact, encouraging the living to help their sinful fathers, through prayer, by asking him for forgiveness on their behalf."[1] The icing on the cake of this subject is the extraordinary gift of having our brothers, sisters, children—members of our own family—able to act as our intercessors in heaven. How many times has this consoled me, especially when I realize I can ask them for special favors for loved ones still living.

Cleansing My Mother's Womb

My therapist told me the unresolved losses of my siblings have spiritually wounded me leaving a residue of guilt and grief which needs healing. She shared how the Lord led her to minister to more than 600 women who have had stillborn, miscarried and aborted babies, many of whose mothers or whose selves had been violated as children.

After a miscarriage or abortion, the next child who is born and lives, can sometimes carry the mother's guilt and fear. I entered a womb that had been a death chamber. *Would I make it or die like the others? Is the sense of dread I've felt most of my life traceable to the womb?* The womb is our spiritual environment for nine months, and new research indicates that the climate of this environment seems to form a pattern in each of us which can influence how we will react to everything else in life. I believe my mother was filled with negativity—with depression, anxiety, and a general feeling of being burdened. *I think I was born feeling like a burden! Unwanted.* I believe I made a vow in the womb never to be a burden and never to be a victim. At birth I was already primed to prove that I was wanted and needed, and developed patterns of behavior to show what a difference I could make in life. There is ample scientific research and evidence today which shows the intimate connection between the child and the mother in the womb, so intimate that the child's memories are linked to its mother's experiences and reactions. The chemical and hormonal changes which are produced in our bloodstream by our emotions are also shared with the fetus of a pregnant woman. In studying thousands of patients, the English psychiatrist Dr. Frank Lake, "came to believe that the most severe personality disorders (psychoses) could be traced to prenatal trauma, especially from conception through the first three months in the womb."[2] There are studies which relate the suicide attempts of patients to abortion attempts by their mothers.

Through guided imagery, we had a cleansing of my mother's womb with me being reborn into a place of love and security. Then I broke the vow I made and destroyed the mother I introjected in the womb, the evil part of her who lived inside of me all these years tormenting me with her negativity, criticism and anger.

Masses Offered for Our Children

Tommy and I decided to have two Masses offered for our deceased children, one for John and one for David. The first of the two Masses was celebrated in our home by our close friend and my editor and spiritual director, Fr. Anselm Romb, OFM Conv., during which we gave John back to the Father praying for his fulfillment in the kingdom of heaven.

*"It was You who created my inmost self, and put me together
in my mother's womb; for all these mysteries I thank You: for
the wonder of myself, for the wonder of Your works. You
know me through and through, from having watched my
bones take shape when I was being formed in secret, knitted
together in the limbo of the womb." (Psalm 139: 13-15)*

It was deeply comforting to know we have done all we possibly can to
bring John Christ's peace and healing. Mass is the most perfect prayer and
vehicle for us to pray healing into our family tree. When we place
ourselves on the altar during the holy sacrifice of the Mass and offer our
needs, problems, fears, and lives to the Father, we are most intimately
united to all our deceased and living loved ones. Christ's love becomes the
matrix for our familial love and is the vehicle for our healing. The Mass is
a prayer of infinite merit because Jesus offers His life to the Father for us.

The Broken Body of Christ on Earth

Yet the lack of understanding of the Mass and faith in the Real
Presence of Christ in the Holy Eucharist is astounding, even among
Catholics, even among priests. Many of our teenagers and children have
not been taught the most important doctrine of our Catholic faith.
According to a 1992 Gallup Survey on the belief of Catholics in the Real
Presence of Jesus in the Blessed Sacrament, only 30% of those surveyed
believe that when they receive Communion they receive the Body and
Blood of the Risen Christ. A majority of Catholics today do not understand
or appreciate their faith nor are they passing it on to their young. A recent
poll of U.S. Catholics by The New York Times and CBS News shows that
60 percent of all Catholic children are not receiving any religious
instruction at all, either through their parishes or in Catholic schools.

In Timothy we read these sobering words:

*"But understand this: there will be terrifying times in the
last days. People will be self-centered and lovers of money,
proud, haughty, abusive, disobedient to their parents,
ungrateful, irreligious, callous, implacable, slanderous,
licentious, brutal, hating what is good, traitors, reckless,
conceited, lovers of pleasure rather than lovers of God, as*

they make a pretense of religion but deny its power."
(2 Tim3:1-5)

Doesn't this reading speak to our times? We have lost sight of God and of our need for a Savior. Indeed, our society is becoming pagan. In this century especially, Jesus and Mary are calling us, begging us to listen to them, to read the signs of the times and to convert, to pray, to fast, to read Scripture, to go to Mass, and to offer our suffering for people who are far from God. *One of the signs by which Jesus is trying to get our attention is through the Eucharistic miracles.* He is trying to show us that He is not a far away Spirit; He is real and alive and living among us reaching out to us through His Eucharistic Presence. He is saying *"This is My Body."* Father George Kosicki says that this rebellious age is a cry against God. "It is a cry of independence and self-determination, most poignantly heard in support of the stance over the issue of abortion. How often we hear the assertion that 'I have a right over my own body!' This rebellious cry is a cry against the Lord; it is a cry in contradiction to the Eucharist. The Lord says over us: *"This is My Body."* But so many are rejecting His sovereign reign over us and say, 'No, this is *my* body!'. . . The present world-wide number of abortions each year is conservatively reported as forty million, and is possibly as high as sixty million. . .There are 125,000 abortions performed daily. We are annihilating the human race. We have broken the body of Christ on earth again. We are in a crisis of Eucharist. The answer to the crisis is the Eucharist — the ultimate humility and mercy of God."³

Our Government Promotes Violence

And the crisis is being fostered by our government which legalized abortion in January, 1973. By 1993 more than 25 million pre-born babies have died. Organizations such as *Planned Parenthood* are federally funded — for example in 1994 to the tune of 350 million dollars a year — and are responsible for eighty percent of the abortions done in the United States. It is all the more horrifying to realize that in that same year 21 million dollars were to be cut out of the health care budget, money which was designated for adoption agencies and abstinence programs. Mother Teresa minced no words in speaking before an audience of 3,000 which included the president, vice president, and congressional leaders at a National Prayer Breakfast in Washington, D.C. America, she said, was once known for its generosity to the world. But it has become selfish and the greatest proof of that selfishness is abortion. "If we accept that a mother can kill even her own child, how can we tell other people not to kill each other? Any country that accepts abortion is not teaching its people to love, but to use any violence to get what they want." Then she delivered her coup de grace: "Many people are very, very concerned with children in India, with the children of Africa where quite a few die of hunger, and so on. Many people are also concerned about all the violence in this great country of the United States. These concerns are very good. But often these same people are not concerned with the millions who are being killed by the deliberate decision of their own mothers. And this is what is the greatest destroyer of peace today—abortion, which brings people to such blindness."

The Truth Will Set Us Free

The Lord mercifully healed me of my own blindness to the violence of abortion, in order, perhaps, to share it with you. Like the blind man who sat begging at the side of the road asking Jesus to restore his sight, Jesus said, "*Receive your sight, your faith has healed you.*" (Luke 19: 35)

I, too, have begged for His healing. He opened my eyes to the anguish that has been brewing inside of me all these years, causing such suffering. The Scripture reading from Exodus which the Lord gave me before the trip (see Introduction) promising to free me from slavery was really a prophecy which has been fulfilled through this pilgrimage. I didn't realize I needed deliverance from the inner enslavement which I suffered for so many years from the wound of abortion.

Feast of Faith is one of the fruits of new life through which I am able to witness to Jesus' promise, "*If you remain in my word, you will truly be my disciples, and you will know the truth, and the truth will set you free.*" (John 8:31-33). The Holy Spirit has been leading me on this inner healing journey and steering me to the root of the brokenness, the sin of abortion and the unexpressed guilt and grief over the loss of my two children. With those children I also lost a sense of myself. Through the dreams I had in Italy, the Lord was pointing out a sick woman in need of a doctor, the lost, separated part of myself, who wandered off, so in need of love and forgiveness. Therapy helped me find her and uncover the wound, but it is Jesus who healed and forgave her. He has heard the cries of my heart and given me spiritual and emotional healing. Like Rachel who mourned her children who were carried off in bondage, God assured her that her children will return from exile and be reunited through His love:

> *"In Ramah is heard the sound of moaning, of bitter weeping! Rachel mourns her children, she refuses to be consoled because her children are no more. Thus says the Lord: Cease your cries of mourning, wipe the tears from your eyes. The sorrow you have shown shall have its reward, says the Lord, They shall return from the enemy's land. There is hope for your future, says the Lord: Your sons shall return to their own borders."* (Jeremiah 31: 15-17)

Living Memorials

Several years ago Tommy gave me a large outdoor statue of the Blessed Mother for my birthday. We placed her in the backyard on the edge of the prairie garden facing the house. She stood by herself for a long time until I had an inspiration to have a cross made for Lent. The young carpenter recommended for the task arrived one evening with his father. While the father supervised, he told us how, early in his own career, he had been asked to make such a cross and learned the technique which he was now passing on to his son. How like Joseph and Jesus they both were, laboring in the vineyard for the glory of God. Soon after the 8 foot cross was erected, I found a tall stone angel who stood in adoration with hands folded in prayer. We then planted six Colorado spruce trees in a semi-circle behind the cross. They are living memorials of our lost siblings and children, standing there in place of Maria, William, Michael, Agnes, John and David, thriving, growing and giving glory to God. Every time I look out the kitchen window and see them, waves of warm love and gratitude wash over me reminding me of the existance of these loved ones. Sometimes Tommy and I look out the window and experience a felt sense of joy and closeness to these souls which words cannot convey.

We Are Living Eucharists

Jesus unites us most intimately to one another—both the living and the dead—through the Holy Eucharist. When I go to Communion, I often go with John or David where I know for those few moments we are bonded in deepest intimacy. In Jesus there are no barriers; we are one in Christ's Mystical Body. *Grant that we, who are nourished by His body and blood, may be filled with His Holy Spirit, and become one body, one spirit in Christ.* At times I bring someone else with me, someone who is suffering and in need of Jesus. But most often, I bring myself, to receive the nourishment which enables me to be Jesus to others. It may not always look like I am trying to live out of His love, but I pray to be transformed in order to be His hands and heart in the world. This is our gift and our burden, to become living Eucharists, so that all who see our light or are touched by our love will give glory to God. When the apostles broke bread with Jesus at the Last Supper, they promised to lay down their lives in memory of Him. They were willing to sacrifice themselves to bring Jesus' risen presence to the community. Thus Christ's sacrifice on the cross which is commemorated in the consecration of the bread and wine at Mass is perpetuated through those who receive Him. The Sacrament challenges us to say, *Lord, this is my body, this is my blood for you,* and to make the sacrifice of Jesus present to the people God puts in our lives.

Choose Life!

For some months now I have been privileged to be part of a small group who goes to the home of a woman who is completely paralyzed from the neck down. Just after her 50th birthday she was thrown from a horse and damaged her spinal cord. She has grown to accept what happened, and offers her suffering for others by literally laying down her life on her bed of paralysis. We take turns bringing lunch, during which we talk and pray the Rosary. Whenever I leave Mary's home I come away feeling so inspired and uplifted by her faith and courage. Her love is deep and strong.

One day Mary asked me to share where the dedication and enthusiasm for my faith came from. I found myself telling my whole story, complete with abortion and all. What happened next was a gift from God. One of the ladies whose judgment I feared, told me how my story opened her eyes to see that all women who have abortions are not "women of the street" as she had thought. She then shared what was heavy on her heart, a painful struggle in her relationship with her husband. The others opened their hearts as well, making themselves completely vulnerable to the group. We meet regularly as a spiritual support group now, nurturing one another by sharing the truth of our lives.

Jesus transforms us with His love, *especially* through the Mass and the Eucharist, because we can reach out, like the woman in Scripture, and touch His Real Presence. Each time we go to Jesus in the Blessed

Sacrament, we touch His heart with our faith. Each holy hour we make in His presence, each Mass we attend and Eucharist we receive, releases power and grace upon us, our families, our parishes, our country, our world. We pay thousands of dollars to doctors and psychiatrists to heal our bodies and minds, yet how often do we make a visit to the Blessed Sacrament, where for free we can receive physical, emotional and spiritual healing from our Divine Physician? A mystic who devoted her life to the Blessed Sacrament and whom the Pope beatified some years ago, Dina Belanger, said that if we really knew and understood Who was residing in the tabernacles of our churches, we would have to have armed guards posted at the entrances to keep the crowds from overrunning the buildings.

I pray that everyone who reads this book will deepen their faith in our Eucharistic Lord and draw closer to Him in the Blessed Sacrament. Through Him you will find the answer to all life's problems, no matter what they are. He has the whole world in His heart, which He gives fully and unconditionally to every living soul out of love.

I also pray that if you have had an abortion, a miscarriage or been sexually abused, my story will encourage you to share it with someone and help you take steps of reconciliation that will free you from the pain these wounds cause. Secrecy and denial prevent healing from happening. Until we can share our burden and release the hidden rage, shame and guilt which usually result from these acts, until we can bring ourselves and our lost children into the light of God's love and mercy, we are bound by sin and darkness. Forgiveness results from facing the truth, which Jesus promised would set us free. There is no healing without forgiveness, and the person who is usually the most difficult to forgive is oneself. Jesus came so that we might have life, and have it to the full. He wants to free us from bondage and fill us with life, but He does not force it on us. Until I was willing to face the truth of my life I was not free. The choice is ours. *"I have set before you life and death, the blessing and the curse. Choose life, then, that you and your descendants may live, by loving the Lord your God and heeding his voice, and holding fast to him. For that will mean life for you, a long life for you to live on the land which the Lord swore he would give to your fathers Abraham, Isaac and Jacob."* – Deut 30: 19-20

Afterword

While praying in front of the Blessed Sacrament to discern God's will as to whether to include the final chapter about the abortion, I begged for guidance. One of my favorite ways to pray is to dialogue with Him in my journal, a practice which I began years ago, dropped for awhile, and took up again recently. The conversations which follow took place over several days and reveal my struggle, which might also be your struggle. Perhaps Jesus will speak to your heart as He did mine through these dialogues.

Joan: Jesus, You have been so patient, so understanding, so generous and loving, so attentive to my needs and desires, so present to me through faith and through the people You've put in my life to love me. Lord, I'm not fit to tie Your sandals, much less be a guest at Your banquet. You invited me to Your Feast when I was a child. I loved You from afar and was glad for the invitation. I believed in You and in Your kingdom of love and I started following. I followed You on my schedule and selfishly, according to what was in it for me. I used You, Jesus, to help me, to guide me to the next step on the journey, to take care of my inner needs which no one else seemed to care about, to get me out of jams, to fill my emptiness with people who would love me. I looked to You for everything I was lacking.

Jesus, You were always there for me, even though I spent 99% of my time ignoring You, running around pleasing myself and others, You never left me and You never stopped loving me. Even in my worst sin, You still held out Your arms to forgive me, waiting only for me to open my heart to You. Lord, it has taken me fifty-plus years to begin to appreciate Your constancy, Your patience, Your generosity, Your unconditional love poured out on me and those I love. Your love is there no matter what I do or don't do, no matter if I sin or hurt You, You don't turn away from me.

Jesus, Jesus, You who know me better than I know myself and can read my mind and heart, help me now to witness to You through my sharing. Please make my words draw people to Your love, Your truth, Your purity, Your charity. Lord, how can I begin? Where? There is so much and yet so little. Help me, Jesus, Holy Spirit, with the right words, to touch people in their experience and allow Your grace through faith and love to fill their pain and emptiness. Right now I'm afraid and feel intimidated by this tremendous task—to share my truth with others. I'm not supposed to preach or lecture or instruct them about abortion.

Jesus: Just give your lived experience, Joan and I will take it from there. Joan, Joan, Joan, how little faith you have in Me! Remember our writings of years ago?

Joan: Yes, Jesus, very well.

Jesus: Well then, you will remember how we used to have conversations which had substance and meaning but which you had no idea about before you sat down to write. This is the same now, Joan. Joanie, My delight, My heart beating with love for you, for your desire to serve Me, your willingness to take time as you are doing to listen to Me, to seek Me, to discern My thoughts for your book. Then, child, listen up close, because My thoughts are filled to overflowing in your book. It is our book, and I wish you to complete it.

Joan: Jesus, please give me the final chapter. You know how important it is. I am afraid of it. Please, Lord, take my pen now and write it.

Jesus: Joan, you have My words already in Your heart. Simply tell the story of your healing, My healing of you, little one, without worrying how it is said. I already gave you a start with the other journal. Joan, when you write it, I will be with you every step of the way.

Joan: Jesus, why must I write this healing into the book?

Jesus: Do you hear the birds singing?

Joan: Yes, Jesus.

Jesus: Listen to them, Joan. Their song gives Me glory. They praise Me by singing, by bringing music to the world. By being true to their life, by utilizing their gift, they give glory and praise to their Creator. They contribute to the fulfillment of the kingdom; they add peace and joy to the world, and in turn, receive life and energy by living out their vocations. And so my precious child, you who are willing to live in the truth of My love and light, and follow in My steps, you also give glory and praise to your Father who created you to reflect His heart. Joan, by telling your story, you bring music to the world so that others can sing. You espouse truth for others to learn of God and you share His justice and mercy through your own experience. Your revelations are God's revelations and many will be moved by your words. As hearts are moved, your God will touch them and draw them to Himself. Joan, you are an instrument, a beautiful instrument which God uses to bring truth, love and healing to people. When you exercise your truth by telling the truth, you "play your instrument" because you were made in truth and love. When you become fully open and let it all out, the music resounds and reverberates. Joan, Joan, peace My little one. Use your gifts of honesty, openness, simplicity, to help dispel Satan's lies. So many of my children are deceived by him. You have been protected and gifted and I want you, beg you, to share the gift you have received. Then will you give the greatest glory to My Father for His creation. Peace and love, little daughter.

Another time:

Joan: So many desires, Lord, things I want to do for You: revise my slide presentation, make the video, publish my book, and write two others which are sitting on the back burner.

Jesus: So much, Joan, and yet so little. How few souls give themselves to My tasks. I ask so little—for hearts to open to Me so that I can fill them and use them. Is this such a burden?

Joan: Oh Jesus, no. It is pure joy. It is life to the fullest. It is sweet and energizing and meaningful and fulfilling. If only people knew the joy of living in the Spirit with You.

Jesus: Joan, you My little heart, can tell them! Go and shout it from the rooftops. Proclaim Me and My love and mercy and My longing for souls, especially My longing that they unite with Me in the Eucharist. It is My most special gift to the world, given to show the depth of My care for every soul. Joan, I offer My life in the Host for each soul, to feed them, nourish them spiritually, empower them to live a life of victory over darkness, and yet they ignore Me, they reject Me, they disregard My presence as if I were not there. Joan, I am there and I yearn to be recognized. Joan, Joan, please, child, know what a gift I've given you in your faith and in your desire to spread your faith to others. You are like a wick which I've lit with My own love and through which you can light the fire in hearts which are cold and distant from Me. Just open your own heart and they will find My love there, ready to warm and comfort them.

Joan: Jesus, this makes me cry. I want so much to convert and draw people to You, especially my own family.

Jesus: Joan, little Joan, I kiss your heart for the love you bear to Me and want others to bear, especially your family. I keep them close to Me even if they do not seem to be. They are My special loves, each one, precious and anointed with My special blessing. Joan, do not fear, only pray for their souls to be on guard, lest the enemy gain a foothold when they are not looking. They are open to Me but they are open to the world, too. Pray that the opening to Me will grow wider and deeper, and the opening to the world will grow smaller.

Joan: Jesus, thank You for these words. I will pray everyday for this. Lord, what else do You want from me?

Jesus: Joan, I want your all, as you are giving Me in your book. I want every ounce of you wrung out to thirsty souls who need to drink in My love. Their thirst is for Me. You will help quench their thirst, and in so doing they will begin to understand that it is really Me who is answering their prayers through you. Then, they will kneel in supplication and in thanksgiving to Me and I will draw them to Myself. Joan, I kiss you with tenderness and joy, a gift from My Father to His special child of grace. He loves you and appreciates the work you are doing for His kingdom and He sends His protection and help on all that you do.

Joan: Jesus, this makes me cry. I believe and feel Your presence through these words. Jesus, let me follow Your lead every minute of every day.

Jesus: Joan, I kiss away your tears.

Another time:

Jesus: Little one, little one! How you yearn for Me, for My presence! I read your heart and find therein a treasured cave of love, receptivity, openness, eagerness, hopefulness, joy, prayer, petition, trust, and a willingness to die to self. Joan, do you hear Me saying these things about you, child of Mine?

Joan: Oh, Jesus, You know my heart's desire is to be close to You. Close, so close, so intimate I will be the music and You the flute. Jesus, I hunger for You and in You and with You and my main desire is to open other hearts to Your reality. Yes, to reach their hearts and turn them on to You!

Jesus: Joan, My Joan, your gift is growing in you like a precious flower. From a tiny seed first planted in your little heart years ago by your mother and the nuns, faith took root in the good soil of solid teaching, Scripture and the Sacraments. Now, you are beginning to see and taste the fruit of our growth. Your faith has matured and ripened like a good fruit. It is ready to be picked so that I can feed others through you. Just let yourself be used by Me, My little Joan, and we will go far together, you and I, touching hearts and setting them on fire for love of Me.

Joan: Jesus, You know me so deeply and You have touched the core of my desire: to minister in Your name and have You fill and heal people through me. But I am such a weak and rusty channel, so full of debris and ego. There's so much of me and so little of You. I fear Your power will be diminished by my humanity.

Jesus: Joan, My Joan, when you will your humanity to Me I transform it into My vessel, which is made pure and whole through My love. Remember, it is nothing that you do that makes you deserving or worthy of Me, it is My love, and My love alone, which makes you light the fire in other hearts. You must only submit to Me, to My desire and will for you. Joan, surrender your life at every moment to Me and I will work powerfully through you.

Joan: Jesus, how can I recognize You better? Please give me a way to know Your wishes, Your urges, Your messages. Jesus, help me to hear Your voice in me so clearly that I will know it is You. Jesus, I beg You for this gift. Please, please give me a sound or something to alert me. I wish You could say words to me like you do to some chosen souls, sentences in my head, clear, precise (as differentiated from these thoughts which form into sentences). But maybe I am asking too much and being presumptuous. Lord Jesus, its just that I want the closeness so much.

Jesus: Joan, My precious child, you already have it! And you have had My closeness your whole life. I walk with you every minute. You have never been out of My sight, even for a second. You have come down the road following My call and now I give you more responsibilities. I give you charge of many more souls who are waiting for you. They are praying to Me to answer their needs and I am going to send you to them because you will guide them to Me.

Joan: Jesus, this makes me cry. I'm weeping with joy.
Jesus: Good. You will weep more, in joy and in sorrow. Your tears will melt hearts.

Joan: Jesus, am I doing right in undressing myself in public sharing about the abortion in the book? Please tell me precisely.

Jesus: Joan, how else will people be able to relate their problems to faith and dependence on Me unless someone like you guides them by relating her own problems to faith and then sharing the answer? *Now that is the bottom line*! Your lived experience is their lived experience. Except many have not given their burdens to Me. They *want* to repent but need the motivation. You can give that because you have experienced My healing of your heart. You will lead them to:

    1) want to repent
    2) want to trust more in Me and My plan for them
    3) hunger for My life in the Eucharist

You, Joan, will bring Me souls who are dying for lack of love, love for themselves and love for Me. I give you My anointing to awaken My love in hearts which are cold and closed and afraid. Your truth and your openness of heart will pierce the steel covering of their hearts and bring warmth and light to their darkness. Joan, this is My gift given to mankind through you. Bring many to Me, little one, many. I wait for them and hunger for their love. I hunger to be this close to you 24 hours a day. Let Me fill you child of My heart, and you will overflow with love and joy. Joan, we are a team, *the Love Team!*

Citations

Chapter 2 - The Miracle of Corpus Christi

1. Bob and Penny Lord, *This Is My Body, This Is My Blood, Miracles of the Eucharist* (Journeys of Faith. P.O.Box 429, Slidell, LA 70459, 1986), 38.
2. Thomas Aquinas. *Summa Theologiae* III. q. 79, a. 1.
3. Herbert J. Thurston, S.J. and Donald Attwater, *Butler's Lives of the Saints* (Christian Classics, Westminster, Maryland), 510.
4. G.K. Chesterton, *Saint Thomas Aquinas "The Dumb Ox"* (Image Books, Doubleday, 666 Fifth Ave, New York, New York 10103, 1956), 136-137.
5. Thurston and Attwater, *op. cit.,* 511.
6. Joan Carroll Cruz *Eucharistic Miracles* (Tan Books and Publishers, Inc. Rockford, Illinois 61105 1987), xvii.
7. SC *Divine Worship, Holy Communion & Worship of the Eucharist Outside Mass.* General Introduction and Chapter 3, Introduction, 21 June 1973. (Vatican Polyglot Press, 1973).
8. Sister Josefa Menendez, T*he Way of Divine Love* (Tan Books and Publishers, Inc. Rockford, IL 61105), 248-249.
9. Cruz, *op. cit.,* xvii.

Chapter 3 - The City of St. Catherine

1. Cruz, *op. cit.,* 91. Some popes and people of nobility did receive these consecrated Hosts until they were forbidden to do so by Rome.
2. *Ibid.,* 90.
3. *Ibid.,* 91.
4. Frances Parkinson Keyes, *Three Ways of Love* (The Daughters of St. Paul, 50 St. Paul's Avenue, Boston, Ma. 02130), 166.
5. Catherine of Siena, *The Dialogue.* Translation and introduction by Suzanne Noffke. O.P. (Paulist Press, 997 Macarthur Blvd. Mahwah, N.J. 07430), 29, 36.
6. Bob and Penny Lord, *Saints and Other Powerful Women in the Church,* (Journeys of Faith. P.O. Box 429, Slidell, LA 70459-0429), 116.
7. *Ibid.,* 117.
8. Catherine of Siena, *op. cit.,* 206.
9. *Ibid.,* 211-212.
10. Bob and Penny Lord, *This Is My Body, This Is My Blood, Miracles of the Eucharist* (Journeys of Faith, P.O. Box 429, Slidell, LA 70459-0429), 172.

Chapter 4 - Eucharistic Miracles in Florence

1. The best resource book I've found to decipher the meaning of dreams is *Dreams and Spiritual Growth, A Christian Approach to Dreamwork* by Louis M. Savary, Patricia H. Berne and Strephon Kaplan Williams (Paulist Press, Ramsey, N.J. 1984).
2. Cruz, *op. cit.,* 290.
3. Fr. Paul O'Sullivan, O.P. *All About Angels* (Tan Books and Publishers, Inc. Rockford, IL 61105), 45-46.
4. Cruz, *op. cit.,* 47-48.

Chapter 5 - The Apple of His Eye

1. I grew up trying to live an idyllic life, free of pain or problems. Through retreats and spiritual mentors, I realized that we have a choice: to unearth our pain and problems and bring them to Jesus for healing, or to remain a victim of them. A book which has been most helpful to me in connecting our brokenness to our spirituality is,

Broken But Loved, Healing Through Christ's Power by George A. Maloney, S.J. (Alba House, New York, 1988).

2.   Books which have been especially helpful to me in seeing how alcoholism and mental illness affected me are: *Adult Children of Alcoholics* by Janet Geringer Woititz. (Health Communications, 1983). *Healing the Child Within* by Charles Whitfield, M.D. (Health Communications, 1721 Blount Road, Pompano Beach, FL 33069) and, *Love Is A Choice, Recovery for Codependent Relationships* by Drs. Robert Hemfelt, Frank Minirth and Paul Meier. (Thomas Nelson Publishers, Nashville, 1989). *Healing the Eight Stages of Life* by Matthew and Dennis Linn and Sheila Fabricant (Paulist Press, New York/Mahwah, 1988) has been my personal "Bible" for showing me how to bring the hurts and brokenness of different stages of my life to Jesus for healing.

3.   Gerald G. May, M.D., *Addiction and Grace* (Harper & Row Publishers, San Francisco, 1988). This book was a real eye-opener for me and enlarged my understanding of addiction to see how subtle are the objects of attachment which rob us of our freedom and become false gods. Addictions, he says, disguise our true longing for God which hides underneath our compulsions etc. Our journey to God is a process of purgation, detachment, purification which is painful but necessary to transform our desires and free us to love.

Chapter 6 - 911–A Call for Help

1.   John Powell, *The Secret of Staying in Love* (Argus Communications, Niles, IL, 60648), 26-27.

2.   *Ibid.*, 103.

3.   Barbara Leahy Shlemon, *Healing the Hidden Self* (Ave Maria Press, Notre Dame, Indiana, 1982). I have attended several retreats given by Barbara Shlemon where I have received deep inner healing of childhood hurts. This book is an invaluable guide to praying our way through the stages of growth, helping us appropriate the healing love of Jesus into the hidden, hurting parts of ourselves.

4.   Chapter 8, "I Am Broken," in *Broken But Loved, Healing Through Christ's Power* by George Maloney, S.J. (Alba House, New York) is so helpful to our understanding of spiritual growth. Treats the demonic in us, that which is a part of our broken state of inauthenticity; how unfree we human beings are to love and receive love and the "pain of prayer" which we must endure if we are to break through the defense barriers to our inner truth. In our center is where God makes His mansion. He calls us to break out of our prisons of narcissism but His call is frightening and takes courage because we must face our darkness. It is a call to live in the freedom of the children of God. Only God is powerful enough to aid us in becoming "re-born." This chapter clarifies the call to holiness and integrates the psychological and spiritual aspects of sanctity with such clarity. Rereading this strengthens my will and encourages me to uncover truth and love in myself and to surrender my all to God.

5.   Ann Ross Fitch and Fr. Robert DeGrandis S.S.J., *Walking In The Light*, (H.O.M. Books, 108 Aberdeen Street, Lowell, MA 01850), 15.

6.   Thomas Merton, *Contemplative Prayer* (Image Books, a division of Doubleday & Company, Inc. Garden City, New York 1969), 70.

7.   Thomas Merton, *New Seeds of Contemplation* (New York: New Directions, 1961) Edition cited: New Directions Paperbook, 1972, 36.

Chapter 7 - Two New Friends

1.   *Perpetual Eucharistic Adoration Newsletter*, Volume 2, Number 1, March, 1989. (P.O. Box 84595, Los Angeles, CA 90073), 11.

2.   Bob and Penny Lord, *This is My Body, This is My Blood, Miracles of the Eucharist*, (Journeys of Faith, P.O. Box 429, Slidell, LA 70459 1986), 82.

3.   Joan Carroll Cruz, *The Incorruptibles* (Tan Book & Pub., Rockford, IL 61105), 33.

4.   *Ibid.*, 34-35.

5.   Herbert J. Thurston, S.J., and Donald Attwater, *Butler's Lives of the Saints* (Christian Classics, Inc. P. O. Box 30, Westminster, MD. 21157) Vol. 1, 537.

6.   *Ibid.*, 537.

7.   Marion A. Habig O.F.M., *The Franciscan Book of Saints* (Franciscan Press, 1800 College Ave, Quincy, IL 62301), 338.

8.   Thurston and Attwater, *op. cit.*, 538.

Chapter 8 - Day of the Bells

1.   *Introduction to the Devout Life*, tr. by Michael Day, (Cong. Orat., Burns & Oates, London, 1956), 81 ff.

2.   This song from *Godspell* is taken from a prayer written by St. Richard of Chicester, and hearkens back to medieval times.

Chapter 9 - Buried Treasure

1.   Theo. Desbonnets, *Assisi in the Footsteps of Saint Francis, A Spiritual Guidebook,* (Casa Editrice Francescana, Frati Minori Conventuali, 06082 Assisi, Italy), 60.

2.   *Ibid.*, p. 63.

3.   Habig, *op. cit.*, 596.

4.   Nesta De Robeck, *The Life of St. Francis of Assisi,* (Casa Editrice Francescana. Frati Minori Conventuali, 06082 Assisi, Italy), 34.

Chapter 10 - Lesson of the Box

1.   Hannah Hurnard, *Hind's Feet on High Places,* (Living Books, Tyndale House Publishers, Inc. Wheaton, IL), 10-11.

Chapter 11 - Assisi

1.   De Robeck, *op. cit.*, 20.

Chapter 12 - The Gift of Tears

1.   De Robeck, *op. cit.*, 34.

2.   St. Peter Julian Eymard, *In the Light of the Monstrance,* (Blessed Sacrament Fathers and Brothers, 5384 Wilson Mills Road, Cleveland, Ohio 44143), 27.

3.   Habig *op. cit.*, 598.

4.   Desbonnets, *op. cit.*, 65.

5.   Joan Carroll Cruz, *Eucharistic Miracles*, (Tan Books and Publishers, Inc. Rockford, IL 61105), 261.

6.   *Ibid.*, 258-259.

7.   St. Catherine of Siena, *op. cit.*, 33.

8.   *Ibid.*, 170.

9.   *Ibid.*, 363.

Chapter 13 - Reconciliation

1.   Julia Green, *God's Fool/The Life and Times of Francis of Assisi* (Harper San Francisco, 1983), 146.

2.   Agnes Sanford, *The Healing Light* (Ballantine Books, New York. 1947), 27.

3.   *Ibid.*, 28.

4.   Jim McManus C.SS.R. *The Healing Power of the Sacraments* (Ave Maria Press, Notre Dame, IN), 42.

5.   Menendez, *op. cit.*

Chapter 14 - Breaking Down Barriers

1. Desbonnets, *op. cit.*, 18.
2. De Robeck, *op. cit.*, 51.
3. Harville Hendrix, Ph.D., *Getting the Love You Want, A Guide For Couples* (Henry Holt & Co. New York, 1988). This book has been very helpful in showing me how I've used marriage to resolve my unmet childhood needs. It illustrates the barriers to intimacy we set up and why. Also, how to take them down.
4. John Powell S.J., and Loretta Brady, M.S.W., *Will the Real Me Please Stand Up?* (Tabor Publishing, Allen, Texas), 43.
5. Fitch and DeGrandis, S.S.J., *op. cit.*, 93, 94.

Chapter 15 - Miracles In Cascia

1. De Robeck, *op. cit.*, 75.
2. *Ibid.*, 105.

Chapter 16 - The Oldest Miracle of the Eucharist

1. Louis Kaczmarek, *Hidden Treasure, The Riches of the Eucharist*, (Trinity Communications, Manassas, VA. 22110), 106.
2. Bob and Penny Lord, *This Is My Body, This Is My Blood, Miracles of the Eucharist*, (Journeys of Faith, P.O. Box 429, Slidell, LA 70459-0429), 20-21.
3. *Santuario Del Miracolo Eucaristico*, Frati Minori Conventuali, Lanciano, Italy. There are detailed chapters in, *This Is My Body, This Is My Blood, Miracles of the Eucharist*, by Bob and Penny Lord, and in *Eucharistic Miracles* by Joan Carroll Cruz.
4. *Ibid.*, 29.
5. Joan Carroll Cruz, *Eucharistic Miracles* (Tan Books and Publishers, Inc. Rockford, IL 61105), xvi.
6. *Ibid.*, xvi.
7. *Ibid.*, xvi.

Chapter 17 - Padre Pio

1. Father Gerardo Di Flumeri, O.F.M. Cap. *The Mystery of the Cross in Padre Pio of Pietrelcina* (Our Lady of Grace Capuchin Friary, 71013 San Giovanni Rotondo (Foggia) Italy 1983), 23.
2. *Ibid.*, 241.
3. Padre D'Alberto D'Apolito, *Padre Pio of Pietrelcina* (Edizioni San Giovanni Rotondo (Foggia) Italy, 1986), 153.
4. *Ibid.*, 155.
5. Di Flumeri, *op. cit.*, 15.
6. *Ibid.*, 20.
7. Alessandro da Ripabottoni, *Padre Pio The Great Sufferer of Gargano,* (Edizioni Convento dei Padri Cappuccini, 71013 San Giovanni Rotondo, Foggia, Italy), 30.
8. De Robeck, *op. cit.*, 59-60.

Chapter 18 - A Continuous Martyrdom

1. D'Apolito, *op. cit.*, 167.
2. *Ibid.*, 163.
3. Malachy Gerard Carroll, *The Mass of Padre Pio.* Immaculata Magazine, Special issue on Padre Pio. (Conventual Franciscan Friars, Marytown, 1600 West Park Avenue, Libertyville, IL 60048), 29.
4. D'Apolito, *op. cit.*, 92-93.
5. *Ibid.*, 93.

6.   *Ibid.*, 165.
7.   *Ibid.*, 172.
8.   *Ibid.*, 173.

Chapter 19 - Spiritual Warfare

1.   Michael H. Brown, *The Final Hour* (Faith Publishing Company, P.O. Box 237, Milford, Ohio. 45150, 1992). This book offers extensive research on the reports of worldwide apparitions and unusual spiritual events which are happening on every continent. It is enlightening, to say the least, especially to read how the varied apparitions in different parts of the world agree. Revelations about the Anti-Christ are especially interesting.
2.   O'Sullivan, O. P. *op. cit.*, 88.
3.   "The Good Angels and Padre Pio." *Immaculata Magazine*, Special issue on Padre Pio, (Conventual Franciscan Friars, Marytown, 1600 West Park Ave., Libertyville, IL 60048), 45.
4.   *Caritas of Birmingham*, (Box 120, 4647 Highway 280 East, Birmingham, Alabama, 35242).
5.   *Immaculata Magazine, op. cit.*, 18.
6.   For more information about a horrifying vision which Pope Leo XIII experienced see: *'Neath St. Michael's Shield*, published by the Daughters of St. Paul, and also *Prophecies! The Chastisement and Purification*, by Rev. Albert J. Hebert, S. M. (P.O. Box 309, Paulina, LA 70763), 152.
7.   D'Apolito *op. cit.*, 77-78.
8.   *Ibid.*, follows p. 32 on back side of a photograph of Padre Pio showing his swollen and bruised face after the Satanic assault.
9.   Fitch and DeGrandis S.S.J., *op. cit.*, 7-9.
10. Padre Pio, *Counsels* Edited by Fr. Alessio Parente, (Our Lady of Grace Capuchin Friary, 71013 S. Giovanni Rotondo, Foggia, Italy. 1984). Also published by the National Center for Padre Pio, Inc. RD #1, Box 134 (Old Rt. 100) Barto, PA 19504. USA
11. *Ibid.,* 32,34.

Chapter 21 - Going Home

1.   Sebastion Moore, *The Crucified Jesus Is No Stranger*, (The Seabury Press, 815 Second Ave, New York, NY 10017), 37.

Chapter 22 - My Sacrifice of Thanksgiving

1.   Dr. Kenneth McAll, *Healing the Family Tree* (Sheldon Press, London), 90-91.
2.   Rev. Matthew Linn, S.J., Dennis and Sheila Linn, *Healing the Greatest Hurt,* (Paulist Press, 997 Macarthur Blvd., Rahway, NJ 07430), 114
3.   Rev, George W. Kosicki, C.S.B., *Living Euchrist, Counter-Sign to Our Age and Answer to Crisis*, (Faith Publishing Company, P. O. Box 237, Milford, OH 45150, 1991), 4-5.

Apostolate for Family Consecration

Mr. & Mrs. Jerry Coniker, Founders, John Paul II Holy Family Center, Route 2, Box 700, Bloomingdale, OH 43910 (614) 765-4301

Dedicated to renewing family and parish life under the Marian spirituality of the Holy Father. Retreat Center. They offer a week-long family retreats: "Family Fest." They originated a program of "Family Hours" in parishes through videos with different themes: the Eucharist, Rosary etc.... Goal is to draw families into the parish in front of the Blessed Sacrament weekly for a year. Write or call for free information. For $10 they will send a video featuring Mother Teresa's endorsement of this idea as well as a look into the "Family Holy Hour." (No charge for priests)

Apostolate for Perpetual Adoration

Fr. Martin Lucia, Director. P. O. Box 46502, Mount Clemens, MI 48046, (810) 949-0046. Attn: Pat Forton

An organization founded to spread Perpetual Eucharistic Adoration around the world. Priest promoters and promotional materials available, including video & audio tapes, English and Spanish pamphlets, and meditation books and booklets. Six page newsletter published monthly.

Blue Army National Headquarters

Ave Maria Institute; World Apostolate of Fatima, Mountain View Road, Box 976 Washington, NJ 07882. (908) 689-1700

Congregation of the Blessed Sacrament

Fr. Donald Jette, S. S. S., Provincial, 5384 Wilson Mills Road, Cleveland, OH 44143-3092. (216) 442-6311

Commonly known as "The Blessed Sacrament Fathers," founded by St. Peter Julian Eymard. Part of their apostolate involves administering parishes to make them into Eucharistic centers of adoration.

Corpus Christi Institute

Fr. Christopher Malachowski, O.S. Director. 703 Pinon Drive, Santa Fe New Mexico 87501.

Emmanuel Magazine

35384 Wilson Mills Road, Cleveland, OH 44143-3092. Published ten times a year, *Emmanuel* explores the meaning of Eucharistic spirituality for all who are interested in developing their spiritual life with the Eucharist as its source.

Eternal Life

William J. Smith, Founder & Fr. John Hardon, S.J., Rev. Edmund McCaffrey, Advisors. P.O. Box 787, Bardstown, KY 40004, (502) 348-3963. A Catholic organization and pro-life movement to end abortion through the Holy Sacrifice of the Mass. Promotes Eucharistic Adoration. Through a Eucharistic Crusade of Prayer they want to organize "Apostles of the Eucharist." Tapes, booklets etc. available.

Franciscan University of Steubenville

(Consecrated to the Sacred Heart)

Franciscan Way, Steubenville, OH 43952 Campus Ministry (614) 283-6276. Perpetual Adoration of the Blessed Sacrament in the *Portiuncula*, Chapel of St. Mary of the Angels (except during summer, winter and spring school breaks) Holy Hours, First Friday and Saturday devotions. Eucharistic and Marian conferences.

Holy Eucharist Apostolate

Deacon Bill Crane, Director

P.O. Box 206, Lombard, IL 60148.

Worldwide organization to encourage frequent visits to the Blessed Sacrament, and foster deeper belief in Jesus' Real Presence in the Eucharist, devotion to Our Lady of the Most Blessed Sacrament and fidelity to the Church. Members make a weekly Holy Hour for at least six months. Monthly Six page newsletter.

Journeys of Faith, Bob and Penny Lord, Directors. Catholic Faith in Action P.O. Box 429, Slidell, LA 70459-0429 504-863-2546 or 800-633-2484. An apostolate dedicated to evangelization through communication: videos, books, *The Good Newsletter*, and pilgrimages to Eucharistic and Marian Shrines.

The Link Magazine
Rev. Roland Huot, S. S. S., editor, Mrs. J. Hoard, 2 Piercefield Rd., Freshfield, Merseyside, L37 7DQ England. An excellent publication with Eucharistic articles on the Holy Sacrifice of the Mass, Holy Communion, and adoration of the Real Presence of Jesus. Devotional & solidly Catholic in theology. The most complete on-going publication on the Eucharist. Published quarterly.

Marytown
Conventual Franciscan Friars, 1600 West Park Ave, Libertyville, IL 60048. (708) 367-7800. Dedicated to Perpetual Adoration of the Blessed Sacrament, the friars have a worldwide ministry of evangelization through books, TV, videos, radio and magazines. They sponsor retreats, Days of Recollection, & a youth program, YMI (Youth Mission for the Immaculata). Their magazine, *Immaculata*, features articles on the Eucharist, Our Lady, St. Maximilian Kolbe and more. Marytown chapel is open for adoration from 6 AM to 11 PM seven days a week. Gift shop.

Our Lady of the Angels Monastery
Mother Angelica, Superior. Eternal Word Television Network; 5817 Old Leeds Rd., Birmingham, AL 35210 (205) 956-5987. The Poor Clare Nuns of Perpetual Adoration and Thanksgiving, Mother Angelica founded Our Lady of the Angels Monastery. Their vocation is Perpetual Adoration of the Blessed Sacrament. They also have a worldwide radio and TV ministry. Monastery Retreats available. Director, Mr. D. Scallon. (205) 956-9537

Our Lady's Missionaries of the Eucharist
Sister Joan Noreen, Director. Magnificat House, 4530 Vera Cruz Road, Center Valley, PA 18034. (215) 797-1950. A Eucharistic and Marian mission and community for women religious, dedicated to Jesus in the Eucharist, consecrated to Mary. Seeks to bring orthodox programs of dynamic spirituality to dioceses and parishes. Established PEACE, Perpetual Eucharistic Centers for Evangelization, in which one parish hosts Eucharistic adoration each month.

Perpetual Eucharistic Adoration
L. Owen Traynor, Founder. 660 Club View Drive, Los Angeles, CA 90024, (310) 273-3856. An international apostolate promoting Perpetual Eucharistic Adoration. Contemplative in nature. Established as a Public Association of the Faithful, and directed to the sanctification of its members, who pledge one Holy Hour weekly and financial support for the apostolate. Devotional booklets available. Monthly twelve page color newsletter.

Witness Ministries
Joan McHugh, Director. Fr. Anselm Romb OFM Conv. Spiritual Advisor. 825 S. Waukegan Road, A8-200, Lake Forest, IL 60045 (708) 735-0556 An apostolate promoting devotion to the Real Presence of Christ in the Holy Eucharist. Through slide presentations, videos, books and pamphlets people are brought into a deeper awareness of this great Sacrament of Love.

YOUTH 2000 Prayer Festival
Ann Browley, Director. 6225 Boca Raton Dr., Dallas, TX 75230 (214) 361-2581. A movement comprised of weekends of prayer, adoration, singing, talks and sharing one's experiences with other youth. Their goal is to promote devotion to Jesus in the Holy Eucharist through a worldwide network of youth gathered in prayer around the Blessed Sacrament.